What people are saying about …

The Fresh Life Series

"I'm touched and blessed by Lenya and Penny's heart for His kingdom."

Kay Arthur, Bible teacher and
author of many best-selling Bible studies

"What a great way for women to learn to study the Bible: interesting stories, thought-provoking questions, and a life-changing approach to applying Scripture. Lenya and Penny provide a great method so women can succeed and grow spiritually in a short period of time. Kudos!"

Franklin Graham, president and CEO of
Billy Graham Evangelistic Association and Samaritan's Purse

"Skip and Lenya Heitzig have been friends of my wife, Cathe, and I for more than twenty years. Lenya loves to study God's Word and teach it to women in a way that is both exciting and accessible. I trust her latest book will be a blessing to you."

Greg Laurie, pastor and evangelist of Harvest Ministries

"Lenya and Penny's love for the Lord and knowledge of His Word uniquely equips them to help other women discover the pathway to God through these in-depth Bible studies."

Kay Smith, wife of Chuck Smith (Calvary Chapel)

"The Fresh Life Series is an insightful and in-depth look at God's Word. Through these Bible studies Lenya Heitzig and Penny Rose lead women to deeper intimacy with God."

K. P. Yohannan, president of Gospel for Asia

"Lenya and Penny have created another wonderful Bible study series that invites participants to spend time in God's Word and then see the Word come to fruition in their lives. What a blessing! These studies are perfect for small groups or personal daily devotions."

Robin Lee Hatcher, women's event speaker
and award-winning author

Live Fearlessly

Fresh Life
Bible Study Series

A 20-MINUTES-A-DAY STUDY

Live Fearlessly

The Book of Joshua

Lenya Heitzig & Penny Rose

David C Cook®

transforming lives together

LIVE FEARLESSLY
Published by David C. Cook
4050 Lee Vance View
Colorado Springs, CO 80918 U.S.A.

David C. Cook Distribution Canada
55 Woodslee Avenue, Paris, Ontario, Canada N3L 3E5

David C. Cook U.K., Kingsway Communications
Eastbourne, East Sussex BN23 6NT, England

David C. Cook and the graphic circle C logo
are registered trademarks of Cook Communications Ministries.

The Web site addresses recommended throughout this book are offered as a resource to you. These Web sites are not intended in any way
to be or imply an endorsement on the part of David C. Cook, nor do we vouch for their content.

Unless otherwise indicated, Scripture quotations are from the New King James Version. Copyright © 1982 by Thomas Nelson,
Inc. Used by permission. All rights reserved. Other Scripture quotations are from the *Holy Bible, New International Version®*.
NIV®. (NIV) © 1973, 1978, 1984 International Bible Society. Used by permission of Zondervan. All rights reserved. And the
Holy Bible, New Living Translation, copyright © 1996. Used by permission of Tyndale House Publishers, Inc., Wheaton, Illinois
60189. All rights reserved. And the Revised Standard Version (RSV), copyright 1952 [second edition, 1971], Division of Christian
Education of the National Council of the Churches of Christ in the United States of America. Used by permission.

Additional material provided by Misty Foster, Maria Guy, and Judy Sutton

ISBN 978-1-4347-9941-8

© 2008 Lenya Heitzig and Penny Rose
Published in association with William K. Jensen Literary Agency,
119 Bampton Court, Eugene, OR 97404

The Team: Terry Behimer, Karen Lee Thorp, Amy Kiechlin, and Jaci Schneider
Maps: Bob de la Peña
Cover/Interior Design: ThinkPen Design, Greg Jackson

Printed in the United States of America
First Edition 2008

2 3 4 5 6 7 8 9 10 11
120808

With Gratitude

In gratitude to our fearless fathers:

Rod Farley, Lenya's dad, a fierce Scotsman and faithful believer who encourages her with the motto "Never, never, never give up."

Jack Pierce, Penny's dad, who has fought a good fight, living by the creed "When the going gets tough, the tough get going."

Contents

Introduction   11

How to Get the Most out of This Study   15

Lesson One

Joshua 1 PASSING THE BATON   19

Lesson Two

Joshua 2 RED BADGE OF COURAGE   45

Lesson Three

Joshua 3—4 STEPPING OUT IN FAITH   67

Lesson Four

Joshua 5 WHEN GOD PULLS RANK   93

Lesson Five

Joshua 6 AN EARTH-SHATTERING SHOUT   117

Lesson Six

Joshua 7—8 SOMETHING IS ROTTEN IN THE STATE OF ISRAEL   145

Lesson Seven

Joshua 9 NOTHING UP MY SLEEVE   173

Lesson Eight

Joshua 10 THE DAY THE SUN STOOD STILL   199

Lesson Nine

Joshua 11—13 & 16—19 THE DIVINE DEVELOPER   227

Lesson Ten

Joshua 14—15 EXPLORING THE NEW LAND   265

Lesson Eleven

Joshua 20—21 THE CITIES DIFFERENT   293

Lesson Twelve

Joshua 22 FAMILY FEUD   321

Lesson Thirteen

Joshua 23—24 PARTING IS SUCH SWEET SORROW   351

Notes   377
Maps of the Promised Land in Joshua 1   388
About the Authors   391

Introduction

LIVE FEARLESSLY

Let's face it, we're all afraid of something. As children many of us were scared of the unseen boogeyman in the dark. Maybe in adolescence we were terrified of not fitting in with our peers. As adults we face the fear of the future for ourselves and those we love. Simply reading the newspaper makes us feel that the world is a ticking time bomb. The threat of terrorism is very real. Costs for food and fuel rise every day. Wars and rumors of wars abound. Fear really does take a toll on our emotional energy. That's why the book of Joshua, though written centuries ago in a land far away, is so relevant for today. In a world that can be terrifying, we can turn to God to *Live Fearlessly!*

GOD'S ENABLEMENTS

In the book of Joshua we will learn that victory comes to faithful people who trust and obey the Lord. We'll see this model of faith lived out in the person of Joshua after he took command of the children of Israel. He passed that faith down to the tribal leaders, and it reached the citizenry. The people received orders to obey and promises to possess. As believers, we can still obey these commands and cling to these promises. Warren Wiersbe wrote, "God's commandments are still His enablements!" When we are enabled by God, victory is certain.

GOD'S PRESENCE

Even more important than achieving victory in the Christian life is the Victor we long for— the one true God. When the Israelites wandered in the wilderness, a cloud of smoke by day and pillar of fire by night revealed God's presence in their midst. Moses declared, "If Your Presence does not go with us, do not bring us up from here" (Ex. 33:14). God gave His people a visible sign to follow. We, too, long to know God is with us wherever we go.

Author: Joshua the son of Nun, with some additions made following his death

Audience: Children of Israel

Theme: Possessing the Promised Land

Timeline: Fourteenth century BC

Setting: Crossing the Jordan River from the wilderness to the land of Canaan

Scripture: "Only be strong and very courageous, that you may observe to do according to all the law which Moses My servant commanded you; do not turn from it to the right hand or to the left, that you may prosper wherever you go" (Josh. 1:7).

Throughout this study we'll discover that we can take comfort in the presence of the living God, who dwells in the hearts of His people.

In Joshua's day the ark of the covenant represented God's presence. It went before the fledgling nation to remind them of their dependence on the Almighty to bring victory. We will see in this study that God's presence spelled victory. With a loud shout, walls fell down! You'll find that as you grow more dependent on God, your walls of sin and sorrow will fall down too.

GOD'S TACTICS

Throughout Joshua, God used unusual means to achieve victory. For instance, unlike the time the Red Sea parted for Moses from a distance as he raised his staff, the leaders in Joshua's day were asked to step into the waters of the raging Jordan River. Only then would the waters recede. It took a step of faith for them to move toward the Promised Land. So, too, must we take the step of faith into the Promised Land, placing one foot in front of another into whatever roiling rivers are churning around us. And rather than using the logical war strategies Moses used, God challenged Joshua's faith by ordering unorthodox battle plans to conquer Jericho by merely marching rather than laying siege or stealthily attacking. We must also learn to follow God's plan for battle. In that way we can see how God will claim the victory and receive the glory.

GOD'S MONUMENTS

We'll also see another recurring theme in the book of Joshua: memorial stones. By ordering these monuments, God hoped the people would remember that He was the One who brought them to the land and delivered their enemies into their hands. Hopefully, the visual memory would help the people fight the temptation to rewrite history or take any credit. At Gilgal and in the midst of the Jordan, Joshua erected two pillars of rocks to commemorate the miraculous river crossing. At the mountains of Ebal and Gerizim, two stones of "blessing and cursing" reaffirmed the laws of Moses. A mound of stones covering Achan's body represented an indictment against his disobedience. A "witness stone" at Shechem recalled the covenant between God and His people. Finally, the Transjordan tribes set up a stone monument to remind their children that they were part of the Israeli nation.

We all face battles in this life. We have obstacles to overcome and enemies to defeat. Joshua shows us that victory comes to those who trust and obey. As we study this wonderful Old Testament book, let's march forward in faith. Our Lord assures us of His presence: "I am with you always, even to the end of the age" (Matt. 28:20). As He gives you the strength to *Live Fearlessly,* you will become more than a conqueror. And you will come to know the Victor, Jesus Christ. So when He shows Himself victorious, place a stone of remembrance at His feet; erect a monument to His holy name.

May you live fearlessly,
Lenya Heitzig and Penny Rose

How to Get the Most out of This Study

Are you living life to the fullest, or are you just going through the motions? The secret to truly living rather than merely languishing is found in God's Word. We know that God reveals Himself through His Word. That's why doing a Bible study like this is so vital—because God's Word has the power to do His work in our lives. It is the catalyst that refreshes your heart, renews your mind, and restores your soul—it makes life worth living!

This study focuses on the book of Joshua. It reminds us time and again of God's faithfulness to keep His promises. Because He is so faithful, we can *Live Fearlessly!* Just as God led His people into the Promised Land, we pray that He will lead you into new promises and help you conquer new spiritual territory.

Each week of the study is divided into five days for your personal time with God. Each day's lesson has five elements. They are designed to help you fully "live" as you apply the truths you learn to your life:

1. Lift up … Here we ask you to "Lift up" prayers to God, asking Him to give you spiritual insight for the day.

2. Look at … This portion of the study asks you to "Look at" the Scripture text, using inductive questions. These questions help you to discover *What are the facts?* You'll learn the basic who-what-when-where-how aspects of the passage as well as some of the important background material.

3. Learn about …The "Learn about" sidebars correlate to specific questions in order to help you understand *What does this text mean?* These sidebar elements offer cultural insight, linguistic definitions, and biblical commentary.

4. Live out … These questions and exercises are designed to help you investigate *How should this change my life?* Here you are challenged to personally apply the lessons you have learned as you "Live out" God's principles in a practical way. We encourage

you to write out all of the answers to the questions in this study. You may want to write the answers to the personal application questions in a journal to ensure privacy. By writing your insights from God day by day, you'll have a record of your relationship with Him that you can look back on when you need a faith boost.

5. Listen to … We finish with inspiring quotes from authors, speakers, and writers. You'll be able to "Listen to" the wisdom they've gleaned in their lives and relate it to your own.

Live Fearlessly is ideal for discussion in a small-group setting as well as for individual study. The following suggestions will help you and your group get the most out of your study time:

PERSONAL CHECKLIST

- Be determined. Examine your daily schedule, then set aside a consistent time for this study.

- Be prepared. Gather the materials you'll need: a Bible, this workbook, a journal in which to write your thoughts, and a pen.

- Be inspired. Begin each day with prayer, asking the Holy Spirit to be your teacher and to illuminate your mind.

- Be complete. Read the suggested Bible passage and finish the homework each day.

- Be persistent. Answer each question as fully as possible. If you're unable to answer a question, move forward to the next question or read the explanation in the "Learn about …" section, which may offer further insight.

- Be consistent. Don't get discouraged. If you miss a day, use the weekend to catch up.

- Be honest. When answering the "Live out …" questions, allow the Lord to search your heart and transform your life. Take time to reflect honestly about your feelings, experiences, sins, goals, and responses to God.

- Be blessed. Enjoy your daily study time as God speaks to you through His Word.

SMALL-GROUP CHECKLIST

- Be prayerful. Pray before you begin your time together.

- Be biblical. Keep all answers in line with God's Word; avoid personal opinion.

- Be confidential. Keep all sharing within your small group confidential.

- Be respectful. Listen without interrupting. Keep comments on track and to the point so that all can share.

- Be discreet. In some cases, you need not share more than absolutely necessary. Some things are between you and the Lord.

- Be kind. Reply to the comments of others lovingly and courteously.

- Be mindful. Remember your group members in prayer throughout the week.

SMALL-GROUP LEADER CHECKLIST

- Be prayerful. Pray that the Holy Spirit will "guide you into truth" so that your leadership will guide others.

- Be faithful. Prepare by reading the Bible passage and studying the lesson ahead of time, highlighting truths and applying them personally.

- Be prompt. Begin and end the study on time.

- Be thorough. For optimum benefit, allot one hour for small-group discussion. This should allow plenty of time to cover all of the questions and exercises for each lesson.

- Be selective. If you have less than an hour, you should carefully choose which questions you will address, and summarize the edited information for your group. In this way, you can focus on the more thought-provoking questions. Be sure to grant enough time to address pertinent "Live out …" exercises, as this is where you and the women will clearly see God at work in your lives.

- Be sensitive. Some of the "Live out …" exercises are very personal and may not be appropriate to discuss in a small group. If you sense this is the case, feel free to move to another question.

- Be flexible. If the questions in the study seem unclear, reword them for your group. Feel free to add your own questions to bring out the meaning of a verse.

- Be inclusive. Encourage each member to participate in the discussion. You may have to draw some out or tone some down so that all have the opportunity to participate.

- Be honest. Don't be afraid to admit that you don't have all the answers! When in doubt encourage ladies to take difficult questions to their church leadership for clarification.

- Be focused. Keep the discussion on tempo and on target. Learn to pace your small group so that you complete a lesson on time. When participants get sidetracked, re-direct the discussion to the passage at hand.

- Be patient. Realize that not all people are at the same place spiritually or socially. Wait for the members of your group to answer the questions rather than jumping in and answering them yourself.

Passing the Baton

Joshua 1

Imagine the pressure. The Olympic Stadium filled with fans waving red, white, and blue. All of the early hours, long workouts, and years of sacrifice had brought the athletes to this moment.

At the 2004 Summer Olympics, four of the fastest women in the world ran the U.S. Women's 4x100 meter relay. Common knowledge held they would take home gold. The American women breezed to a win in the semifinals. They were well on their way to victory when disaster struck. The final baton pass between Marion Jones and Lauryn Williams went terribly awry. The women couldn't make the pass. It's unclear exactly what went wrong. Williams wonders if she took off too early. Spectators say Jones was tired and broke form by the end of her leg. Whatever happened, the baton pass was bungled, and the team didn't even medal.

When I [Penny] was a little girl, my daddy coached West Texas football in the fall and track in the spring. He taught me that the baton pass is the most crucial part of a relay. He decided which runners could handle the pass. He didn't always choose the fastest; he wanted team players with strong legs, sound minds, steady hands, and a solid reach. I remember watching the relay team practicing the handoff for hours on hot, windy days—endlessly repeating the takeoff, timing, and technique of the baton pass.

As it is in sports, so it can be in life. After forty years in the Sinai desert, the time came for Jehovah God to make His choice for passing the baton following Moses' brilliant years of leadership. God had spoken to him "face to face, as a man speaks to his friend" (Ex. 33:11). This servant leader guided the people to freedom from slavery throughout their long wilderness wanderings.

Moses had diligently obeyed God in every detail *except* for one instance: God told

Moses to speak to a rock to produce water, but Moses struck the rock. Because of his disobedience, God denied Moses entrance to the Promised Land (see Num. 20:7–13). But Moses and his successor had spent hours, days, and years preparing for this time.

Who would God choose to lead the headstrong Israelites? Someone with experience. Someone who could stand up to pressure. Someone steadfast. Someone faithful. Someone who would courageously reach for the future. Someone like Joshua.

Day 1: Joshua 1:1–2	COMMANDER IN CHIEF
Day 2: Joshua 1:3–5	COMMISSION AND COMFORT
Day 3: Joshua 1:6–9	CALLED TO COURAGE
Day 4: Joshua 1:10–15	COLLECTING COMRADES
Day 5: Joshua 1:16–18	COMPLIANCE TO COMMANDS

Hebrews 3-4 live in God's rest
Moses served God directly
Joshua served thru man (Moses)
Courage - Presence of faith in midst of fear

DAY 1

Commander in Chief

LIFT UP ...

Lord, I know You are my Commander in Chief. Help me to be Your servant, to obediently follow Your directions so that I may obtain all that You have for me. Amen.

LOOK AT ...

The children of Israel wandered forty years in the wilderness. Years earlier, God had miraculously set them free from slavery in Egypt and sent them to claim their inheritance in the Promised Land. Sadly, the generation that had witnessed God's miraculous works and experienced His amazing deliverance died in the desert, afraid of the people in the land. Of all the people who escaped Egypt, only two would enter the Land of Promise: Joshua and Caleb. Today we see that God named Joshua as commander in chief.

Joshua is the first book in the Bible named after a person. But this book isn't merely the story of a man; it is the history of Canaan's conquest. A transitional book, Joshua takes us from the patriarchal age where we witness the birth of the Hebrew people to the settlement of the Promised Land where we witness the birth of a nation. More than five hundred years had passed since God had promised Abraham, "To your descendants I will give this land" (Gen. 12:7). Now the next generation would take the baton of faith and move forward. As you move forward in the book of Joshua, look for God to move you to new and exciting territories on your journey of faith.

READ JOSHUA 1:1–2.

After the death of Moses the servant of the LORD, it came to pass that the LORD spoke to Joshua the son of Nun, Moses' assistant, saying: "Moses My servant is dead. Now therefore, arise,

LEARN ABOUT ...

1 Moses' Death

A leader's death can trigger a crisis. However, when Moses died, Jehovah was alive with plans for succession. After Moses led the Israelites to the borders, his work was done. God honored Moses with an unusual funeral: "He buried him in a valley in the land of Moab … but no one knows his grave to this day" (Deut. 34:6).

2 Servant's Servant

Joshua, "Moses' assistant," received a promotion. Moses' servant became the servant of the Lord. This was not expected, nor was Joshua unprepared. The people also knew who would lead them: "The LORD said to Moses: 'Take Joshua … a man in whom is the Spirit, and lay your hand on him … inaugurate him in their sight'" (Num. 27:18–19).

6 What Land?

The Israelites would cross into the land of Canaan. Situated on the trade routes that stretched from Egypt to Syria and from Phoenicia to the Babylonian Empire, this was a strategic position in the ancient world. After capturing Canaan, the Israelites developed a thriving trade route with other nations along these routes.[1]

go over this Jordan, you and all this people, to the land which I am giving to them—the children of Israel." Joshua 1:1–2

1. What sad event introduces the book of Joshua?
   Moses death.

2. Moses is described as "the servant of the LORD." How lofty or lowly a title does that sound like to you? Why?

3. Explain who ensured the succession of authority and who He spoke to. *The Lord spoke to Joshua.*

4. Why do you think God began his instructions to Joshua by stating something Joshua already knew: "Moses My servant is dead"?

5. What did God command Joshua and the children of Israel to do? *Go to land which I am giving you.*

6. What property did God promise the children of Israel? (See the maps on pages 388–89. The exact boundary lines are uncertain, but the maps gives a general idea of the broad territory Joshua 1 discusses.)

LIVE OUT ...

7. Just as Moses' death inaugurated a fresh start for the children of Israel, at times death can spark new life for us as well.

   a. Based on your personal observations, describe some instances in the natural world.

   b. Now transition your thoughts from the natural world to your personal life. Describe how you have experienced new life after a terrible loss (For example: The death of a dream brought new possibilities).

c. Move your thoughts one step deeper in your spiritual life. Describe how death can bring new life to your heart and soul (For example: Dying to my desires made me better able to meet the needs of others).

8. a. God chose Joshua to become the next leader of the Hebrew people. Fill in the table to discover how some of Joshua's life experiences prepared him for his role as leader of the people.

SCRIPTURE	JOSHUA'S PLACE & ROLE
Exodus 17:8–13	
Exodus 24:13–18	
Exodus 33:7–11	
Numbers 14:1–38	

b. Now think back over your life. List some of the events that God has used to prepare you for the role you occupy today.

9. The people had to wait a long time to obtain God's long-awaited promises. But God's delays don't necessarily mean "no"; they could mean "not now." Write down a promise from Scripture that you have been waiting for God to fulfill.

o o ● o o

George Washington, the first commander in chief of the Continental Army, didn't take the job to achieve fame or fortune. In fact, General Washington refused even to take a salary. He humbly said, "Lest some unlucky event should happen, unfavorable to my reputation, I beg it may be remembered, by every Gentleman in the room, that I, this day, declare with the utmost sincerity, I do not think myself equal to the Command I am honored with."

LEARN ABOUT ...

7 Death to Life

Jesus Christ's death on the cross made it possible for all who believe to live abundant life on earth and eternal life in heaven. Jesus said, "Unless a grain of wheat falls into the ground and dies, it remains alone; but if it dies, it produces much grain" (John 12:24).

9 Never Late

The time between God's pledge to provide the Promised Land and the fulfillment of their inhabiting it was five hundred years. The children of Israel learned that good things come to those who wait. While they murmured and doubted, they should have known that God never lies and He is never late—He's always right on time.

Since then, every U.S. president has served as commander in chief of the armed forces, outranking all military officers. However, of more than forty presidents, only George Washington and James Madison have faced battle. Frustrated with his generals' incompetence in the Civil War, Abraham Lincoln considered taking command of the Union Army. He actually came under enemy fire in 1864 during the Confederate attack on Fort Stevens in the District of Columbia but never exercised battlefield authority.

Joshua was on par with George Washington. He held the position of both military commander and head of state. He also exhibited the humility of the "gentleman from Virginia." Joshua is often overlooked for his spiritual greatness, as those who follow in the footsteps of great men often are. Phillip Keller said, "[Joshua] has seldom been given the full credit he deserves as perhaps the greatest man of faith ever to set foot on the stage of human history. In fact, his entire brilliant career was a straightforward story of simply setting down one foot in front of another in quiet compliance with the commands of God."[2]

LISTEN TO ...

I would say to my soul, O my soul, this is not the place of despair; this is not the time to despair in. As long as mine eyes can find a promise in the Bible ... as long as there is a moment left me of breath or life in this world, so long will I wait or look for mercy, so long will I fight against unbelief and despair.

—John Bunyan

Commission and Comfort

Has anyone ever told you, "I've got your back"? Perhaps it was a parent, a player on your baseball team, or a private in the military. On a recent trip to the Holy Land, I (Lenya) saw a T-shirt hanging from a shop in the Old City of Jerusalem that read, "Don't worry America, Israel's got your back." It made me chuckle knowing that, in fact, the United States has got Israel's back. Suddenly it occurred to me that no human *or* army, past *or* present, possesses enough strength to deliver Israel from her enemies. God alone watches Israel's back.

The phrase "I've got your back," which probably originated with pilots in World War II, has been popping up a lot lately from movies on YouTube to sweatshirts made by military wives. If you Google the phrase, you'll discover it denotes a sense of protectiveness. It's someone's way of saying, "Go ahead, I'll watch out for you." A good definition for the term might be: An expression that assures someone that you are watching out for them. A promise made by someone assuring that you are protected from what's behind while you're busy looking ahead.

Although the Promised Land was God's gift to Israel, the people would be victorious only through vigorous battle. God gave them title to the territory, but in order to possess it, they had to march upon every part of it. Thankfully, with God's divine commissions come His great comforts. God gave Joshua a command and a promise: lifetime victory over his enemies based on His unfailing presence. Joshua knew he could march forward because God truly had his back!

LIFT UP ...

Lord, help me to walk in Your promises with confidence. I trust You to stay with me through good times and bad, never to leave nor forsake me. Thank You for "having my back." Amen.

I Every Place

God promised the Israelites immense physical territory, but they have never claimed every place He offered. God also promises us spiritual territory and triumph: "Now thanks be to God who always leads us in triumph in Christ, and through us diffuses the fragrance of His knowledge in every place" (2 Cor. 2:14). Have you claimed every area He offers?

4 Invincible

God's promise of invincibility extends to all of His servants: "No weapon formed against you shall prosper, And every tongue which rises against you in judgment You shall condemn. This is the heritage of the servants of the LORD" (Isa.54:17). Though bad things may happen, God watches over His people and will ultimately prevail, if not here, then in the hereafter.

LOOK AT ...

God passed command to Joshua, one of the original members of the exodus. Next, He commissioned Joshua to take a step of faith into the land and comforted the people with His presence.

God made some astounding promises to Joshua for both the present and future; however, these promises were not given carte blanche. They came with some faith-building conditions. As we move forward with Joshua and the Israelites, remember that your faith-walk will progress on two feet. Take one step planted in the promises of God and the other step possessing the promises by faith.

READ JOSHUA 1:3–5.

"Every place that the sole of your foot will tread upon I have given you, as I said to Moses. From the wilderness and this Lebanon as far as the great river, the River Euphrates, all the land of the Hittites, and to the Great Sea toward the going down of the sun, shall be your territory. No man shall be able to stand before you all the days of your life; as I was with Moses, so I will be with you. I will not leave you nor forsake you." Joshua 1:3–5

1. God promised to give the Israelites "every place" they stepped on in the land. What does this promise say about God's character?

   Generous   faithful

2. Read Deuteronomy 11:24–28 to discover what God had promised Moses. Explain why God would bless the people and what would cause Him to curse them.

   Blessing - Obey   Curse - Disobey

3. a. Describe the specific boundaries of the Promised Land:

   From

   As far as

   All

To

Toward

b. Find these places on the map on page 388.

4. What promise did God make concerning the enemies in the land?

5. How did God confirm that He would treat Joshua as He had treated Moses?

6. What twofold promise did God make to Joshua?
   Will not leave you nor forsake you.

LIVE OUT ...

7. God promised the children of Israel that every piece of land they treaded upon would belong to them. Yet they never fully possessed all of it.

   a. Describe the places your feet trod on before salvation. (Example: bar rooms or the backseat of a car.)

   b. List some of the places you have visited as a Christian. (Example: church or convalescent homes.)

   c. Think of a place God would want to conquer. This week take a walk of faith around that place and ask God to be victorious. (Example: your prodigal's apartment or a needy neighborhood.)

8. Some of God's promises are conditional; they come with an offer as well as an obligation. God reminded Moses that obedience is the key to unlocking either blessing or curse. Use the letters in the word OBEY to describe some areas in your life where you have

LEARN ABOUT ...

6 Inseparable

People may pass on, but God's promises are eternal. God's promise of inseparability to Moses was passed on to Joshua. His promise to Joshua has extended from the Old Testament Israelites to New Testament believers: "He Himself has said, 'I will never leave you nor forsake you'" (Heb. 13:5).

7 Promised Land

Many people think that crossing the Jordan River is a metaphor for death and that entering the Promised Land stands for heaven. However, if the Promised Land were heaven, we wouldn't encounter enemies. Instead, the book of Joshua depicts a faithful life in the world, claiming our inheritance in Christ. What Paul's letter to the Ephesians teaches doctrinally, the book of Joshua depicts practically.

Learn about ...

9 Stand in Awe

When Joshua and the people entered the land, God assured him that no one could stand before them. Why? Because they served the mighty God who said: "Who then is able to stand against Me? Who has preceded Me, that I should pay him?" (Job 41:10–11). When we stand with God, He will always stand up for us.

experienced God's blessing. For instance, the letter O might stand for the blessing you feel when you have been openhanded.

O

B

E everyday –

Y

9. a. God's assurance of victory over His enemies must have caused Joshua to rejoice. We as believers have great reason to rejoice. Read 1 Corinthians 15:56–57 and describe humanity's greatest enemy and the conqueror of this enemy.

b. Journal about what this means to you personally and spend some time giving thanks to God for His victory in your life.

○ ○ ● ○ ○

Unlike Joshua, who took power at an old age (probably around eighty), William Pitt, Pittsburgh's namesake, became prime minister of Great Britain at the young age of twenty-four. A popular ditty scoffed: "A sight to make all nations stand and stare: a kingdom trusted to a schoolboy's care."

Known for oratorical skills and mental acuity, Pitt encountered many obstacles—he suffered from ill health and fought political enemies at home and foreign enemies abroad. When Napoleon threatened to conquer the world, Pitt allied with Russia, Austria, and Sweden. Following the Battle of Trafalgar, Pitt was hailed as the savior of Europe.[3]

The story is told that Pitt was eventually forced to walk on crutches. One day, a man came to him complaining of an impossible task he'd been assigned. Pitt picked up his crutches and shook them at the man. "Impossible, sir?" he shouted. "I walk on impossibilities."

We who walk by faith walk on impossibilities. We face enemies from all sides. The world, the flesh, and the Devil conspire to keep us from claiming the inheritance God has staked for us both here and in the hereafter. Whether we are young or old, we need the true Savior to lead us to victory. Joshua—the Hebrew name for Jesus—foreshadowed the One who came at just the right time to save humanity from sin and death. He is the Conquering King, who helps us fight both the enemies without and the enemies within.

LISTEN TO ...

God's promises are, virtually, obligations that he imposes upon himself.

—*Friedrich Wilhelm Krummacher*

DAY 3

Called to Courage

During the 1950s, America was exploring new territory in aeronautics. George Smith was a courageous test pilot willing to face anything. On February 26, 1955, he became the first person to survive a supersonic ejection. When he was forced to bail out from an F-100 Super Sabre going Mach 1.05 (over 675 miles per hour) from six thousand feet, *TIME* magazine reported that the wind hit his body with a force of eight thousand pounds. His helmet, shoes, socks, gloves, and watch were stripped off. The deceleration of forty g's made his organs weigh forty times more than normal. It was thought his arms and legs must have flailed like propeller blades.[4] He survived with grave injuries and feared flying again. Later he discovered the antidote to fear. One of his caregivers told him, "Courage is knowing the worst—and discovering that, in God's world, the very worst can't really hurt you."[5]

Joshua was exploring new territory too. Willing to face anything, he, too, knew the worst. A former Egyptian slave, a veteran wilderness wanderer, and witness to a generation of his countrymen dying in the desert, Joshua had every reason to be afraid. But he was a daring soldier during the exodus. When the majority of spies sent on reconnaissance returned quaking in their sandals, Joshua courageously said: "Do not be afraid of the people of the land, because we will swallow them up. Their protection is gone, but the LORD is with us. Do not be afraid of them" (Num. 14:9 NIV).

You might think forty years of wandering in the wilderness discouraged Joshua. Maybe trying to fill Moses' shoes was intimidating. Perhaps mustering an army from a group of vagabonds was daunting. But God ensured Joshua had the antidote to fear.

LIFT UP ...

God, help me to be courageous regardless of what may come my way. Help me to turn to Your Word as the source of my strength. Amen.

LOOK AT ...

We've seen how Joshua received God's promises of His presence and protection before venturing into the land. But before the people entered the Land of Promise, God instructed Joshua on the people's spiritual needs. He reminded him that the Word of God would be the source of their strength.

The newspaper *Israeli Insider* said, "Our sages say that more than the Jewish People kept the Torah, the Torah kept the Jewish People."[6] Some critics argue that Scripture didn't appear in written form until centuries after the events in this book, but today's lesson clearly shows that the people had a written text to read and rely on. They probably at least had the Torah, known to us as the Pentateuch, the first five books of the Bible, which were attributed to Moses. When you need help, know that you can find solace by reading God's Word.

LEARN ABOUT ...

I Courage

Courage is the strength that enables one to withstand fear or difficulty. Physical courage is based on moral courage, which is a reliance on the presence and power of God and a commitment to His commandments.[7] "Wait on the LORD; Be of good courage, And He shall strengthen your heart" (Ps. 27:14).

READ JOSHUA 1:6–9.

"Be strong and of good courage, for to this people you shall divide as an inheritance the land which I swore to their fathers to give them. Only be strong and very courageous, that you may observe to do according to all the law which Moses My servant commanded you; do not turn from it to the right hand or to the left, that you may prosper wherever you go. This Book of the Law shall not depart from your mouth, but you shall meditate in it day and night, that you may observe to do according to all that is written in it. For then you will make your way prosperous, and then you will have good success. Have I not commanded you? Be strong and of good courage; do not be afraid, nor be dismayed, for the LORD your God is with you wherever you go." Joshua 1:6–9

1. Describe in your own words what God told Joshua to "be."

LEARN ABOUT ...

3 Very Courageous

This second command is stronger than the first, adding "very" to courageous. The implication is that it takes more fortitude of heart to obey God's Word than to wage a war. It's true; personal conformity to God's laws allows us to conquer new territory.

---

5 Down & Out

Afraid means to dread, fear, or to be terrified. However, to be dismayed is much worse, coming as the result of continual fear. Dismayed means to be beat down, broken down, or fallen prostrate. It portrays an individual who has given up or completely fallen apart.[8]

---

8 Cowardice?

Three times God said, "Be strong," to a man probably feeling weak. Three times He repeated, "Take courage," to a timid leader. Twice Joshua was told not to be afraid. God gives power to the faint. Admitting weakness gives way to God's strength. Courage is not the absence of fear but the presence of faith despite fear.

2. What reason did God give "for" this? Explain in your own words.

3. "Observe to do" (Josh. 1:7) means "carefully do." Why do you think it would take great courage for Joshua to carefully do everything God's Word commands?

4. Describe the three ways the book of the law should be experienced.
   ~~Meditate~~

5. What two things did God promise if they observed the book of the law?

6. What commands did God repeat?

7. What promises did He affirm? Why do you think He repeated Himself?

LIVE OUT ...

8. a. Scan through Joshua 1 and circle the words "courage" or "courageous."

   b. How many times do they appear?

   c. List each verse you've discovered. Beside each passage, list who was exhorted to be courageous and by whom they were exhorted.

   d. Now journal about a situation in which *you* were encouraged to be courageous, who encouraged you, and how you responded.

9. God told Joshua that God's Word should be experienced in three different ways: 1) say it, 2) pray it, 3) display it. With this in mind complete the following exercise.

a. Say it! Read today's Scripture text aloud, once during the day and once at night.

b. Pray it! Rewrite Joshua 1:6–9 into a personal prayer.

c. Display it! Resolve to act up one truth from today's lesson and record it in your journal.

∘ ∘ ● ∘ ∘

LEARN ABOUT …

9 Prosperity

God's definition of prosperity differs drastically from humanity's definition. Society often measures success by possessions, power, and popularity. Spiritual prosperity encompasses progress in knowledge, purity, and joy. It arises from participating in divine blessing and is evidenced by frequent prayer and love of God's Word.[9]

"Some good book is usually responsible for the success of every really great man," wrote author and pastor Roy L. Smith. Was he right?

Alexander the Great carried Homer's epic *The Iliad* as he sought to conquer the world, but he died young, depressed, and disillusioned. Gandhi was influenced by the Hindu poem *The Bhagavad Gita*. Yet Gandhi's call to pacifism has not ended war in this world. Napoleon read Plutarch's *Lives* repeatedly but met his Waterloo and was exiled to the island of Saint Helena.

Only one book stands the test of time and holds the secret to true success: the *Good Book*. The Bible has been responsible for the success of many great men and women; Joshua is no exception. Though he probably had only the first five books of the Bible penned by Moses, we'll witness Joshua faithfully saying, praying, and displaying God's Word throughout his life. This helped make him a true success story.

All of us hope to be successful. Yet we often fall short of our dreams because we take shortcuts. We skip the steps to spiritual success. Take heart! If you, like Joshua, say God's Word, pray His Word, and display it on a daily basis, then you, too, will find strength and courage to overcome whatever comes your way. You'll find that the *Good Book* is responsible not only for a full life, but a successful life as well.

LISTEN TO ...

One man with courage makes a majority.

—Andrew Jackson

DAY 4

Collecting Comrades

Even today, Israel has mandatory military service for young men and women. All Israeli citizens are conscripted except for ultraorthodox Hasidic Jews, married or pregnant women, Israeli Arabs, or people with physical or mental illnesses.

Israel is surrounded on all sides by enemies, so the army stands at a constant state of military alert. The conscripts are immersed in the military culture, with its own set of rules and codes. The soldier is trained to understand that the individual is less important than the whole. Commanders emphasize the greater good at every opportunity. It is instilled into every new recruit as absolute truth.

Soldiers are trained to blindly trust their comrades in arms just as their comrades trust them. Otherwise, a combat unit will be unable to perform its mission. *Esprit de corps* (the spirit of the group) is not merely a phrase; it is their code of conduct. Combat soldiers are closer than brothers; they are brothers in arms ready, willing, and able to die for one another. They put their lives on the line to protect one another and their homeland.[10]

All adult Israelite men were conscripted into the armed services in Joshua's day, as well. They were needed to accomplish the task of conquering the seven nations inhabiting the land. They didn't have modern weapons or strength of numbers, but they had one advantage—God was on their side. And so Joshua meticulously prepared his troops for battle.

LIFT UP ...

Lord, I want to truly possess those things You've given me to possess. Help me to be prepared spiritually, emotionally, and physically. Help me to remember that the battles are not mine alone; let me rely on my brethren and on You as I walk through this world. Amen.

LEARN ABOUT ...

2 Threes

In Scripture the number three speaks of *completeness*: beginning, middle, and end; of *time*: Jesus spent three days in the tomb and Moses was hidden three months from Pharaoh; and of *persons* or *spirits*: Noah's three sons and Abraham's three visitors. The most profound and mysterious three is the Holy Trinity: Father, Son, and Holy Spirit.

LOOK AT ...

The years of wandering were over; the Israelites would cross the Jordan River. Joshua received his orders from God, his Commanding Officer, to move into the Promised Land. In turn, he collected comrades to establish a chain of command.

Most conservative scholars agree that Moses was the living representative of the law. Alan Redpath wrote, "Observe, from the opening verses of the first chapter of the book of Joshua, that it was impossible for the law to lead into the land of Canaan ... the law could not inherit the promises of God because of human infirmity and sin."[II] Joshua, then, became the living representative of grace. For the remainder of the study, look for the many ways Joshua foreshadowed Jesus Christ. Jesus—the One filled with grace, the One who fulfilled the law—the One who divinely exhibited every characteristic of His name: "the Lord is salvation."

READ JOSHUA 1:10–15.

Then Joshua commanded the officers of the people, saying, "Pass through the camp and command the people, saying, 'Prepare provisions for yourselves, for within three days you will cross over this Jordan, to go in to possess the land which the LORD your God is giving you to possess.'" And to the Reubenites, the Gadites, and half the tribe of Manasseh Joshua spoke, saying, "Remember the word which Moses the servant of the LORD commanded you, saying, 'The LORD your God is giving you rest and is giving you this land.' Your wives, your little ones, and your livestock shall remain in the land which Moses gave you on this side of the Jordan. But you shall pass before your brethren armed, all your mighty men of valor, and help them, until the LORD has given your brethren rest, as He gave you, and they also have taken possession of the land which the LORD your God is giving them. Then you shall return to the land of your possession

and enjoy it, which Moses the LORD'*s servant gave you on this side of the Jordan toward the sunrise." Joshua 1:10–15*

1. To whom did Joshua turn to fulfill God's commands?

2. How long would it take the people to get ready to cross the river into the Promised Land?

3. Of what did he remind the Reubenites, Gadites, and people of Manasseh?

4. What would become of their families?

5. Describe how they would help their brethren.

6. After the occupation, explain what would happen and whose authority this was based upon.

7. a. Scan through today's passage (verses 10–15) and circle the words "possess" and "possession." Record how many times these words occur.

   b. Look back through verses 1–9. In what other ways is the idea of possession alluded to? Write down any similar words or concepts you see.

LIVE OUT ...

8. God has given you, too, an inheritance that He wants you to possess. How should this truth affect the way you conduct your life?

LEARN ABOUT ...

4 Two and a Half Tribes

Numbers 1:3 explains that *all* men twenty years and over would "go to war." However, two and a half tribes were allotted good grazing land east of the Jordan River (see Num. 32:5). The men in these tribes crossed the river to help their fellow Israelites win their land west of the river, while the women and children stayed on the eastern land.

6 One Goal

Joshua repeatedly focuses on the theme of possession. The word recurs fifteen times throughout the book and 260 times in the Bible. It literally means to occupy; to drive out previous tenants and take their place; to inherit. Regarding the Promised Land, *yarash,* or possess, means to take over by conquest as a permanent possession.[12]

7 Possess Your Possessions

The children of Israel were promised a literal land if they would go forward to possess their inheritance. As children of God, we have much greater promises: the earth (see Matt. 5:5); eternal life (see Matt. 19:29); a blessing (see 1 Peter 3:9); and all things (see Rev. 21:7). "Imitate those who through faith and patience inherit the promises" (Heb. 6:12).

9 Chain of Command

Joshua learned about leadership from Moses, who gained insight from his father-in-law, Jethro. Moses was trying to do everything himself, so Jethro said, "The thing that you do is not good .... You will surely wear yourselves out" (Ex. 18:17–18). So "Moses chose able men out of all Israel, and made them heads over the people" (Ex. 18:25).

9. a. In question 1 we discovered that God established a chain of command in His army. Describe who was in charge of whom.

   b. Journal about your personal chain(s) of command. Who do you lead—and who do you follow—at home, at work, at church, or elsewhere? How would you rank yourself as a leader? How would you rank yourself as a follower?

○ ○ ● ○ ○

Throughout history great leaders have established chains of command to create order within governments, armies, and businesses. A chain of command is a system of authority that descends through a series of executive positions or military rank. Each position is accountable *to* the person directly above and accountable *for* those directly subordinate.[13]

The chain of command is important because it establishes clear lines of authority and responsibility through which orders are passed. The orders proceed from higher-ranked officers, who give orders directly to lower-ranked soldiers. Military personnel give orders only to those who serve directly under them in the chain of command. They receive orders only from those serving directly above. In fact, a soldier is likely to be disciplined for not observing the chain of command if he bypasses his commanding officer or appeals to a higher-ranking officer in his chain of command.

The concept of chain of command doesn't give higher-ups free rein. Higher rank does not entitle a person to give commands. An officer of a given military unit does not have the authority to directly command soldiers of another unit because he is outside their chain of command.

A good chain of command is necessary to keep armies, governments, businesses, and families from spinning into chaos. God is a God of order, Who wisely establishes chains of command where He is at the top. Joshua needed this wisdom to conquer the Promised Land. We all need this wisdom to walk in this world.

LISTEN TO ...

I do not want merely to possess a faith; I want a faith that possesses me.

—*Charles Kingsley*

DAY 5

Compliance to Commands

Children learn from an early age to comply with commands. Even schoolyard games affirm the value of following the leader. Remember the rules? A leader is chosen as "head of the line." The other kids line up behind the leader. The game begins when the leader moves around, marching, waving his arms, and performing tricky maneuvers. The children's challenge is to follow and mimic the leader's activities. Any player who "messes up" or refuses to do what the leader does is out of the game. At the end of the game, the last person standing becomes the new leader.

Moses led the children of Israel through forty years of wandering in the wilderness. But not all of the children followed their leader. Some murmured and complained. Others worshipped the golden calf. Sadly, the entire generation that escaped during the exodus fell out of line, except for Joshua and Caleb.

God tapped Joshua to be the new leader. It became his task to teach the people to march, not meander. The newly appointed leader stood before the people and instilled confidence for their new venture of faith. And like the childhood game, those who fell out of line would be forced out.

People follow a leader like Joshua because to follow him is to tacitly follow God. They were able to put their trust in Joshua because they ultimately trusted in God.

LIFT UP ...

Father, help me to be obedient to whatever You command. I want to be so obedient that wherever You send me, I go. May I heed You in all things. Amen.

LOOK AT ...

Joshua gathered his troops, preparing them to conquer the land. Now we see the people's response to their new commander in chief as they mobilized for action.

Scholars disagree whether it was the Transjordan tribes (Reuben, Gad, and half of

Manasseh) who responded, the leaders of the tribes, or all the people in unison. Regardless of who it was, we know that they voiced the people's will. In today's lesson we see two characteristics of this nation: 1) they were willing to sacrifice their own lives for the national good, 2) they were willing to submit their own rights to Joshua's leadership. We also see two concerns expressed by the leaders: 1) that Joshua follow God's leading, 2) that he live up to God's command to be strong and courageous. As you study this passage, examine your heart to see whether you're willing to submit and sacrifice for the greater good of your church and community.

2 Wherever

The Israelites promised to go "Wherever." Unknown to them, this would include crossing a flooding river, entering a harlot's house, stopping for a mass circumcision, going longer than they thought they could go, and fighting many battles. Are you willing to say, "Lord, I will follow You wherever You go" (Luke 9:57)?

READ JOSHUA 1:16–18.

So they answered Joshua, saying, "All that you command us we will do, and wherever you send us we will go. Just as we heeded Moses in all things, so we will heed you. Only the LORD your God be with you, as He was with Moses. Whoever rebels against your command and does not heed your words, in all that you command him, shall be put to death. Only be strong and of good courage." Joshua 1:16–18

3 However

The Israelites promised to obey. *However,* Moses' return was delayed. Often, when a strong leader is away, the people will stray. God solved the problem. Jesus said, "If you love Me, keep My commandments. And I will pray the Father, and He will give you another Helper, that He may abide with you forever" (John 14:15–16).

1. In your own words, recount how many commands they promised to obey.

2. They promised to go wherever Joshua sent them. Why was "wherever" important?

3. At Mount Sinai, the previous generation of Israelites had promised to do "all" that the Lord commanded (see Ex. 19:8). Then Moses climbed the mountain to receive the Lord's commands. Skim Exodus 32. Describe how the people broke their promise and the results of their actions.

4. What two things "only" did the people ask of Joshua (see Josh. 1:17–18)?

Only

Only

5. Describe the sentence for treason.

LIVE OUT ...

6. The people vowed to heed Joshua's commands. Since Joshua was God's representative to the nation, to obey him was to obey the Lord. Read Psalm 81.

   a. Who is this psalm written to?

   b. What historic events does it recall (see verses 4 and 10)?

   c. What command are they to heed (see verse 9)?

   d. How do the people respond to the Lord's cries (see verse 11)?

   e. What fate befalls those who disobey (see verse 12)? Why might that fate be more painful than the disobedient expect?

   f. What does God promise those who obey (see verses 13–16)?

7. a. We've discovered some of the things Moses and Joshua asked the children of Israel to heed. Fill in the following chart to discover some things that the Lord commands you to heed.

SCRIPTURE	COMMANDS TO HEED
Luke 8:18	
Luke 12:15	
Luke 17:3–4	
Luke 21:34–35	

b. Which, if any, of these commands are you failing to heed?

c. How will you "follow the leader" in the future?

8. a. The Israelites had two great concerns for their leader: that he follow God and that he be strong and courageous. In what areas of life do you have people in authority over you (church, government, family, business, etc.)?

b. What expectations do you place upon these people? Which of these seem realistic, and which seem unrealistic?

c. Journal a prayer for those you named based on the two "onlys" in today's lesson.

LEARN ABOUT ...

8 Expectations

The people declared that they would obey Joshua as long as he met their expectations. Of course, they hadn't completely obeyed Moses, and Joshua didn't expect them to completely obey him either. Nevertheless, Joshua willingly took the responsibility the Lord laid on his shoulders and did his duty to the very end.

o o ● o o

We've all seen the elegant signatures at the bottom of the Declaration of Independence and read the stories about the Revolutionary War. But have you ever wondered what happened to the fifty-six men who signed the document? Five were captured by the British as traitors and tortured before they died. Twelve had their homes ransacked and burned. Two lost sons in the Revolutionary War. Another two had sons taken as prisoners of war. Nine fought and died during the war. The stories are heartbreaking and tragic. Yet they fought on until they achieved victory.

These men weren't anarchists or criminals. Twenty-four were jurists; eleven were merchants; nine worked the land. The founders of our nation were well-educated men of means. But they willingly signed the Declaration of Independence, knowing that the penalty would be death if they were captured. They pledged: "For the support of this declaration, with a firm reliance on the protection of the Divine Providence, we mutually pledge to each other, our lives, our fortunes, and our sacred honor."[15]

The Israelites trusted Divine Providence to lead them to a good and pleasant land. They pledged to one another and to Joshua that they would follow him to the death. You will find their tales as heartrending as the tales of the American Revolution. And you will see God's hand of providence lead them through battle after battle into the Land of Promise. Even today, the battles are not easy, but when God stands with you, victory is assured.

LISTEN TO ...

The longer I live, the more convincing proofs I see of this truth, that God governs in the affairs of man; and if a sparrow cannot fall to the ground without his notice, is it probable that an empire can rise without his aid?

—*Benjamin Franklin*

LESSON TWO

Red Badge of Courage
Joshua 2

What color is courage? Throughout Stephen Crane's classic novel *The Red Badge of Courage,* courage is bloodred. At the beginning of his foray into war, Henry Fleming "regarded battles as crimson blotches on the pages of the past." Sadly, during his first battle, Henry turned yellow and ran.

Henry returned to the battle and grew to manhood, gaining the strength of will to fight for the infamous "red badge of courage" (a battlefield wound). But it was not his to win. He walked away a hero in name only. Nevertheless, "he felt a quiet manhood, nonassertive but sturdy and strong of blood.... He had been to touch the great death, and found that, after all, it was but the great death. He was a man."[16]

At one time or another, we all reach a moment of decision. It may be on a real battle-field where we decide to fight or take flight. It may be in a relationship that we decide whom to marry. The ultimate point of decision is where we place our faith. Will we follow Jesus, the One who bore the ultimate "red badge of courage" on a cross, or will we turn and walk the way of the world?

This week we'll meet Jesus' ancestress Rahab, who faced her own conflict. Would she remain loyal to her pagan king and people, or would she follow Jehovah and save her soul and household? We'll rejoice together as we see how Rahab hung a "scarlet flag of faith." She was a woman of courage.

Day 1: Joshua 2:1–3	HOUSE OF SECRETS
Day 2: Joshua 2:4–7	HIDING THE ENEMY
Day 3: Joshua 2:8–13	HEARING BRINGS FAITH
Day 4: Joshua 2:14–20	HOUSE OF SAFETY
Day 5: Joshua 2:21–24	HERALDS OF HOPE

DAY 1
House of Secrets

LIFT UP ...

Father, let my home be known as a house of faith. Let me host and protect those who love and serve You. May I reflect Your love and forgiveness that came through the shedding of Jesus' blood. In His name, Amen.

LOOK AT ...

A strategic planner, Joshua sent two spies on a reconnaissance mission to the fortified city of Jericho. God used this event not only for military intelligence, but to accomplish another divine purpose—to reward and redeem Rahab the harlot for her faith. Today's lesson reveals the lengths to which God was willing to go to protect her and those she held dear from judgment.

When Joshua sent the spies, it was unlikely they would meet an ally, because the Canaanites were known as fierce and mighty warriors (see Deut. 7:1). However, the two men providentially stopped at the house of a woman who was predisposed to help them as they gathered information. When you are facing an unknown future, remember that God will providentially guide you to the places you should go too.

READ JOSHUA 2:1–3.

Now Joshua the son of Nun sent out two men from Acacia Grove to spy secretly, saying, "Go, view the land, especially Jericho." So they went, and came to the house of a harlot named Rahab, and lodged there. And it was told the king of Jericho, saying, "Behold, men have come here tonight from the children of Israel to search out the country." So the king of Jericho sent to Rahab, saying, "Bring out the men who have come to you, who have entered your house, for they have come to search out all the country." Joshua 2:1–3

1. Chapter 2 begins with the transitional word *Now*. Review Chapter 1 and recount what happened to bring us to where we are *Now*.

2. Describe what action Joshua took.

3. a. Read Numbers 13, where Moses sent men to spy out the land. How was that spy mission like and unlike the spy mission in Joshua 2?

   b. What aspects of that earlier spy mission would Joshua likely not want to see repeated?

4. Where did Joshua's spies wind up?

5. Explain who learned of their presence and how he heard of it.

6. Who did he go to, and what did he ask?

LIVE OUT ...

7. Rahab's name is linked with the label "the harlot." Fill in the following chart to discover other biblical characters who were labeled.

SCRIPTURE	NAME & LABEL
Matthew 10:3	
Matthew 26:6	
Acts 13:8	

8. Today we saw Joshua send out two soldiers to "secretly spy" in the city of Jericho and hide out in Rahab's house. With this in mind, read Psalm 31:19–21.

LEARN ABOUT ...

2 Jericho

Jericho could mean "fragrant city," derived from the local herbs. During Joshua's time, Jericho was situated at the foot of the Judean mountains. One of the oldest inhabited cities in the world, it was large and impressive. Its size and location made it one of the most important cities in the Jordan Valley.

4 Hiding Place

Why did the God-fearing spies hide in a harlot's home? Some say that Rahab was an innkeeper as well as a harlot. It is believed that she bore the title "harlot" from a profession she no longer engaged in. The foreigners would not draw suspicion by visiting a well-frequented establishment. They were hiding out in the open.

6 Counterintelligence

Jericho was one of many city-states in Canaan ruled by a king. Likely, the whole city was nervous about the army encamped outside their walls. Apparently, the king had a few spies of his own since he became aware of the spies' presence.

LEARN ABOUT ...

7 Namesake

The Israelites were fond of playing on names. To them, the name was a sign of something outward, like a job, a physical trait, or an occupation. The tendency to use names to find analogies or contrasts is seen throughout the Bible.[17] For the writer of Joshua, it was probably quite natural to link Rahab with her profession.

---

8 Secret Place

The best place to hide is in God. Has He become your secret place? "He who dwells in the secret place of the Most High Shall abide under the shadow of the Almighty. I will say of the LORD, 'He is my refuge and my fortress; My God, in Him I will trust'" (Ps. 91:1–2).

a. Who does God show His great goodness to (see v. 19)?

b. Based on your knowledge of Scripture, what does it mean to fear God?

c. God promises to "hide them in the secret place of [His] presence" (see v. 20). What picture of God's presence does this phrase give you?

d. What shall He protect them from (see v. 20)?

e. How is this like what God did for Joshua's spies?

f. How does the psalmist respond and why (see v. 21)?

9. Journal about how God could be a secret place of refuge for you. What do you need to do to take advantage of God's offer?

○ ○ ● ○ ○

On May 18, 1965, a close "friend" of the president of Syria was executed. Many believe he saved the State of Israel from being destroyed. More than any other man, Eli Cohen, an Egyptian-born Jew, earned the Israeli Secret Service's reputation as the best intelligence operative in the world and paved the way for Israel to win the Six-Days War in June 1967.

Cohen adopted the persona of a rich Arab immigrant, Kamal Amin Taabes, who had returned from Argentina to his Syrian homeland. The Mossad agent joined the revolutionary Ba'ath Party and befriended many officials in the new government.

Cohen was one of few civilians allowed to inspect Syrian installations in the Golan Heights. He secretly sent pictures of the Syrian frontlines to the Mossad. In one case he radioed Israel of an impending attack by Syria across the border.

Cohen was exposed when the KGB discovered his radio equipment. After two trials he was sentenced to death by hanging. It turns out he was no friend of the Syrians—his loyalty was with Israel. His advice was heeded by Menachem Begin in 1981, when the Israeli air force bombed Iraqi nuclear plants. Eli Cohen had cautioned, "Against the Arab you mustn't defend yourself. You must attack."[18]

Israeli spies have existed since time immemorial. God has used them to protect the nation from attack as well as inform them of the enemy's vulnerabilities. Joshua's spies took one they thought was an enemy, Rahab, into their confidence. She knew who they were and became their true friend. How she responded determined her destiny.

LISTEN TO ...

Great supplicants have sought the secret place of the Most High, not that they might escape the world, but that they might learn to conquer it.

—*Samuel Chadwick*

DAY 2
Hiding the Enemy

Corrie ten Boom's book *The Hiding Place* tells how she became a member of the Dutch underground until her arrest by the Gestapo. Maybe one of the least recognized characters in this World War II drama was Father ten Boom, who allowed a "secret room" to be built in Corrie's bedroom in Haarlem, Holland. Nazi Germany was bent on exterminating the Jews, but Father ten Boom had an abiding love for God's chosen people and was willing to risk his life to protect them.

Her father inspired Corrie to help Holland's persecuted Jews. She recalled asking a pastor to help shield a mother and her baby. He replied, "No definitely not. We could lose our lives for that Jewish child." She recalls, "Unseen by either of us, Father had appeared in the doorway. 'Give the child to me, Corrie,' he said. Father held the baby close, his white beard brushing its cheek, looking into the little face with eyes as blue and innocent as the baby's. 'You say we could lose our lives for this child. I would consider that the greatest honor that could come to my family.'"[19]

Since the time of Genesis, there has been insidious opposition to God's people. They have faced persecution in many forms from enslavement to the Inquisition to the gas chamber. But God has promised to "bless those who bless you, And … curse him who curses you" (Gen. 12:3). Ultimately, Rahab was not hiding the enemy—she was hiding God's friends.

LIFT UP ...

Lord, I want to be hidden in You. You are my refuge and strength. Help me to love those You love and protect Your people from harm. Amen.

LOOK AT ...

Joshua's spies needed a place of respite. They found one in an unlikely place. But Rahab's loyalty to king and country was put to the test. Would she be found hiding the enemy?

Last week we learned that Joshua's men promised they would put to death any man who fled from battle. It is also commonly known that treason against a king was grounds for the death penalty. This week we will see Rahab struggle with the concept of civil disobedience, putting her loyalty to God and His people above loyalty to her nation.

READ JOSHUA 2:4–7.

Then the woman took the two men and hid them. So she said, "Yes, the men came to me, but I did not know where they were from. And it happened as the gate was being shut, when it was dark, that the men went out. Where the men went I do not know; pursue them quickly, for you may overtake them." (But she had brought them up to the roof and hidden them with the stalks of flax, which she had laid in order on the roof.) Then the men pursued them by the road to the Jordan, to the fords. And as soon as those who pursued them had gone out, they shut the gate. Joshua 2:4–7

1. Yesterday we saw what happened *Now*. Today, we see another transitional word: *Then*. Describe what happened *Then*.

2. What fabrications did Rahab tell the king's envoys about the Israelite men?

3. Describe the action she encouraged the envoys to take and why.

4. Explain what had really happened to the spies.

5. Describe the actions of both the king's men and the gatekeepers.

6. Rahab the former prostitute lied and broke the law to help the Israelites invade her corrupt city. What does it say about God that He worked through such a person and welcomed her into the community of His people?

LEARN ABOUT ...

2 White Lies?

Scripture condemns lying. "Lying lips are an abomination to the LORD, But those who deal truthfully are His delight" (Prov. 12:22). Although the Bible affirms Rahab's faith, it does not condone her fibs. She risked her life to protect the spies. But do the ends justify the means?

3 Civil Disobedience

Believers are exhorted to obey civil authorities. We should be the most law-abiding citizens in the land. However, when men's statutes conflict with God's commands, believers have no choice but to obey God: "Whether it is right in the sight of God to listen to you more than to God, you judge" (Acts 4:19).

5 Gates

The city gates in ancient city walls were massive wooden doors through which traffic passed. They were often reinforced with brass or iron for greater security. The gates were opened by day, but they were generally closed at night for safety.[20]

LEARN ABOUT ...

6 Faith That Works

According to James, Rahab proved she had living faith by hiding the spies. She manifested her faith by her works: "Likewise, was not Rahab the harlot also justified by works when she received the messengers and sent them out another way?" (James 2:25). Faith and works always go hand in hand.

8 Governing Authorities

God established governing authorities to benefit society. He places them in powerful positions for the common good: "Let every soul be subject to the governing authorities. For there is no authority except from God, and the authorities that exist are appointed by God" (Rom. 13:1). We must have a very godly reason for resisting them.

LIVE OUT ...

7. Rahab told untruths to protect the spies who sought refuge in her home. Scripture is honest to portray the highs and lows of the great men and women of faith. Fill in the following chart to discover who else stretched the truth.

SCRIPTURE	LIARS AND THE LIES THEY TOLD
Genesis 12:10–20	
Genesis 26:6–11	
Genesis 27:1–29	
1 Samuel 21:1–6	

8. Quickly skim Daniel 3 to review one of the most memorable cases of civil disobedience in Scripture as Shadrach, Meshach, and Abed-Nego faced King Nebuchadnezzar. In your own words, describe the political environment, their response, and the results.

9. a. Today we saw some instances of civil disobedience for God's higher good. Recount a contemporary example of Christians who obey God rather than men.

   b. Would you, like Rahab, lie or break the law in service to God? If so, under what circumstances? If not, why not?

○ ○ ● ○ ○

Another Dutchman, Andy Van Der Bijl, born in 1928, dreamed of becoming an undercover spy. A born daredevil, he had visions of one day working behind enemy lines. The man we've come to know as Brother

Andrew grew to manhood and found himself working undercover for God. His life's mission was fraught with danger, financed by faith, and filled with miracles.

His book, *God's Smuggler*, recalls how people told him it was impossible to minister behind the Iron Curtain because of their laws against the Christian faith. But Brother Andrew knew that nothing was too hard for God. When he crossed "closed" borders, he prayed, "Lord, in my luggage I have Scripture to take to Your children. When you were on earth, You made blind eyes see. Now, I pray, make seeing eyes blind. Do not let the guards see those things You do not want them to see." And they never did.

Rahab must have prayed a prayer like Brother Andrew's when the king's men came to her home searching for Joshua's spies. Her faith was rewarded when she hid them among the flax on her roof and the ruse proved successful. Both Brother Andrew and Rahab "loved not their lives unto the death" (Rev. 12:11 KJV), risking life and limb to further the kingdom of God.

Interestingly, Rahab's descendant Solomon would write that a virtuous woman "seeks wool and flax" (Prov. 31:13). Could it be that he had his brave great-great-grandmother in mind?

Listen to ...

Thank God you don't have to be flawless to be blessed! You need to have a big heart that desires and wants the will of God more than anything else in the world.

—*A. W. Tozer*

DAY 3
Hearing Brings Faith

"She was scared to death," echoes somewhere in your past—a ghost story, a horror flick, or some creepy Stephen King novel. It seems to be the stuff of make-believe. Just maybe someone suffering from a heart condition could drop dead due to trauma. But honestly, could a healthy person be scared to death?

Strangely, fiction writers and doctors concur: It *is* possible to die of fright. In the 1971 *Annals of Internal Medicine,* George Engel, MD, noted how, in the New Testament, the apostle Peter told Ananias, "You have lied not to man but to God," whereupon Ananias, and later his wife, Sapphira, fell down dead. Over a six-year period, Engel compiled press accounts of 170 deaths due to "disrupting life events." Twenty-seven percent of the time (the largest category), the precipitating event involved fear. Here are some examples from the study: "A 63-year-old security guard died after being bound by robbers; A woman seeing some teenagers outside her apartment beating and robbing a bus driver died while phoning the police; A 35-year-old man accused of robbery told his lawyer, 'I'm scared to death,' then collapsed and died."[21]

Rahab confessed to the spies hiding on her rooftop that the citizens of Jericho were "scared out of their wits." Hearing about God's terrifying triumph over the Egyptians and the Amorites had them "shaking in their boots." For some, the news brought terror and faintheartedness. For Rahab, fear brought faith in the mighty God of Israel.

LIFT UP ...

God, You are mighty and awesome! May my heart, like the mountains, melt like wax at the sound of Your voice. Bring me to greater faith as I hear of Your wondrous works. Amen.

LOOK AT ...

Rahab had a great deal going against her: She was a Gentile, an Amorite (Israel's sworn enemy), a woman, and a prostitute. The one thing she had going for her was that she had heard about Israel's God. Where would she have heard of His exploits? Perhaps from the

very men who frequented her establishment. As a result of listening, she began to believe that this God was the one true God.

Hearing brings faith into the lives of those who listen with their hearts as well as their ears. Rahab's faith came by hearing, in contrast to the Israelites who had actually seen God's wonders in the wilderness. The entire generation that witnessed God's wonders perished because of unbelief. Scripture tells us that "faith comes by hearing, and hearing by the word of God" (Rom. 10:17). Won't you be a woman, like Rahab, who believes what she hears?

READ JOSHUA 2:8–13.

Now before they lay down, she came up to them on the roof, and said to the men: "I know that the LORD has given you the land, that the terror of you has fallen on us, and that all the inhabitants of the land are faint-hearted because of you. For we have heard how the LORD dried up the water of the Red Sea for you when you came out of Egypt, and what you did to the two kings of the Amorites who were on the other side of the Jordan, Sihon and Og, whom you utterly destroyed. And as soon as we heard these things, our hearts melted; neither did there remain any more courage in anyone because of you, for the LORD your God, He is God in heaven above and on earth beneath. Now therefore, I beg you, swear to me by the LORD, since I have shown you kindness, that you also will show kindness to my father's house, and give me a true token, and spare my father, my mother, my brothers, my sisters, and all that they have, and deliver our lives from death." Joshua 2:8–13

1. *Now* what happened next?

2. In your own words describe how the inhabitants of the land felt about the Israelites.

3. Describe the events that the residents had heard about.

LEARN ABOUT …

2 Terror

Several Hebrew words are rendered as "terror." All describe tremendous fear capable of agitating both body and mind. Terror can either be the cause or effect of fear.[22] The Canaanites' terror was a fulfillment of God's previous promise: "The LORD your God will put the dread of you and the fear of you upon all the land where you tread" (Deut. 11:25).

LEARN ABOUT ...

4 Territory

The king of Jericho heard the same rumors but never conceded that the land belonged to Israel. However, the Lord had promised this land to the patriarchs and their offspring. And it was God's land to give: "The LORD made a covenant with Abram, saying: 'To your descendants I have given this land'" (Gen. 15:18).

6 A Token

Rahab requested a token and an oath—that they would swear safety to herself and her household by the name of Jehovah, the only true God. This further revealed her faith in Him and devotion toward Him. She truly believed that He would live up to His name as the covenant-keeping God.

7 Fearsome God

The fear of God is expressed three ways: 1) *Superstition* is the fruit of ignorance. 2) *Servile* fear leads to abstinence from many sins because one expects punishment. 3) *Relational* fear springs from love and prompts one to care and therefore not offend God, to please Him in all things.[23]

4. What future event did Rahab know would occur?

5. What did the rumors about the events in Egypt and across the Jordan make Rahab believe about God?

6. What did she ask of the spies?

LIVE OUT ...

7. a. Fear is a powerful motivator. The fear of the Lord is the best type of fear. It describes an awesome respect for God that triggers holy living. List three ways other people have caused you to fear.

    b. Has God ever made you tremble? If so, in what situations?

    c. Is it hard for you to both love and fear God? Why or why not?

8. Rahab's faith was built upon hearing about God's deeds and believing that He would fulfill His promises. Journal about a time when your faith floundered and what restored your heart. What role did Scripture play in restoring you?

9. Rahab revealed an unselfish faith. Her concern for her personal problems did not eclipse her concern for her family. What about you? List the family members you know who need the scarlet thread of redemption. Pray for their salvation.

∘ ∘ ● ∘ ∘

Jason Jones heard the apartment's smoke detector sounding about noon on January 12, 2007. When the detectors in the hallway started to blare,

Jones herded his family down the enclosed stairwell. Suddenly they heard cries from a nearby apartment. Swinging the door open, he spotted a tiny girl through thick gray smoke. Jones grabbed her and pushed her out the front door into the manager's arms.

Somewhere from a back bedroom he heard another child's muffled cry. But flames in the kitchen blocked Jason's path. Scrambling back to his apartment, Jones grabbed a fire extinguisher and ran into the burning apartment. Dousing the flames, he crawled to the bedroom to discover a two-year-old girl. He scooped her into his arms and hurtled out the backdoor. Jones said that he "hates fire," but rescuing the children "was just the right thing to do."[24]

Rahab foresaw the conquest of her country and was as concerned about others as she was about herself. Her concern reflects the heart of other great heroes of the faith. Abraham interceded with God, hoping to rescue as many as possible from Sodom and Gomorrah, including his family members in Lot's household. Others, like "Noah, being divinely warned of things not yet seen, moved with godly fear, prepared an ark for the saving of his household, by which he condemned the world and became heir of the righteousness" (Heb. 11:7).

Saints who honestly believe that God's judgment awaits all sinners will surely seek salvation not only for themselves, but also for those they love. This week, warn those you love about the wrath to come. Beg them to join you on your journey of faith.

LEARN ABOUT …

9 Household

The only thing you can take to heaven is other souls. Make sure those in your household are saved. "And he brought them out and said, 'Sirs, what must I do to be saved?' So they said, 'Believe on the Lord Jesus Christ, and you will be saved, you and your household'" (Acts 16:30–31).

LISTEN TO …

Shame arises from the fear of men, conscience from the fear of God.

—*Samuel Johnson*

DAY 4

House of Safety

On the home front during World War II, slogans urging citizens to do their part to help the war effort flooded the nation. Posters encouraged people to "Carry On, Buy War Bonds"; "Save Your Cans, Help Pass the Ammunition"; and "Plant a Victory Garden: Our Food is Fighting." The war was as much a part of everyday life to those at home as to those who served overseas.

My [Penny's] maternal grandparents did their part. My grandfather built airplanes and my grandmother planted gardens, saved cans, and rationed food. But they took it one step further. Every holiday, my grandfather would go downtown to the train station and pick up two soldiers and bring them back for a home-cooked meal. The soldiers would be treated to my grandmother's delicious turkey, egg noodles, dressing, mashed potatoes, and gravy. To top it off, she'd offer them pie. And my grandmother made the best pie in the world! My grandparents gave the soldiers a little taste of home, then sent them off with fervent prayers.

My grandparents were sad that they had only enough rations to feed two soldiers. But the two were always grateful for a taste of home. Joshua wisely sent only two spies. Perhaps he knew that only two could surreptitiously enter Jericho. A larger presence might be captured. Perhaps Joshua figured that more than two would bring back differing answers, as when he himself had spied out the land. For whatever reason, sending two spies was a wise decision. They found their answers in Rahab's house and made plans to report to Joshua.

LIFT UP ...

Lord God, let my home be a place of sanctuary for those who enter it. Let everyone know that You dwell in the midst of my home. Let me be a faithful friend to those who honor me with their presence. Amen.

LOOK AT ...

Rahab welcomed the two spies and proved her allegiance to God by protecting them from the king of Jericho. Of all the citizens in Jericho who had heard of the wonders of the Hebrew God, she alone came to saving faith and shared it with others. Today we see her make a covenant with the spies about the Hebrew army's return to her town. She learned how she and her family could stay safe in her home.

God had instructed the people through Moses, "When the LORD your God delivers them over to you, you shall conquer them and utterly destroy them. You shall make no covenant with them nor show mercy to them" (Deut. 7:2). The Hebrew spies were faced with negotiating a verbal agreement to show mercy to Rahab despite her heritage as a Canaanite. Perhaps they recalled God's promise to Abraham that "in your seed *all* the nations of the earth shall be blessed" (Gen. 22:18, emphasis added). Or maybe they recalled the time God hid Moses in the cleft of the rock and declared Himself "the LORD, the LORD God, merciful and gracious, longsuffering, and abounding in goodness and truth" (Ex. 34:6). Let's follow the example of these brave men and remember to choose mercy over judgment.

READ JOSHUA 2:14–20.

So the men answered her, "Our lives for yours, if none of you tell this business of ours. And it shall be, when the LORD has given us the land, that we will deal kindly and truly with you." Then she let them down by a rope through the window, for her house was on the city wall; she dwelt on the wall. And she said to them, "Get to the mountain, lest the pursuers meet you. Hide there three days, until the pursuers have returned. Afterward you may go your way." So the men said to her: "We will be blameless of this oath of yours which you have made us swear, unless, when we come into the land, you bind this line of scarlet cord in the window through which you let us down, and unless you bring your father, your mother, your brothers, and all your father's household to your own home. So it shall be that whoever goes outside the doors of your house into the street, his blood shall be on his own head, and we will be guiltless. And whoever is with you in the house, his blood shall be on our head if a hand is laid on him. And if you tell this business of ours, then we will be free from your oath which you made us swear." Joshua 2:14–20

1. Describe how the men promised to protect Rahab for keeping their secret and what they expected in return.

LEARN ABOUT ...

I Pledge

The spies made a verbal contract with Rahab to give their lives in return for hers if they did not keep their end of the bargain to protect her family from their assault on Jericho. This compact involved each party agreeing to do certain things in return for the other party fulfilling their part of the bargain.

---

3 Protection

Also known as the Moon City because the people practiced lunar worship, Jericho was the key to Canaan. As such, two walls highly fortified it. Villages were unwalled, but cities were protected with defensive barricades made of stones or brick: "Cities were fortified with high walls, gates, and bars" (Deut. 3:5).

---

5 Poster

The scarlet cord was the signal the spies arranged with Rahab to ensure she was keeping her part of the contract. It could be that the scarlet cord was her signage advertising her business and that it normally hung from her window. Thus, it would go unnoticed by the king's men.

2. How did they promise to treat her?

3. Describe how she helped the spies escape and what made her job easier.

4. What instructions did Rahab give the spies? How did this match Joshua's timeline for crossing the Jordan?

5. What sign would Rahab give to indicate she was keeping her oath?

6. Describe who would fall under the oath and who would be exempt.

7. What would nullify their verbal contract?

LIVE OUT ...

8. a. Verbal contracts are a part of everyday life. Describe some of the things you promise people and the conditions you place on these promises.

   b. On a scale of one to ten, how would you rate your promise-keeping ability?

   c. What is one thing God has promised you? What passage in the Bible states that promise?

   d. Find a Scripture verse that speaks of how God keeps His promises. How has He proven this to you?

9. The city walls protected ancient people *from* their enemies. God spoke figuratively of walls called Salvation that protect us *for*

eternity (see Isa. 60:18). According to Philippians 4:7 and 2 Thessalonians 3:3, summarize some ways God protects us. Can you think of others?

10. God doesn't ask us to tie scarlet cords outside our homes, but He does ask us to show evidence of living faith. If a guest visited your home, how would they know you were a follower of Christ?

o   o   ●   o   o

The color of blood is a scarlet thread woven through the history of God's people. It began with the first animal sacrifice in the garden of Eden, offered by God Himself, to cover Adam and Eve's nakedness and restore fellowship with their Maker. Later the blood of a ram took the place of Abraham's beloved son on the altar of sacrifice.

The scarlet thread is woven through time to the captivity in Egypt when the River Nile turned crimson. It is woven through the day that doorposts were stained with lambs' blood so that God would pass over the homes and spare the Hebrews' firstborn sons. Then onward it went to the dripping altars of sacrifice made to atone for the sins of a wandering people.

The Israelite spies found shelter in the house of Rahab, a "scarlet woman," who heard what the God of Israel had done when he parted the Red Sea, how blood had covered the battlefield when the Israelites encountered the despicable Amorites. This courageous woman was protected by the scarlet cord and ultimately became part of the bloodline of Jesus Christ.

Artists know that red is a dominant color. Even a small dab in a painting will draw your eyes toward it. Rahab tossed a scarlet cord to capture the spies' attention: *Hands off this house!* God threw out the

LEARN ABOUT ...

8 Promises

Isn't it wonderful to live in relationship with a God who keeps *all* of His promises? "All the promises of God in Him are Yes, and in Him Amen" (2 Cor. 1:20). The Promise-Maker helps us to become promise-keepers: "His divine power has given to us all things that pertain to life and godliness" (2 Peter 1:3).

9 Protection

In Philippians 4:7, *guard* is a military term. It means to keep by guarding with a garrison, to provide protection against an enemy. It implies the sense of security the believer has when he or she places all that matters into God's hand. It also speaks of inward garrisoning or fortification by the Holy Spirit.[25]

scarlet lifeline of salvation, so when He looks at us through Jesus' blood, all He sees is white—pure white.

LISTEN TO ...

My case is bad, Lord, be my advocate, My sin is red; I'm under God's arrest.

—*Edward Taylor*

DAY 5
Heralds of Hope

Gathering information about the enemy is as old as warfare itself. People chosen for work in military intelligence are screened for high intellect and psychological stability. Intelligence agents gather, analyze, protect, and disseminate information about the enemy, terrain, and weather in places of interest. Intelligence activities are conducted at both tactical and strategic levels during both peacetime and war. Most militaries throughout the world maintain a military intelligence corps with specialized intelligence. Military intelligence has four phases:

- ❏ Collection: This consists of assessing an adversary's capabilities and vulnerabilities, such as the population, ethnic makeup, and main industries of a region.
- ❏ Analysis: This consists of analyzing an adversary's capabilities and vulnerabilities, looking for threats and opportunities.
- ❏ Processing: Critical vulnerabilities are indexed in a way that makes them easily available to advisors and intelligence personnel who package the information for policy makers and fighters.
- ❏ Dissemination: Policy makers are ultimately presented with a list of threats and opportunities. They approve some action whereby the professional military personnel plan the detailed act and carry it out.[26]

We've observed the spies in Joshua go through the first two stages of intelligence gathering: They have collected and analyzed their enemy's weaknesses. Now they must return to their top military advisor to process the enemy's vulnerabilities so he can come up with a plan. Joshua will disseminate the information to the troops so they can cross the Jordan and conquer Jericho.

LIFT UP ...

Father, help me to be a messenger of hope to those I encounter. May I trust You to deliver me into all of the promises You have for me. Amen.

LEARN ABOUT ...

1 Covenant

A covenant is simply an agreement; a contract between two or more parties with certain conditions laid down for all parties to obey. Covenants are found throughout Scripture. "I have also established My covenant with them, to give them the land of Canaan, the land of their pilgrimage, in which they were strangers" (Ex. 6:4).

---

4 Comprehensive

The two spies were thorough in recounting to Joshua all the details of their encounter with Rahab. Unlike their predecessors, they returned full of faith that inspired the entire nation to believe God's deliverance was at hand: "Faith is the substance of things hoped for, the evidence of things not seen" (Heb. 11:1).

LOOK AT ...

We've seen how Rahab made a contract with the spies to protect her household from harm, then developed a signal so the Israelites would know which house was hers. Today we see the spies go on their way and become heralds of hope to Joshua.

Many people presume that Joshua wrote this historic book himself. If so, perhaps he wanted to emphasize that God welcomed the faith of a Canaanite female. How gracious of God to receive Rahab into His new nation and into His family without arms or bloodshed. We find that Joshua only reenters the story at the end of this chapter when the spies make their analysis and report.

READ JOSHUA 2:21–24.

Then she said, "According to your words, so be it." And she sent them away, and they departed. And she bound the scarlet cord in the window. They departed and went to the mountain, and stayed there three days until the pursuers returned. The pursuers sought them all along the way, but did not find them. So the two men returned, descended from the mountain, and crossed over; and they came to Joshua the son of Nun, and told him all that had befallen them. And they said to Joshua, "Truly the LORD has delivered all the land into our hands, for indeed all the inhabitants of the country are fainthearted because of us." Joshua 2:21–24

1. In what two ways did Rahab confirm the contract?

2. Describe how the spies followed Rahab's instructions.

3. What three vivid verbs does the text use to describe how the men returned to Joshua?

4. The spies told Joshua "all that had befallen them." Think back over what they learned at Rahab's house. What details would a military commander particularly benefit from knowing?

5. What did the spies "truly" believe?

6. Upon what did they base this conviction?

7. God made covenants with several people in the Bible. Fill in the table below to discover who He entered into covenant with. Note whether the covenant was conditional or unconditional.

Scripture	Covenant With	Conditional or Unconditional
Genesis 9:8–17		
Genesis 15:12–17		
Exodus 34:10–34		
2 Samuel 7:11–16		

Live out ...

8. The spies told Joshua *all* that had befallen them. Their witness bolstered the commander's faith and rallied a nation to advance on enemy territory. Journal about a faith-building circumstance in your life. Don't leave out the important details!

9. The spies reported that the Canaanites were fainthearted. Perhaps if they had turned their fainthearts to faithhearts, they would have been saved like Rahab. Reword 1 Thessalonians 5:14 into a prayer for someone you know who is fainthearted.

Learn about ...

6 Cowards

Rahab had reported that the hearts of the people had melted within them. The spies conveyed the Canaanites' emotional state of mind as "fainthearted." Fainthearted literally means "little spirited." It signifies one who is laboring under such trouble that his heart sinks within him.

7 New Covenant

The new covenant was promised so God could accomplish what the old covenant (based on the Law) had failed to do: "The days are coming, says the LORD, when I will make a new covenant" (Jer. 31:31). This new covenant was fulfilled in the death of Jesus. Now God writes His Law on our hearts.

9 Conversion

Joshua wandered in the wilderness for forty years. Why did he need three additional days before entering the land? To send two spies on a reconnaissance mission so they could meet Rahab, comfort her fearful heart, and reassure her of the Lord's promises. God was patiently waiting for one more soul's conversion.

o o ● o o

How were you saved? Did you convert during a foxhole confession? Were you wooed into the kingdom as an impressionable child at Sunday school? Or did you utter a silent prayer in the privacy of your own room? Whatever the circumstance of the sacred moment, there was a faithful witness (or more than one) who led you to that moment. Someone somewhere told you about the Savior and the scarlet blood He shed for you. Thank God for those bold enough to tell us the truth!

The two spies told Joshua *all* that had befallen them. They did not leave out a single detail of their deliverance from the king or the dedication of Rahab the harlot. Through their faithful witness, Rahab became a proselyte to God's precious covenants. As a result, her blood would not be on their hands. Instead, a scarlet cord would hang from her home and link her forever to the Messiah.

Paul, too, was a faithful witness sharing the entire counsel of God with the church in Ephesus. Therefore he wasn't accountable for the fate of those who would not believe. "Therefore I testify to you this day that I am innocent of the blood of all men. For I have not shunned to declare to you the whole counsel of God" (Acts 20:26–27).

This week you have been exhorted to list those unbelievers who are dear to you and to pray for their salvation. You've also been challenged to make sure that those entering your home know of your faith through your decor or decorum. However, the most powerful witness includes a verbal testimony that imparts the gospel in its entirety to those who are lost in sin. Make sure that you impart the entire counsel of God to those around you.

LISTEN TO ...

The church as a whole must be concerned with both evangelism and social action. It is not a case of either-or; it is both-and. Anything less is only a partial gospel, not the whole counsel of God.

—*Robert D. Dehaan*

Stepping Out in Faith

Joshua 3—4

Our founding fathers stepped out in faith. On December 21, 1620, the Mayflower dropped anchor in Plymouth Bay with Captain Christopher Jones at her helm. The grueling journey across the Atlantic had taken sixty-six days. Disease and hardship afflicted the 102 passengers.

Sadly, the first bleak New England winter claimed over half the travelers. When spring unfolded, Captain Jones stood before the forty-one surviving Pilgrims to thank them for their kindness in nursing his crew back to health. Before heading home he offered, "If any of you wish to return to England, I will give you free passage."

Governor William Bradford replied, "Men, you have heard the captain's offer…. Do any of you wish to return to England?"

"No," they answered. "Our homes are here and here we will stay."

Not even those who had been orphaned or widowed accepted the offer. Instead, they all signed the Mayflower Compact, which stated, "In the name of God Amen…. Having undertaken for the glory of God and Advancement of the Christian Faith," the pioneers dedicated themselves to the new land and to the political and religious freedom that life in America offered. Faith prompted their voyage; faith sustained them through hardship; and faith sustained them in the new land.[27]

Israel's founding fathers also stepped out in faith for God's glory and to further His kingdom. They didn't sail across an ocean; they passed over the dried-up Red Sea and through the harrowing wilderness. And by faith they would cross the mighty Jordan River to reach their new land.

Day 1: Joshua 3:1–6   **MARCHING ORDERS**

Day 2: Joshua 3:7–11   **MAGNIFYING JOSHUA**

Day 3: Joshua 3:12–17; 4:10–18   **THE MIRACLE**

Day 4: Joshua 4:1–9; 4:19–20   **MANUFACTURING MONUMENTS**

Day 5: Joshua 4:21–24   **MAKING MEMORIES**

DAY 1
Marching Orders

LIFT UP ...

Lord, teach me to wait on You for instruction. I want to be so attuned to Your voice and to see You work wonders in my life. Thank You for Your promise to guide me. Amen.

LOOK AT ...

Throughout the wanderings in the wilderness, a pillar of smoke and fire revealed God's presence in the midst of His people. By the time Joshua took command, the ark of the covenant represented God's presence. The priests carried it before the fledgling nation as a constant reminder of their dependence on almighty God. Unlike at the parting of the Red Sea, the priests bearing the ark needed to faithfully step into the raging Jordan before its waters would recede. Then the people would file through on dry land.

Because the ark introduced the presence of the holy God in their midst, the Lord required the people to make special preparation. The people were asked to sanctify themselves through ritual bathing and a change of clothing. Out of reverence, they were commanded to keep a respectable distance between themselves and the ark.

We, too, can march forward in faith, rather than meandering in the wilderness of unbelief, because our Lord assures us of His presence. He said, "I am with you always, even to the end of the age" (Matt. 28:20). No matter what obstacle you face, launch out in faith. And when God prevails by accomplishing the impossible on your behalf, give Him all of the glory.

READ JOSHUA 3:1–6.

Then Joshua rose early in the morning; and they set out from Acacia Grove and came to the Jordan, he and all the children of Israel, and lodged there before they crossed over. So it was,

LEARN ABOUT ...

1 Early to Rise

Joshua is an Old Testament type of Jesus Christ delivering his people from their enemies. His devotional life displayed similar habits to those of our Lord: "Now in the morning, having risen a long while before daylight, He went out and departed to a solitary place; and there He prayed" (Mark 1:35).

3 The Ark

The ark was a portable chest made of acacia wood and overlaid with gold. The two cherubims with outstretched wings facing each other comprised the cover, known as the "mercy seat." They marked the place where the Lord dwelt, where the Lord communicated with Moses.[28] The ark represented God's holiness and presence among His people.

6 Sanctification

Rather than sharpening their swords, Joshua commanded the people to sanctify their hearts because the battle would be spiritual, not physical. Sanctification represented a new start, which was accomplished through bathing and changing clothes. The distance the people were to keep reminded them of the sacredness of the ark and of God's holiness.

after three days, that the officers went through the camp; and they commanded the people, saying, "When you see the ark of the covenant of the LORD your God, and the priests, the Levites, bearing it, then you shall set out from your place and go after it. Yet there shall be a space between you and it, about two thousand cubits by measure. Do not come near it, that you may know the way by which you must go, for you have not passed this way before." And Joshua said to the people, "Sanctify yourselves, for tomorrow the LORD will do wonders among you." Then Joshua spoke to the priests, saying, "Take up the ark of the covenant and cross over before the people." So they took up the ark of the covenant and went before the people.
Joshua 3:1–6

1. How did the people demonstrate they were waiting for God to show them how to cross the Jordan River?

2. How long was it before they were ready to cross?

3. What signal did the people look for before they proceeded farther?

4. What warning did Joshua give the people concerning the ark of the covenant?

5. Why were they told to follow the Levites?

6. Describe what action was required of the people and how God planned to respond.

7. In what sequence were the people to cross the Jordan?

LIVE OUT ...

8. Joshua did not hurry across the Jordan or rush into battle.

Instead, he waited on the Lord to prepare his heart as well as the people's hearts and minds. Are you hasty when facing your battles? Using the word WAIT as an acrostic, list four ways you'll wait on God before your next conflict. For instance, you might consider *Working* on your relationship.

W

A

I

T

LEARN ABOUT ...

8 Time to Wait

Time spent waiting is never wasted. God uses it to strengthen us for what is to come. Waiting provides time for a perspective check, seeking to see things through the eyes of faith rather than the flesh. "Wait on the LORD; Be of good courage, And He shall strengthen your heart; Wait, I say, on the LORD!" (Ps. 27:14).

9. The ark of the covenant represented God's holiness and presence. It contained three mementos of their desert wandering (see Heb. 9:4). Look up the following passages and write down what lessons the people were to remember from each of these items:

   A golden jar of manna (see Deut. 8:2–3)

   Aaron's rod that had budded (see Num. 17:1–11)

   The stone tablets of the covenant (see Ex. 31:18)

10 Set Apart

To sanctify means to set apart for God's purpose. The articles of the tabernacle were set apart for worship, not work. Both items and individuals can be sanctified. Jesus asks His people to be set apart: "That He might sanctify and cleanse it with the washing of water by the word" (Eph. 5:26 KJV).

10. Reflect on the precautions the people took so God would manifest His presence, and think about some symbolic ways you can sanctify yourself. Journal about the ways in which you prepare yourself to seek the Lord.

o o ● o o

A good leader leads by example. Leaders don't require anything from their followers that they would not ask of themselves. Jesus embodied this philosophy throughout His ministry. He endured persecution and so did His disciples: "'A servant is not greater than his master.' If they persecuted Me, they will also persecute you" (John 15:20). Jesus laid down His life to save the lost. Eventually most of the apostles died gruesome deaths. John imparted this philosophy to Christ's followers: "By this we know love, because He laid down His life for us. And we also ought to lay down our lives for the brethren" (1 John 3:16).

Joshua was well able to lead by example. He faithfully followed Moses for forty years, and now he asked the priests and tribal leaders to follow his lead. Joshua's example of going on a reconnaissance mission surely inspired the two spies to scout out the land. Having crossed the Red Sea with Moses, Joshua could encourage the priests to be the first to step into the overflowing Jordan.

There's a noticeable difference between a boss and a leader: "A boss creates fear; a leader creates confidence. Bossism creates resentment; leadership breeds enthusiasm. A boss says, 'I'; a leader says, 'We.' A boss fixes blame; a leader fixes mistakes. A boss knows how; a leader shows how. Bossism makes work drudgery; leadership makes work interesting. A boss relies on authority; a leader relies on cooperation. A boss drives; a leader leads."[29]

LISTEN TO ...

Faith is the person stepping out into the unknown, obeying God's commands.

—Unknown

DAY 2

Magnifying Joshua

Chuck Smith, founder of the Calvary Chapel movement, passed on this motto to those considering the ministry: "Whom God anoints, man appoints." This clever aphorism challenges fledgling ministers that before they seek a title or position there must be evidence of God's hand on their lives. That's good advice and godly counsel. Paul exhorted Timothy, "Do your best to present yourself to God as one approved, a workman who does not need to be ashamed and who correctly handles the word of truth" (2 Tim. 2:15 NIV).

For four decades the younger generation had watched Joshua serve under Moses. They knew him as a mighty warrior. They knew that he had ascended Mt. Sinai. They knew that he sat outside the tent when Moses talked with God. But perhaps they wondered, "Will God still be with us now that Moses has departed?" Perhaps they even wondered if they should follow Caleb or one of the younger promising leaders from their own generation.

But God has a way of making His divine appointments known. When choosing a wife for Isaac, Abraham's servant prayed that the one who said, "Drink, and I will also give your camels a drink," would be "appointed for … Isaac" (Gen. 24:14). In the book of Acts, when the apostles grew overwhelmed with the heavy workload, they sought "out from among [them] seven men of good reputation, full of the Holy Spirit and wisdom [to] … appoint over this business" (6:3).

God doesn't always use the same means to make his appointments known, but He *does* make them known so that we can follow His lead.

LIFT UP …

Lord, help me to follow those You exalt. Help me to know what You have appointed me to do. Amen.

LOOK AT …

Yesterday we saw the Israelites prepare themselves for crossing the Jordan by setting out from

LEARN ABOUT ...

1 Exalted

To exalt literally means to magnify, promote, or make large. It speaks of a position of dignity, honor, or rank. In this case, God was affirming Joshua's rank as commander and governor of the people. Jesus taught that "whosoever shall exalt himself shall be abased, and he that shall humble himself shall be exalted" (Matt. 23:12 KJV).

3 Priests

Priests were the official worship leaders who represented the people before God and conducted rituals to atone for sin. God appointed Aaron as the first high priest. Thus, Aaron and his descendants were established as the priestly line carrying out important duties as a special class devoted to God's service.[30]

Acacia Grove and sanctifying themselves unto the Lord. Today we see God magnify Joshua as the leader of the Hebrew nation.

God promised to honor Joshua and publicly confirm his position. Acting in accordance with his responsibility as leader of the nation, Joshua took command not only of the people, but also of the priests, placing them into marching position. He would lead the entire nation into battle. Crossing the Red Sea was indeed miraculous and faith building. But the people wound up only in the Sinai wilderness. By crossing the Jordan, the people would find themselves in a place of no return, in a land filled with strong enemies, iron chariots, and walled cities. They would need a strong leader to guide them against their foes and help them take the land. The leader would need God's wisdom to guide him.

READ JOSHUA 3:7–11.

And the LORD said to Joshua, "This day I will begin to exalt you in the sight of all Israel, that they may know that, as I was with Moses, so I will be with you. You shall command the priests who bear the ark of the covenant, saying, 'When you have come to the edge of the water of the Jordan, you shall stand in the Jordan.'" So Joshua said to the children of Israel, "Come here, and hear the words of the LORD your God." And Joshua said, "By this you shall know that the living God is among you, and that He will without fail drive out from before you the Canaanites and the Hittites and the Hivites and the Perizzites and the Girgashites and the Amorites and the Jebusites: Behold, the ark of the covenant of the Lord of all the earth is crossing over before you into the Jordan." Joshua 3:7–11

1. Explain who chose to honor Joshua, where, when, and why.

2. Who was Joshua instructed to approach first?

3. What was Joshua to command them to do?

4. Then who would Joshua address?

5. What enticement did Joshua use to summon the people?

6. What would the people come to know about their God and His ability to conquer their enemies?

7. Describe what would precede the people on their crossing.

LIVE OUT …

8. God promised to exalt Joshua at the Jordan River. Read Matthew 3:13–17 and describe who else was exalted there and the circumstances surrounding this event.

9. a. In the days of Joshua, Aaron's descendants were the only people qualified to be priests. Read 1 Peter 2:9–10. Who does God now consider priests?

   b. What should we accomplish in this role?

   c. Contrast the difference between what we once were and what we are now.

10. a. One sign of God among His people was the ark of the covenant. Read Colossians 1:3–8 and summarize the evidence of God "among" His people today.

    b. Describe some evidence you've seen of God's presence recently.

LEARN ABOUT …

8 Well Pleased

Joshua was exalted by God and men. Jesus was exalted by God but humiliated by men's treatment of Him when they failed to see Him as Messiah. The book of Joshua tells us that "Israel served the LORD all the days of Joshua" (Josh. 24:31). Sadly, when the true Joshua—Jesus—was born, "He came to His own, and His own did not receive Him" (John 1:11).

9 Priesthood

Priests have four characteristics: 1) Chosen of God; 2) Property of God; 3) Holy to God; and 4) Offer gifts to God. Since Christ came as High Priest and King, believing Jews and Gentiles are called priests and kings: "[Jesus Christ] has made us kings and priests to His God and Father" (Rev. 1:6).[31]

o o ● o o

Elaborate processions and parades date back centuries. They have been memorialized on ancient monuments such as Egyptian hieroglyphics, the great Panathenaic procession of the Parthenon, and Roman triumphal reliefs like the famous Arch of Titus in Rome.

Such processions serve a number of important purposes. Some processionals are commercial. Think of the Olympic parades that advertise the "thrill of victory and the agony of defeat." The opening and closing pageants are big moneymakers for network television and for the host countries. Other parades are celebratory, commemorating past events such as war victories. These help instill national pride and remind people of their shared history. Still other processionals are for the purpose of conquest. Usually countries display their arms in order to instill fear in their enemies. Another reason to hold a parade is ceremonial: to perform religious services such as weddings, funerals, or church services.

When God initiated the processional across the Jordan River, it served several functions. Gathering the people consolidated the Israelites into a unified team so they could move forward as a new nation. It also set them into the proper order for their ceremonial crossing of the river, ensuring that the ark of the covenant, carried by the priests, would be given the preeminence it deserved. The parade set the precedent that the visible presence of God would lead the way. The stage was set for a victory parade.

Listen to ...

However exalted our position, we should still not despise the powers of the humble.

—Periander of Corinth

DAY 3

The Miracle

Travelers to Maui are likely to journey along the twisting-turning Highway 36 down the northeastern shore to capture a small glimpse of heaven. They drive past miles of mesmerizing seascape, view majestic waterfalls, observe the beauty of creation at botanical gardens, see a wealth of foliage at the verdant rain forests, and peek at bleak black lava flows. This heavenly highway leads to the tropical village of Hana.

Some jest that God was working overtime when He created the natural wonders of Hana, Hawaii. But locals say God went out of His way to work a miracle when their ancestors began building a church in 1860. Legend says men were diving for coral to make stone for the church, but the process was difficult and dangerous since the coral was deep offshore. They were forced to swim out far, dive deep, and come up with only small amounts of coral each dive. Then a storm hit and swept coral from the deep onto the beach. This allowed the community to gather what they needed and finish their building. When the church was completed, another storm came and washed the coral back out to sea. They decided to name the church The Coral Miracle Church.[32]

A miracle is an event or phenomenon that seems to violate natural laws. Parting a sea, raising the dead, or healing the lame reveals God's glory, power, and love to His people.[33] Throughout the book of Joshua, we'll see God work miracles on behalf of His chosen people. Today, we see God start at the Jordan River.

LIFT UP ...

Lord, I'm amazed at the miracles You perform that defy explanation. Help me to have complete confidence when I go into those places You have prepared for me. Amen.

LOOK AT ...

Yesterday we saw God promise to magnify Joshua in the presence of the people. In response, Joshua gathered the people and the priests, instructing them to prepare for the crossing of the Jordan River. Today, we see Joshua initiate the activity leading to the first miracle of the Canaanite conquest.

While the Red Sea parting and the heaping of the Jordan both involved the people miraculously crossing large bodies of water, the miracles were different in several respects. In the first place, at the exodus they were heading away from Egypt, but at the Jordan they were heading home to the Promised Land. Second, they were escaping captivity at the exodus, but here they were conquering enemies. Third, Pharaoh's army perished when the Red Sea returned to its natural condition, but no one perished during the miracle at the Jordan River. Fourth, God worked the miracle at the Red Sea despite the people's murmuring. At the banks of the Jordan, we see the Israelites walking forward in faith.

There are both similarities and differences that could be elaborated on concerning the miracles in the desert. But the important thing to remember is that God is still in the miracle business. He is not limited to performing miracles in the same way He always has. His ways are always fresh, always new, and always perfect for the occasion. Won't you trust God to part whatever river you are facing today?

READ JOSHUA 3:12–17.

"Now therefore, take for yourselves twelve men from the tribes of Israel, one man from every tribe. And it shall come to pass, as soon as the soles of the feet of the priests who bear the ark of the LORD, the Lord of all the earth, shall rest in the waters of the Jordan, that the waters of the Jordan shall be cut off, the waters that come down from upstream, and they shall stand as a heap." So it was, when the people set out from their camp to cross over the Jordan, with the priests bearing the ark of the covenant before the people, and as those who bore the ark came to the Jordan, and the feet of the priests who bore the ark dipped in the edge of the water (for the Jordan overflows all its banks during the whole time of harvest), that the waters which came down from upstream stood still, and rose in a heap very far away at Adam, the city that is beside Zaretan. So the waters that went down into the Sea of the Arabah, the Salt Sea, failed, and were cut off; and the people crossed over opposite Jericho. Then the priests who bore the ark of the covenant of the LORD stood firm on dry ground in the midst of the Jordan; and all Israel crossed over on dry ground, until all the people had crossed completely over the Jordan. Joshua 3:12–17*

1. Joshua told the people to select one man from each of the twelve tribes (see 3:12), but he didn't plan to explain those men's job until 4:2, after the people experienced something amazing. At what moment did he predict that the waters would be cut off?

2. The ark was a heavy wooden chest overlaid with gold. Poles were threaded through rings attached to the ark. The priests could hoist the ark by the poles and carry it. Try to picture the scene as the priests headed down the steep riverbank toward the roiling waters. Describe the scene from there step-by-step in detail.

3. What would have been the challenging parts of this situation for a priest carrying the ark?

LOOK AT ...

As He had with the Red Sea, God miraculously made a way for the chosen people to move forward on dry land. Now let's move ahead to Joshua 4:10–18 to learn more about this miraculous moment in Israel's history.

So the priests who bore the ark stood in the midst of the Jordan until everything was finished that the LORD had commanded Joshua to speak to the people, according to all that Moses had commanded Joshua; and the people hurried and crossed over. Then it came to pass, when all the people had completely crossed over, that the ark of the LORD and the priests crossed over in the presence of the people. And the men of Reuben, the men of Gad, and half the tribe of Manasseh crossed over armed before the children of Israel, as Moses had spoken to them. About forty thousand prepared for war crossed over before the LORD for battle, to the plains of Jericho. On that day the LORD exalted Joshua in the sight of all Israel; and they feared him, as they had feared Moses, all the days of his life. Then the LORD spoke to Joshua, saying, "Command the

Learn about ...

4 Finished

The priests stood in the middle of the Jordan River "until everything was finished." This foreshadowed the death of Christ on the cross: "He said, 'It is finished!' And bowing His head, He gave up His spirit" (John 19:30). The phrase literally means paid in full or accomplished completely.

priests who bear the ark of the Testimony to come up from the Jordan." Joshua therefore commanded the priests, saying, "Come up from the Jordan." And it came to pass, when the priests who bore the ark of the covenant of the LORD had come from the midst of the Jordan, and the soles of the priests' feet touched the dry land, that the waters of the Jordan returned to their place and overflowed all its banks as before. Joshua 4:10–18

4. Explain what happened during the time the priests stayed "in the midst of the Jordan."

5. "Then" recount what "came to pass."

6. What do you think the text means when it says that the forty thousand soldiers crossed over "before the LORD"?

7. Explain in detail what the passage says happened "on that day." Try utilizing transitional words like *then* to help tell the story.

Live out ...

8. a. Today we saw that Joshua described God as "Lord of all the earth." Fill in the following chart to discover other things God is Lord of.

Scripture	Lord Of
Deuteronomy 10:17	
1 Samuel 1:11	
Matthew 11:25	
Mark 2:28	
Acts 10:36	
2 Thessalonians 3:16	
Revelation 19:16	

b. Which area in your life do you need to allow God to be Lord of? Use one of the Scriptures in the chart to write a personal prayer giving Him lordship over that area of your life.

9. The priests carrying the ark into the Jordan River could symbolize Christ's death on the cross. In order for us to cross into victorious Christian living, we, too, must put some things to death. What is one thing you sense God wants to put to death so you can live a godly life? (Think of a sin, an unloving attitude, or an attachment to something that you treat as more important than God. You don't have to name this thing to your group.)

10. Just as the priests stayed in the Jordan until their work was finished, Jesus stayed on the cross until His work was finished. Talk about the work God has given you to do and how He is empowering you to complete it.

∘ ∘ ● ∘ ∘

I (Penny) vividly remember getting baptized. I was a young girl attending church camp at Glorieta, New Mexico, when I heard God call my name. I went home and told my parents about my personal experience with God. I wanted Him to be Lord of my life. In the denomination we belonged to, the next step was to "make a public profession of faith." But I was too shy to walk to the front of the church. For weeks my parents sat me on the aisle, hoping I'd have the courage to go forward. After about a month, I finally had the courage to walk forward. The moment I set my foot down, I wasn't afraid anymore. I knew I had a heavenly companion.

That afternoon I met with my pastor, who told me the meaning of baptism. He held up his hands in the shape of a cross and explained that my body was like the vertical line of the cross. My going down into the

LEARN ABOUT …

8 Lord

The title *Lord* speaks of power or authority. In the Old Testament the root word is *adonai.* The New Testament root word is *kurios.* It speaks of possession or ownership and signifies placing the disposal of anything at His feet.[36] It's been said that if Christ is not the Lord *of* all, He is not the Lord *at* all.

_____

9 Life

Christ's death, resurrection, and ascension allow us to live a resurrected life in this world. When we recognize our sins and confess them, Jesus puts them behind us so we don't have to keep blaming ourselves: "For godly sorrow produces repentance leading to salvation, not to be regretted; but the sorrow of the world produces death" (2 Cor. 7:10).

water was symbolic of dying to my old life. Rising from the water would be like rising to new life in Christ. That visual illustration has always stayed with me.

In the same way, crossing the Jordan River was a visual illustration for the Hebrew nation of baptism into a new life. When they walked down into the riverbed, they were "dying" to their old life; when they walked out on the other side of the river, they were baptized into a new life.

LISTEN TO ...

A baptism of holiness, a demonstration of godly living is the crying need of our day.

—*Duncan Campbell*

DAY 4

Manufacturing Monuments

Throughout history, monumental circumstances have inspired civilizations to erect monuments of varying shapes. Columns with statues often celebrate great leaders like Admiral Nelson at Trafalgar Square in London. Triumphal arches are another form of monument. Napoleon Bonaparte commissioned the Arc de Triomphe in Paris after a great victory. Made of a single piece of stone, an obelisk is a tall, thin, four-sided, tapering monument that ends in a pyramidal top. Obelisks originated in ancient Egypt and were placed in pairs at the entrance of pagan temples. In more modern times, monuments represent an individual's influence on a community. Washington, D.C., is chock-full of them: The Lincoln Memorial, Jefferson Memorial, and the obelisk-shaped Washington Monument are just a few of the monuments that dot our nation's capital.

Similar to monuments, memorial stones represent one of the recurring themes in Joshua. At Gilgal and in the midst of the Jordan, Joshua erected two pillars of rocks commemorating the miraculous river crossing. At the mountains of Ebal and Gerizim, two stones of "blessing and cursing" reaffirmed the laws of Moses. A "witness stone" at Shechem recalled the covenant between God and His people. Finally, the Transjordan tribes set up a stone monument to establish their children as part of the Israelite nation.

We all face battles to win, obstacles to conquer, and enemies to defeat. Like Israel, victory comes to those who trust and obey. Our Lord assures us of His presence: "I am with you always, even to the end of the age" (Matt. 28:20). And when God prevails, we should give Him the glory by remembering His work in our midst and erecting a monument to His holy name.

LIFT UP ...

Lord, You have done great things at different moments in my life, the greatest of which is saving me. Help me to remember these moments in tangible ways. May I share them with the people around me so they, too, will see Your faithfulness. Amen.

LOOK AT ...

Yesterday we saw the people cross the Jordan River on dry ground while the priests stood with the ark of the covenant in the midst of the riverbed. Today we see God command Joshua to build two memorials to commemorate this important crossing.

Some people believe that when John the Baptist was baptizing in the wilderness of Judea and rebuked the Pharisees by saying, "God is able to raise up children to Abraham from these stones" (Matt. 3:9), John pointed to the very stones Joshua had raised up when crossing the Jordan River. J. Vernon McGee said, "Some of the important things in this chapter are that the ark goes before and divides the Jordan River—not the rod of Moses. The ark goes before, carried by priests. Christ goes before us through death but also through this life. Jordan is typical of Christ's death, not ours."[37]

READ JOSHUA 4:1–9.

And it came to pass, when all the people had completely crossed over the Jordan, that the LORD spoke to Joshua, saying: "Take for yourselves twelve men from the people, one man from every tribe, and command them, saying, 'Take for yourselves twelve stones from here, out of the midst of the Jordan, from the place where the priests' feet stood firm. You shall carry them over with you and leave them in the lodging place where you lodge tonight.'" Then Joshua called the twelve men whom he had appointed from the children of Israel, one man from every tribe; and Joshua said to them: "Cross over before the ark of the LORD your God into the midst of the Jordan, and each one of you take up a stone on his shoulder, according to the number of the tribes of the children of Israel, that this may be a sign among you when your children ask in time to come, saying, 'What do these stones mean to you?' Then you shall answer them that the waters of the Jordan were cut off before the ark of the covenant of the LORD; when it crossed over the Jordan, the waters of the Jordan were cut off. And these stones shall be for a memorial to the children of Israel forever." And the children of Israel did so, just as Joshua commanded, and took up twelve stones from the midst of the Jordan, as the LORD had spoken to Joshua, according to the number of the tribes of the children of Israel, and carried them over with them to the place where they lodged, and laid them down there. Then Joshua set up twelve stones in the midst of the Jordan, in the place where the feet of the priests who bore the ark of the covenant stood; and they are there to this day. Joshua 4:1–9

1. Explain what task was completed before the Lord spoke to Joshua.

2. God commanded Joshua to "take for yourselves" twelve men. Describe step by step what the men were commanded to do.

3. Based on this text, explain how the twelve stones served as a memorial and for how long.

4. What do you think later generations were supposed to understand about God—His nature and character—when they looked at those stones?

5. Where did Joshua have a twin monument built? Why do you think he did this?

LOOK AT ...

We've seen the people cross the Jordan at flood stage. Now we discover the exact time of the crossing and the location where they landed. It's interesting, too, that the day the people crossed over, the tenth day of the first month, is the same day the Passover lamb is selected: "On the tenth of this month every man shall take for himself a lamb, according to the house of his father, a lamb for a household" (Ex. 12:3). The people who had been passed over by the death angel were now passing into a new life (see Ex. 12:1–3). Once again, we see that God's timing is perfect. Now let's move to Joshua 4:19–20 to learn about how the Israelites began to settle in.

Now the people came up from the Jordan on the tenth day of the first month, and they camped in Gilgal on the east border of Jericho. And those

LEARN ABOUT ...

1 Crossover

At the time the people crossed over the Jordan, they were nearly two million strong. The priests stood in the midst of the river for nearly a day. The crossing meant that there was no turning back. Israel was now committed to fight against armies, chariots, and fortified cities.

5 Twin Towers

On his own initiative, Joshua replicated the twelve-stone memorial in the place where the priests had stood. Perhaps he was commemorating the time God ratified Joshua's leadership as He had Moses' at the Red Sea. Or if the memorial in Gilgal (the "lodging place") was removed or vandalized, the one in the midst of the Jordan would remain.

LEARN ABOUT ...

6 Gilgal

Gilgal means "rolling" or "circle of stones." Several events in Israel's history occurred at Gilgal. The first Passover in Canaan was held there. It also became Joshua's base of military operations during the conquest of Canaan. From there, he began allotting the Promised Land to the tribes.[38]

---

8 Uncarved Monuments

Pagans carved stone into images of people, beasts, or symbols of nature to represent gods. God declared that no image shaped by human hands could depict Him (see Ex. 20:4, 22–25). He made humans in His image (see Gen. 1:27), and Jesus would come as a man in the image of the invisible God (see Col. 1:15).

---

9 Holiday Traditions

Holidays are a good way to pass on God's great deeds. "When your children say to you, 'What do you mean by this service?' ... you shall say, 'It is the Passover sacrifice of the LORD, who passed over the houses of the children of Israel in Egypt when He struck the Egyptians and delivered our households'" (Ex. 12:26–27).

twelve stones which they took out of the Jordan, Joshua set up in Gilgal. Joshua 4:19–20

6. Describe what happened at Gilgal.

7. God timed the crossing of the Jordan to coincide with Passover. Why do you think He did this?

LIVE OUT ...

8. a.   The memorials at Gilgal and the Jordan were uncarved stone. Why did God object to carved images (see Ex. 20:3–6, 22)?

   b.   What does it say about God that a lifeless stone carving can't adequately depict him?

   c.   Jesus is "the image of the invisible God" (Col. 1:15). What does that mean?

9. a.   The monuments were memorials to future generations. God is concerned with our parenting, making sure we help our children remember what He has done. Why is that important?

   b.   Journal about the ways that your family passes down biblical truths to the next generation. What new methods might you use?

⚬ ⚬ ● ⚬ ⚬

Bishop G. Bromley Oxnam was honored to give the annual Memorial Day address at the National Monument at Gettysburg. He concluded his speech by reciting Lincoln's famous address. Afterward he felt satisfied with his performance. That is, until an elderly man remarked, "Son, you made an awful mess of Lincoln's speech."

Oxnam asked, "What do you mean? I didn't miss a word. Look at my notes."

The old man interrupted, "Oh, I don't need your notes. I know it by heart. I heard it the first time around."

The bishop was humbled to realize that this man was present when Lincoln originally delivered his address. He was curious about how his delivery had differed from the president's. The old-timer explained, "Abe put his hands out over the people like a benediction, and said, 'That the government of the *people*, by the *people*, and for the *people*, should not perish from the earth.'" He went on to admonish, "You got the words right, son, but you missed the message. You emphasized government, Lincoln talked about people."

Stone monuments sometimes recall situations with a harshness that fails to recall the emotion of the original eyewitness. Bishop Oxnam read Lincoln's words precisely but not passionately. There is a danger in knowing the letter of the law without embracing the spirit of its intent. As we look back at these monuments, let's remember that they are much more than piles of rocks. They are tributes to almighty God, who delivered His people with great signs and wonders. May you stand in awe and wonder, remembering the love of your strong Savior for His people.

Listen to ...

Let your home be your parish, your little brood your congregation, your living room a sanctuary, and your knee a sacred altar.

—Billy Graham

DAY 5

Making Memories

A little boy came to the Washington Monument and said to the guard, "I want to buy it."

The guard replied, "How much money do you have?"

The boy pulled a quarter from his pocket.

The guard said, "That's not enough. In fact, $25 million is not enough to buy the Washington Monument. Second, the Washington Monument is not for sale. If you're an American citizen, the Washington Monument already belongs to you."

It's true, the Washington Monument located on the National Mall stands as one of the enduring symbols of liberty. Parents proudly point out the monument to their children and recount the exploits of our first president to their children when they visit the site. No one can own it, but all Americans have a stake in the Monument.

Interestingly, the Washington Monument houses 193 memorial stones. Beginning in July 1848, the Washington National Monument Society invited states, cities, and patriotic societies to contribute stones that were durable, from the states' soil, and at least four feet long, two feet high, and eighteen inches thick. These stones pay tribute to the character and achievements of George Washington. Perhaps they had the Old Testament memorials in mind when they asked for the stones for the Washington Monument.

We don't know the size and depth of Joshua's memorial stones, but we do know that they were intended to remind the generations to come about the faithfulness of their God and the stories of their founding fathers.

LIFT UP ...

Lord, it is important to You that I share with my children the amazing things You have done. Help me to take advantage of divine opportunities when they inquire about You. Bless these conversations that they may walk away knowing how mighty and awesome You are. Amen.

LOOK AT ...

We've seen Joshua and his twelve men build two memorials so the people would always remember what the Lord had done at the Jordan River. Today we discover that a visual display was not enough—God also instructed the people to verbally remind their descendants of God's mighty work.

At the time of the crossing to Gilgal, the people had been completely obedient and did all that the Lord commanded. Later in time, this memorial at Gilgal lost its meaning, and the Jewish people sinned against God by worshipping there rather than at Jerusalem. Both Hosea and Amos warned the Israelites against this sin of making Gilgal a shrine that would turn the people's hearts from true worship. Sadly, the people failed to learn this lesson and later turned from the Lord. Let's follow the Lord's commands in this passage and impart to future generations the meaning of true worship.

LEARN ABOUT ...

I Memorials

We know memorials are monuments, statues, or holidays that serve as reminders. Passover memorialized God sparing the firstborn of the Israelites (see Ex. 12:14). Twelve stones commemorated crossing the Jordan. The story of the woman anointing Jesus with oil was "a memorial to her" (Matt. 26:13). The Lord's Supper is an ongoing memorial that reminds us of Christ's sacrifice (see Luke 22:19).

READ JOSHUA 4:21-24.

Then he spoke to the children of Israel, saying: "When your children ask their fathers in time to come, saying, 'What are these stones?' then you shall let your children know, saying, 'Israel crossed over this Jordan on dry land'; for the LORD your God dried up the waters of the Jordan before you until you had crossed over, as the LORD your God did to the Red Sea, which He dried up before us until we had crossed over, that all the peoples of the earth may know the hand of the LORD, that it is mighty, that you may fear the LORD your God forever." Joshua 4:21–24

1. Joshua again stressed the importance of sharing what happened with the younger generations. What question were they likely to ask?

LEARN ABOUT ...

3 Moving Waters

The parting of the Red Sea was considered the greatest miracle in the history of the Hebrew nation. The psalmists spoke of it five times, Nehemiah referred to it once, and New Testament writers referenced it twice: "By faith they passed through the Red Sea as by dry land" (Heb. 11:29).

5 Fear the Lord

The fear of God springs from love, prompting us to desire not to offend God and to endeavor to please Him in all things. It is produced in the soul by the Holy Spirit. Fear of the Lord dreads God's displeasure, desires His favor, reveres His holiness, submits cheerfully to His will, and is grateful for His benefits.[39]

6 Alms

Alms speak of aid or money given out of mercy to the poor. Jesus warned: "Take heed that you do not do your charitable deeds before men, to be seen by them. Otherwise you have no reward from your Father in heaven" (Matt. 6:1). God encourages us to feed the hungry and show compassion to those in need.[40]

2. Recount how the people were expected to respond to this question.

3. What past miracle would they compare this to?

4. Explain what the miracle would prove to the people of the earth.

5. Explain what the dried-up waters would cause the Israelites to experience.

LIVE OUT ...

6. a. This week we have been studying about memorials and memorial stones. Read Acts 10:1–5 and describe two other things God considered memorials.

   b. How are alms (gifts to the poor) memorials? What do they show that we remember?

   c. Journal a memorial of prayer to God, thanking Him for delivering you from your past and asking Him to protect you as you move forward in faith.

   d. Now write about some ways you can give alms.

7. The drying of the Red Sea and the Jordan were intended to demonstrate the hand of the Lord. Read the following Scriptures and describe what you learn about the hand of the Lord.
   Psalm 118:15–16
   Proverbs 21:1
   Isaiah 41:18–20
   Isaiah 66:14

8. Describe a time when you've seen God's hand at work. Based on sidebar 7, describe how you've seen Him work. What does He reveal about Himself when He extends His hand?

7 Hand of God

The expression "hand of God" refers to His great power. It often emphasizes His great power in creation. Sometimes His power in judgment is emphasized, especially in the phrase, "The hand of the LORD has gone out against me!" (Ruth 1:13). However, God may also extend His hand to express His mercy and for-giveness (see Ps. 37:24).[41]

○ ○ ● ○ ○

Where we live in Albuquerque, New Mexico, the Native American Pueblo communities have a wonderful tradition. They place storytellers in a position of great importance in their communities. The tribe's older members help preserve the culture and heritage of their people by telling folktales and stories to the next generation.

These Pueblo people are also famous for their clay sculptures. They are skilled at creating small figurines of people and animals. Sometimes they combine these artistic qualities by creating "storyteller dolls."

A storyteller doll is usually a small clay sculpture of a woman. The figure is always depicted openmouthed to show that it is entertaining listeners with songs and stories, passing down tribal culture. The miniature figurines on the storyteller's lap represent the children hearing stories and learning lessons from the wise storyteller.

Oral storytelling is one of the most effective ways of passing on important values and history. Joshua made sure his people knew the value of passing on the values and lessons learned by older generations. Rather than dolls, they used memorial stones to initiate the conversation between generations. You can be creative. Books, photographs, and other mementos can be a wonderful way to pass on your spiritual heritage to the next generation. Be a storyteller.

LISTEN TO ...

The mother's heart is the child's schoolroom.

—*Henry Ward Beecher*

When God Pulls Rank

Joshua 5

Pulling rank occurs when a superior officer uses his or her position of authority to gain advantage. In the military, a direct order may never be willfully disobeyed or ignored by one in an inferior position unless it is an immoral or unlawful order. For instance, if a captain says, "Private, establish a side business selling heroin on the black market so I can buy a new home," the private would not have to obey.

Often, when one pulls rank, the authority forces the person below them to be quiet, obey, or agree. This is useful in time of war to stop a drawn-out debate or to compel action when it is needed. But at other times it may simply be an abuse of authority.

The military isn't the only place where people pull rank. Parents can do it with children, as when a father ends an argument with, "Because I said so." Or when an employer tells a new hire, "You're stuck with the swing shift until you've paid your dues." Sometimes teachers pull rank with students by requiring them to stay after school or write, "I will obey my teacher," a hundred times on the chalkboard. All that is required to pull rank is a position of recognized authority.

This week we'll see Captain Joshua pace the outskirts of Jericho, perhaps pondering a military strategy when the Commander of the army of the Lord suddenly appears. Theologians believe this apparition was a theophany or a Christophany—the manifestation of God or Jesus in the Old Testament. Joshua fell prostrate before the Commander (a clear act of reverence) and asked for instructions. He humbly submitted to God, as He was rightfully about to pull rank and give Joshua instructions to take the town.

Day 1 Joshua 5:1–3   **CONFIDENCE REQUIRED**

Day 2 Joshua 5:4–9   **CIRCUMCISION REQUESTED**

Day 3 Joshua 5:10   **COMMEMORATION REINSTATED**

Day 4 Joshua 5:11–12   **CONSUMPTION REVISED**

Day 5 Joshua 5:13–15   **COMMANDER REVEALED**

DAY 1
Confidence Required

LIFT UP ...

Lord, Your enemies hear about You and tremble with fear. Help me to trust You when it seems that I am vulnerable. You are always aware of where I am and You protect me while I wait. Amen.

LOOK AT ...

Previously we witnessed the children of Israel, led by the priests, cross over the Jordan on dry land. When the kings of Canaan heard of this strange event, their morale hit an all-time low. Perhaps the military leaders would have favored striking out hard and fast while they enjoyed the psychological advantage. But God's ways are rarely our ways. Never hasty, He established important priorities before facing new battles.

First, God reminded the people about His covenant of circumcision, which debilitated Joshua's entire army and might have tested their confidence in their leader. Secondly, the fledgling nation remembered the Passover by holding its first celebration in the new land. Next, they learned to eat local foods rather than the daily manna that had been provided in the wilderness. Finally, they waited for instruction from the Commander of the Lord's army.

How about you? Do you feel like you're in a hurry to make a decision or venture out into unknown territory before consulting the Lord or living up to the commands you already know? Don't make decisions without taking the time to pray, ponder, and personally practice all that is written in His Word.

READ JOSHUA 5:1–3.

So it was, when all the kings of the Amorites who were on the west side of the Jordan,

LEARN ABOUT ...

1 Amorites and Canaanites

The Amorites were warlike mountaineers. They are represented on Egyptian monuments with fair skin, light hair, blue eyes, aquiline noses, pointed beards, and great stature. The Canaanites were descendants of Ham and were known as merchants and seamen as well as artisans. They worshipped the sun-god who they called Baal.[42]

---

2 Word of Mouth

Gossip is quick to spread and difficult to contain. Israel's enemies heard up in the mountains and down to the seas about God's strength and this caused them to lose heart. When Pharaoh heard about God's wonders, he hardened his heart. On the other hand, Rahab heard of God wonders and experienced a change of heart.

---

5 Circumcision! Now?

Circumcision is the surgical removal of the foreskin of the male genitals. An adult male needs days to recover from such a procedure, especially one done without anesthetic and with a flint (stone) knife. While it appears that Israel risked being overcome by making themselves so vulnerable in enemy land, God knew the Amorites and Canaanites were so paralyzed by their despair that there was no danger of their attacking Israel.

and all the kings of the Canaanites who were by the sea, heard that the LORD had dried up the waters of the Jordan from before the children of Israel until we had crossed over, that their heart melted; and there was no spirit in them any longer because of the children of Israel. At that time the LORD said to Joshua, "Make flint knives for yourself, and circumcise the sons of Israel again the second time." So Joshua made flint knives for himself, and circumcised the sons of Israel at the hill of the foreskins.
Joshua 5:1–3

1. In this passage, note who heard of the Israelites and where they were located. (Also, see if you can find these places on the map on page 389.)

2. How did they respond when they heard about the supernatural Jordan crossing?

3. Why do you think they responded like that?

4. Who was responsible for terrifying the Amorites and Canaanites? Why does this matter?

5. With Israel's enemies in a state of despair, what two instructions did God give to Joshua?

6. What did the Israelites name this place? What have you learned about names in previous lessons that helps you understand this?

LIVE OUT ...

7. Put yourself in the shoes of the Israelites. How would you feel if those who opposed you became discouraged? Describe what response you might want to make.

8. It was God, not the Israelites, who terrified the Canaanites. The Israelites needed to be clear on this. Read Jeremiah 9:23–24 below.

Thus says the LORD:

"Let not the wise man glory in his wisdom,

Let not the mighty man glory in his might,

Nor let the rich man glory in his riches;

But let him who glories glory in this,

That he understands and knows Me,

That I am the LORD, exercising lovingkindness, judgment,

and righteousness in the earth.

For in these I delight," says the LORD.

Jeremiah 9:23–24

a. Circle all forms of the word *glory* in this passage.

b. Underline what we should not glory in.

c. Draw parentheses around what we should glory in.

d. List those things the Lord delights in.

e. What are some things that bring you delight? How do they compare with the things that delight God?

9. Reflect on any times you might have taken credit for something God has done on your behalf. Spend time journaling a prayer giving God all the glory. Reword Jeremiah 9:24 as your personal praise.

○ ○ ● ○ ○

In Lesson 1 we learned that God had Israel's back. Today we find that He was also giving Israel His divine backing. To give one's backing is to

LEARN ABOUT …

7 Enemies

An enemy is one who opposes or mistreats another person. The enemies of the Hebrew people were regarded as God's enemies. In the New Testament, enemies are primarily spiritual in nature. The New Testament foresees a day when Christ's redemptive work will overcome all enemies of righteousness.[43]

9 Glory

We were born to give God glory. To glorify God means to magnify, extol, and praise Him. We can do this by ascribing honor to Him and acknowledging Him as to His being, attributes, and acts.[44] "I will praise You, O Lord my God, with all my heart, and I will glorify Your name forevermore" (Ps. 86:12).

provide approval and support. For example, politicians back one another's bills when they go to a vote. Another definition of backing is to strengthen with force. Think of athletes who get behind their teammates, forming a back and strengthening the team. Financially, entrepreneurs offer backing via resources to make difficult projects possible.

God loves to back His people. Let's look at the life of Elisha the prophet when Syria and Israel were at war to understand how miraculous His backing can be. When Elisha prophesied about the placement of Syria's troops, the Syrian king feared he'd been infiltrated by a spy. But his counselor revealed, "Elisha, the prophet who is in Israel, tells the king of Israel the words that you speak" (2 Kings 6:12).

The ruler was furious and surrounded Elisha's home with his army. When the prophet's servant arose, he discovered their predicament and lamented, "What shall we do?" (2 Kings 6:15). Confident of the Lord's backing, Elisha replied, "Those who are with us are more than those who are with them" (2 Kings 6:16). Then he prayed that his servant's eyes would be opened to God's backing. The servant saw that "the mountain was full of horses and chariots of fire all around Elisha" (2 Kings 6:17).

Like Joshua, Elisha had God's backing. The Canaanites, like the Syrians, were fearful not of an earthly leader but of the Lord of the earth. As you face troubling circumstances, may your eyes be open to see the many ways in which the Lord is backing *you*!

LISTEN TO ...

You can't glorify self and Christ at the same time.

—Unknown

DAY 2

Circumcision Requested

God established circumcision with Abraham as a sign of His everlasting covenant, promising that Abraham and his seed would possess the land of Canaan. He stated that those who refused to cut their flesh would be cut off from God's covenant: "The uncircumcised male child … that person shall be cut off from his people; he has broken My covenant" (Gen. 17:14).

Alan Redpath wrote this about Joshua circumcising his troops: "The rite of circumcision was an outward testimony to the fact that the land was to be possessed in the weakness of the flesh, through the suffering, very often, of the body. It symbolized the weakness and almost death, as it were, of everything that man can be, in order that the possession of the land should be given to them unmistakably in the sovereign grace of God."[45]

Jews still celebrate circumcision as a religious ceremony rather than a surgical procedure. The *brit mila* (ritual circumcision) is held the eighth day after a boy's birth. Typically, a *Mohel*—a person trained in the physical and religious procedures—performs the circumcision. When the baby is brought forward, the *Mohel* recites this blessing, "Praised be Thou, O Lord, our God, King of the Universe, who hast sanctified us with Thy commandments, and commanded us concerning the rite of circumcision." Then the circumcision is performed. The father recites another blessing, "Praised be Thou, O Lord our God, King of the Universe, who has sanctified us by Thy commandments, and hast bidden us to make him enter into the covenant of Abraham our father."[46]

LIFT UP …

Lord, please keep me from those situations that cause me to be disobedient. I so want to be in a covenant relationship with You. Cut away anything that is hindering my obedience to You. Amen.

LOOK AT …

Yesterday we saw Joshua make a surprising strategic decision to have every man circumcised before going into battle. Providentially, all of the Canaanites were paralyzed with fear because

Learn about ...

I Kept Out

Disobedience denied the children of the exodus access to the Promised Land. Instead, the unbelievers perished during forty years of wandering. "Do not harden your hearts as in the rebellion ... Where your fathers tested Me, tried Me, And saw My works forty years.... So I swore in My wrath, 'They shall not enter My rest'" (Heb. 3:8–11).

3 Kept Count

To punish the people's unbelief, God gave them one year of wandering for each day that Moses' spies had spent in Canaan: "According to the number of the days in which you spied out the land, forty days, for each day you shall bear your guilt one year, namely forty years, and you shall know My rejection" (Num. 14:34).

of the wonders God had done. Today we gain insight into Joshua's decision to circumcise his soldiers.

Though other nations of the day practiced circumcision, it didn't carry the spiritual significance that it did for the Israelites. Circumcision marked the Hebrew nation as a people set apart in relationship with God.

Read Joshua 5:4–9.

And this is the reason why Joshua circumcised them: All the people who came out of Egypt who were males, all the men of war, had died in the wilderness on the way, after they had come out of Egypt. For all the people who came out had been circumcised, but all the people born in the wilderness, on the way as they came out of Egypt, had not been circumcised. For the children of Israel walked forty years in the wilderness, till all the people who were men of war, who came out of Egypt, were consumed, because they did not obey the voice of the LORD—to whom the LORD swore that He would not show them the land which the LORD had sworn to their fathers that He would give us, "a land flowing with milk and honey." Then Joshua circumcised their sons whom He raised up in their place; for they were uncircumcised, because they had not been circumcised on the way. So it was, when they had finished circumcising all the people, that they stayed in their places in the camp till they were healed. Then the LORD said to Joshua, "This day I have rolled away the reproach of Egypt from you." Therefore the name of the place is called Gilgal to this day. Joshua 5:4–9

1. By this time, what had happened to all the men of war who came out of Egypt? Why?

2. Describe the physical difference between the males who came out of Egypt and those born in the wilderness.

3. Describe how long the Israelites wandered in the wilderness and what happened to them.

4. Explain why they weren't permitted to see the "land flowing with milk and honey."

5. Why did Joshua circumcise all the boys and men? (Consider the meaning of circumcision described above. You might also look at Genesis 17:9–14.)

6. Note how long the circumcision process and recovery took. Why might this have seemed illogical from a military point of view?

LIVE OUT …

7. The Israelites were asked to undergo circumcision, which could lay them up for at least a week, a seemingly illogical request. Has God ever asked you to do something that seemed illogical to the outside world? If so, how did you respond and what was the result?

8. Unbelief in God's promises prevented the exodus generation from entering God's rest. Doubt is honest uncertainty, but unbelief is a stubborn refusal to trust God and act on that trust. What helps you keep the faith when you're tempted toward unbelief?

9. God kept count of the days the spies were in Canaan to number the years of their wilderness experience. Imagine if the Lord punished you with one year of trial for each day of your unbelief in His promises. How long would you suffer? How would that make you feel? What lesson would you learn?

10. Journal about a season when you failed to keep God's commands. Perhaps you stopped praying or your love for others went cold. What signaled your return to obedience? What helped you get there?

LEARN ABOUT …

5 Cut Off

Circumcision literally means "cut off" or "cutting around." During the wilderness journey, boys weren't circumcised. Because of the people's disobedience, God was temporarily rejecting them. They were therefore prohibited from using the sign of the covenant.

8 Unbelief

Unbelief does not hinder God's faithfulness (see Rom. 3:3), but it does affect the individual's capacity to receive the benefits of His faithfulness. The unbelief of one generation of Israelites prevented them from seeing the Promised Land (see Heb. 3:19). The skeptic is limited to what he or she experiences, while "all things are possible to him who believes" (Mark 9:23).

○ ○ ● ○ ○

Aesop told a fable about "The Bat, the Birds, and the Beasts." A war was brewing between the Birds of the air and the Beasts of the field. When the two armies were choosing sides, the Bat hesitated about which side to join.

The Birds passed his perch and cawed at him: "Come with us."

But he replied, "I am a Beast."

Later, the Beasts passed below him and howled: "Come join us."

The Bat called, "I'm a Bird."

Finally, a peace treaty was forged and no battle took place. The Bat wanted to join the Bird's party, but they told him to fly away. He went to the Beasts, but they told him to beat a retreat.

"Ah," said the Bat, "I see: He that is neither one thing nor the other has no friends."

God made sure the Hebrew nation exhibited an outward sign of their inward friendship with Him through the covenant of circumcision. Obedience to His laws and commands is necessary to retain a relationship with God. Those wandering in the wilderness experienced God's rejection because they failed to be true to the covenant despite all outward appearances.

As a child of the new covenant, you can mark yourself as different and set apart from this world. When you walk in faith, "the LORD your God will circumcise your heart and the heart of your descendants, to love the LORD your God with all your heart and with all your soul, that you may live" (Deut. 30:6).

LISTEN TO ...

Christ never failed to distinguish between doubt and unbelief. Doubt is can't believe; unbelief is won't believe. Doubt is honesty; unbelief is obstinacy. Doubt is looking for light; unbelief is content with darkness.

—John Drummond

DAY 3
Commemoration Reinstated

For the devout Jew, the calendar was more than a way of marking time. It provided a timely way to commemorate God's dealings in the life of the nation. The month of Nisan marked Passover, the time of Israel's deliverance from Egyptian bondage. Sivan brought the Feast of Pentecost, the celebration of another bountiful harvest from God. Tishri took the people back to their wilderness wanderings through the Feast of the Tabernacles. Each holiday became a holy day—a time of recalling, repenting, and renewing old commitments to follow the God of Israel.[47]

Holidays really can be holy days. The word *holy* means set apart for divine service or purposes. Our modern calendar can remind us as believers to commemorate what God has done for us. Even the so-called secular holidays can be holy days when observed by followers of the Holy One.

At Thanksgiving we can celebrate God's gracious provision by thanking Him for all He has done. One of His names is *Jehovah-Jireh,* which means "the Lord will provide." At Christmas we can celebrate how Christ the Savior was born—to save us from sin. We can unwrap the "indescribable gift" of God's dear Son. At New Year's we can celebrate a new beginning and make resolutions to live more biblically. Also, we can ring in the New Year by thanking Him for making all things new.

Joshua knew it was time to make Passover a holy day once again. Before reaching into the future, he reminded the people to reflect on the past. Since God's arm had delivered them from Pharaoh, He was more than able to bring victory in whatever lay ahead.

LIFT UP ...

Lord, You prepare a table before me in the presence of my enemies. It is pleasing to You that I celebrate what You have done regardless of the circumstances surrounding me. May I always find time to praise You for my deliverance. Amen.

LOOK AT ...

Yesterday we saw how the Israelites reinstated the ritual of circumcision before embarking on their conquest of Canaan. Today we'll see them celebrate the Passover as they commemorate their deliverance from the bondage of Egypt.

The first Passover included the following provisions: 1) selecting a lamb without blemish for each household on the tenth of the month; 2) sacrificing the lamb at twilight on the fourteenth day; 3) sprinkling the blood on doorposts and lintels of the home where it was eaten; 4) roasting the entire lamb with fire—none of it could be eaten raw, boiled with water, or offered with bones broken; 5) eating the lamb with unleavened bread and bitter herbs; 6) eating swiftly with girded loins, shod feet, and staff in hand; 7) staying inside the house until morning; 8) burning all meat that remained; 9) eating Passover only during the night (see Ex. 12:1–23).[48]

New Testament believers realize that Jesus is our Passover Lamb. He was a sacrificial Lamb without blemish (see 1 Peter 1:19). The sprinkling of His blood allows God to "pass over" our sins (see 1 Peter 1:2). Since He was sacrificed wholly, not one of His bones was broken (see John 19:36). Therefore, Christians as well as Jews can celebrate Passover: "For indeed Christ, our Passover, was sacrificed for us. Therefore let us keep the feast, not with old leaven, nor with the leaven of malice and wickedness, but with the unleavened bread of sincerity and truth" (1 Cor. 5:7–8).

READ JOSHUA 5:10.

Now the children of Israel camped in Gilgal, and kept the Passover on the fourteenth day of the month at twilight on the plains of Jericho. Joshua 5:10

1. The people were still camped at Gilgal, where the men were recovering from the circumcision ceremony. Look back at 4:19. How long had they been at Gilgal?

2. What holiday did the children of Israel celebrate on the fourteenth day?

3. Read Deuteronomy 16:1–8. Why did Moses command the Israelites to "keep the Passover" (Deut. 16:1)?

4. Why were they were instructed to "eat no leavened bread" during the Passover (Deut. 16:3)?

5. When did Joshua's celebration occur, as commanded in Deuteronomy 16:4?

6. According to Deuteronomy 16:5–7, where could the sacrifice take place? Where did the Passover take place for Joshua?

7. What activity was forbidden during the Passover (see Deut. 16:8)? Why do you think this was the case?

LIVE OUT ...

8. a. Joshua reestablished the celebration of the Passover. Jesus, too, celebrated it. Read Luke 22:7–20. Who prepared the Passover? At whose request? What preparations were involved?

   b. Describe how Jesus felt about celebrating the Passover at that time and in the future (see Luke 22:14–16).

   c. What Christian ritual was birthed at this Passover (see Luke 22:17–20)? What elements were included? Why do we continue this activity today?

9. a. Read 1 Corinthians 5:6–8. In Paul's analogy here, what does leaven represent?

LEARN ABOUT ...

2 Passover

In New Testament times, Passover became a pilgrim festival. Large numbers gathered in Jerusalem to observe the annual celebration. Jesus was crucified during a Passover celebration. He and His disciples ate a Passover meal together on the eve of His death.[49] "So the disciples did as Jesus had directed them; and they prepared the Passover" (Matt. 26:19).

4 Leaven

In Scripture, leaven symbolized good or evil. "The kingdom of heaven is like leaven, which a woman took and hid in three measures of meal till it was all leavened" (Matt. 13:33). Here, it portrayed the kingdom of heaven as hidden, powerful, and pervasive. In an evil sense it illustrates corruption: "Beware of the leaven of the Pharisees" (Matt. 16:6, 12).[50]

5 Twilight

According to Leviticus 23:5, Passover began at twilight on the fourteenth day of the month. A Jewish day begins and ends at sundown. Though the holy day started at the end of the day as we see it, it actually started at the beginning of the day as the Jews saw it.

LEARN ABOUT ...

9 Unleavened

Although leaven symbolizes either good or evil, most biblical references carry a negative connotation. Leaven causes fermentation of the original dough, creating "sour dough." Because fermentation suggested corruption, God required that many sacrifices include unleavened bread, which represented purity and holiness.

10 Communion

Communion is an ordinance usually observed during a worship service. Christians partake of bread and wine to remember Christ's death, by which our sins are taken away. His church is to observe it until He returns: "As often as you eat this bread and drink this cup, you proclaim the Lord's death till He comes" (I Cor. 11:26).[51]

b. Paul points to Christ as the Passover lamb. As followers of Christ, what sort of unleavened behavior should we exhibit?

c. What type of leavened behavior should we *not* exhibit?

d. In what current situation will you put this instruction into practice?

10. The Passover could only be celebrated in the place of the Lord's choosing. For Joshua that was at Gilgal. For the disciples it was the upper room. Journal about a specific time when you celebrated the Lord's Supper. Where did it take place? Why did you partake? What was the attitude of your heart?

○ ○ ● ○ ○

Frederick the Great, the third and last king of Prussia, invited some notable people to dine at his royal table. He included his top-ranking generals; however, General Hans von Zieten declined the king's invitation to take communion at his church.

Later, at another banquet, Frederick and his guests mocked the general for his religious fervency, making jokes about the Lord's Supper. Boldly, the general rose to his feet to address the monarch, "My lord, there is a greater King than you, a King to whom I have sworn allegiance even unto death. I am a Christian man, and I cannot sit quietly as the Lord's name is dishonored and His character belittled."

The guests fell silent, knowing that von Zieten's interruption might warrant a death sentence. Instead, Frederick grasped the hand of his faithful officer and asked for forgiveness. The great king promised never again to allow the mockery of sacred things.[52]

Holidays really are holy days. Joshua and Jesus understood the importance of commemorating them. In fact, neglecting the Passover would have made a mockery of God's commands and His faithfulness.

By celebrating the Passover, Jesus instituted a new feast for New Testament believers: the Lord's Supper. When we participate in this ritual, we commemorate the blood shed by our Passover Lamb, Jesus Christ. Every time you drink of the cup and eat of the bread, you honor Him. Make sure that you never neglect the Lord's Supper.

LISTEN TO ...

The holiest of all holidays are those kept by ourselves in silence and apart: the secret anniversaries of the heart.

—*Henry Wadsworth Longfellow*

DAY 4

Consumption Revised

We conducted a nonscientific poll and asked some friends, "What comes to mind when you think about holidays?" Christy said, "Love them!" Barb said, "Stressed." Barb's husband said, "Memories." Barb's stress must work—she makes the holidays memorable for those she loves! One lady replied, "Sad," because a death in her family means the holidays will be a time of mourning. Most of us probably respond, "Cooking." Some might say, "Gathering together"; others might say, "Traditions." However, no one said, "Thankful."

Maybe this isn't surprising. Thankfulness isn't our natural response, it's a learned behavior. We train our children to say "thank you" after a kindness is offered. God commands us to "give thanks to the LORD, for He is good!" (Ps. 118:1).

The Israelites weren't thankful for God's provision of manna in the wilderness—they grumbled! "The children of Israel also wept again and said: 'Who will give us meat to eat? We remember the fish which we ate freely in Egypt, the cucumbers, the melons, the leeks, the onions, and the garlic; but now our whole being is dried up; there is nothing at all except this manna before our eyes!'" (Num. 11:4–6). How tragic that God provided angel food while the Israelites longed for onions.

The Passover celebration marked the end of the manna. Now the people would eat from the fruit of the land once again. The people were called to celebrate God's goodness for a few more days before embarking upon their conquest. Would they gladly gather their own grain, or would they grumble instead?

LIFT UP ...

Lord, You are my faithful provider, who gives me everything I need, including rest and refreshment. Thank You for taking care of all of my needs. Amen.

LOOK AT ...

We saw yesterday that the Israelites completed their consecration to the Lord by celebrating the feast of Passover. Their new life in the Land of Promise was beginning with the proper spiritual focus. Now we see that God was able to provide for the people's daily bread.

Isn't it good to know that God is a very practical God, who takes such good care of us? In the wilderness He provided for the Israelites in miraculous, supernatural ways. But once they reached Canaan—the land of milk and honey—He chose to provide for them in a natural way through the land's agricultural produce. Whether by natural or supernatural means, we can always trust our God to be Jehovah-Jireh, the Lord will provide.

READ JOSHUA 5:11–12.

And they ate of the produce of the land on the day after the Passover, unleavened bread and parched grain, on the very same day. Then the manna ceased on the day after they had eaten the produce of the land; and the children of Israel no longer had manna, but they ate the food of the land of Canaan that year. Joshua 5:11–12

1. What did the children of Israel use as their new food source?

2. When did they see a change in their food supply?

3. Describe what the people stopped receiving. What, if anything, do you know about this substance?

4. This generation of Israelites had been raised on food provided supernaturally. The only work they had to do was to gather it. How do you think they felt about eating "ordinary" food instead?

5. Summarize the eating habits of the Israelites that year.

LEARN ABOUT …

1 Grain

The principal crops of Palestine/Canaan were grain, mostly wheat and barley, that could be parched (roasted) or baked into flatbread. Harvest began with barley, which ripened two to three weeks before wheat. The Israelites probably learned how to work these crops in Egypt. Since God had given them the land, its cultivation was under obedience to the Lord's commands.

2 Feast of Unleavened Bread

The week following Passover was the Feast of Unleavened Bread. The text doesn't mention it, but the people were probably celebrating this feast as part of the larger Passover celebration. Only unleavened bread was eaten during this feast to commemorate Israel's haste in leaving Egypt.[53]

5 Harvest

A change in diet marked the passage from the Israelites' old life in the desert to their life in the Promised Land. Since they entered the land at harvest season, they took possession not only of the land, but also the "food of the land." The psalmist praised, "You provide their grain" (Ps. 65:9).

LEARN ABOUT ...

7 Not Our Ways

God ways are truly "higher than your ways" (Isa. 55:9). Circumcision and feasting seem counterintuitive when we're set on conquest. Joshua's decision might have turned out like the time Dinah's brothers had her fiancé and his men circumcised and then slaughtered them when they were weakened after the surgery (see Gen. 34:25–26). Instead, God gave the Israelites rest.

8 Bread of Life

Jesus, the "bread of life," came to do the will of the Father. In Israel there were two types of bread: sweet bread (*massa*), which was unleavened, and sour bread (*hames*), which was leavened.[54] On the cross, Jesus became broken bread so that we may taste the sweetness of forgiveness.

LIVE OUT ...

6. a. Many Old Testament passages foreshadowed things to come in the New Testament. Read the two passages below and describe how Jesus fulfilled the passage we read today.

   John 6:35
   John 12:23–24

   b. In what ways is Jesus the bread of your life?

7. a. The Israelites were asked to continue to celebrate the Feast of Unleavened Bread rather than start conquering their enemies. Which comes more naturally to you: taking time to celebrate God, or getting busy accomplishing things? How does that natural bent play itself out in your life?

   b. Has God ever asked you to stop to rest or worship when you had some task to accomplish? If so, talk about how you responded spiritually, emotionally, and physically.

8. a. The Israelites experienced a change in their diet. We, too, have been asked to change our diet. Read John 4:31–34 and recount what Jesus said about His diet.

   b. Does doing God's will nourish you? If so, how?

   c. The "work" Jesus talks about in this passage suggests connecting a broken person with God. Name someone you'd like to share the gospel with. How can you help that person take one step toward God?

o o ● o o

A biology professor stood before his students and held up a tiny seed between his thumb and forefinger and bowed reverently before the seed. His students were mystified. The university professor had spent his career studying the origins of life and acknowledged that it remained a mystery. He said, "I know exactly what this seed consists of in the exact proportions of water, carbon, and other elements. I can mix these individual elements and make a seed that will look exactly like this one. But if I plant the seed I have compounded, it will rot. The various elements I have put together will be absorbed by the ground. However, if I sow the seed that God made, it will spring up into a plant; because it contains that mysterious element we call life."[55]

This story makes us realize that God's provision of grain and bread was just as miraculous as His provision of manna. But the greatest miracle was when God stepped out of eternity in the form of a man and, like a grain of wheat, died so that we could experience new life. It is truly miraculous that He uses flawed human beings like us to sow the gospel message so that others can come to a saving knowledge of Him, rather than rotting in unbelief. Won't you help spread the Word to an unbelieving world?

LISTEN TO ...

Every believer is God's miracle.

—*Philip James Bailey*

DAY 5

Commander Revealed

Battlefields throughout the world have been strewn with soldiers who have died in wars. Because of the horrific nature of war, many soldiers' remains have gone unidentified. As a result, nations have built memorials with names like "The Tomb of the Unknown" to represent the war grave of these unidentified soldiers. These monuments usually contain the remains of a dead soldier who is unidentified or "known but to God," as the stone is sometimes inscribed.

It is believed that the first memorial of this kind is the 1858 Landsoldaten or "Foot Soldier" monument of the First War of Schleswig in Fredericia, Denmark. Another early memorial of this kind is the 1866 memorial to the unknown dead of the American Civil War at Arlington National Cemetery on land once owned by Robert E. Lee. The Arc de Triomphe in Paris is the largest such monument. Located on the Champs Elysée, it was designed as a triumphal arch for the Emperor Napoleon, but underneath it stands the monument for France's unknown soldiers. Today, DNA testing makes it uncertain whether more unknowns will be buried in the tombs of the unknowns as identification becomes easier through more sophisticated scientific methods.

When Joshua was going to war, he encountered an unknown soldier. However, this soldier was vibrantly alive, and after encountering this soldier, Joshua's life would never be the same. The soldier is a great and mighty warrior who wants to make Himself known to you. He will fight battles on your behalf, and when you encounter Him, your life will not be the same, either.

LIFT UP ...

Lord, thank You for revealing Yourself through Your Word, Your Spirit, and Your people. Help me to enter my time with You with holy reverence. You are an awesome and holy God. Amen.

LOOK AT ...

The previous verses in Joshua 5 showed the spiritual preparations required by God before the children of Israel would be ready to take Jericho. First, the men submitted to circumcision, which showed a spirit of *consecration*. Next, the people participated in the Passover, reinstituting the spirit of *celebration*. Then, they celebrated the Feast of Unleavened Bread, initiating the period of *possession*. Now, we see God prepare Joshua, their leader, via personal *revelation*.

As you conclude this week's study, examine whether God has taken you through these steps along with the Israelites. Has He cut away something in your life, calling you to a consecrated and holy life? In return, have you felt a stronger sense of celebration, knowing that God has passed over your sin? Have you gained possession of new spiritual territory by feasting on His Word? If so, you can rest assured that God will reveal Himself to you in new and powerful ways.

READ JOSHUA 5:13–15.

And it came to pass, when Joshua was by Jericho, that he lifted his eyes and looked, and behold, a Man stood opposite him with His sword drawn in His hand. And Joshua went to Him and said to Him, "Are You for us or for our adversaries?" So He said, "No, but as Commander of the army of the LORD I have now come." And Joshua fell on his face to the earth and worshiped, and said to Him, "What does my Lord say to His servant?" Then the Commander of the LORD's army said to Joshua, "Take your sandal off your foot, for the place where you stand is holy." And Joshua did so. Joshua 5:13–15

1. Where did this scene take place? Why do you suppose Joshua was there?

2. Describe the person Joshua saw. What hints in the text lead you to believe that this was no ordinary man?

3. a. When he saw the man, how did Joshua react physically, and what did he ask verbally?

Learn about ...

2 Extraordinary Man

Most scholars agree that Joshua experienced a theophany or Christophany. A theophany is a direct visual manifestation of God's presence. A Christophany is a manifestation of Christ before His birth in Bethlehem. Such experiences aren't given for their own sake or to satisfy curiosity about God, but to convey some revelation or truth about Him.[56]

---

4 Commander of the Army

Throughout Scripture, God revealed Himself as Lord of hosts (Jehovah-Sabaoth), which means "Lord of armies." The army referred to here does not necessarily speak of earthly armies. It could speak of celestial or spiritual armies. "Holy, holy, holy is the LORD of hosts; The whole earth is full of His glory!" (Isa. 6:3).

---

7 Barefoot General

To take off one's shoes is an Eastern custom denoting reverence. Taking shoes off prevents an area from being defiled and expresses respect for the place and/or the person one is approaching. In Israel people wore sandals when undertaking some business, such as a military expedition.

b. What insight do these responses give you into Joshua's character?

4. The person called Himself "Commander of the army of the LORD." What do you think this title signified to Joshua?

5. The Commander gave an enigmatic answer to Joshua's question, "Are you for us or for our adversaries?" Why do you suppose He didn't say He was for the Israelites? Can you back up your answer with Scripture?

6. Describe how Joshua responded, both physically and verbally, when the Commander identified Himself. What attitudes toward the Commander do his words and actions reflect?

7. Describe what the Commander asked Joshua to do and why.

Live out ...

8. a. When Joshua saw the Commander, he fell facedown in worship. Fill in the following chart to discover other ways to worship God.

Scripture	How to Worship
Psalm 5:7	
Psalm 29:1–2	
Psalm 66:4	
Psalm 95:6	
Psalm 138:2	

b. Physical gestures (kneeling, bowing, lifting the hands, falling facedown) were common elements in Hebrew worship, as the body expressed what the heart was doing. Spend some time worshipping God in some of the ways you listed above. What have you learned this week that motivates you to worship?

9. Just as He had with Moses, God told Joshua that the place where he was standing was holy. With this in mind, read the passage below.

> Who may ascend into the hill of the LORD?
> Or who may stand in His holy place?
> He who has clean hands and a pure heart,
> Who has not lifted up his soul to an idol,
> Nor sworn deceitfully.
> He shall receive blessing from the LORD,
> And righteousness from the God of his salvation.
>
> Psalm 24:3–5

a. Underline the two questions the psalmist asks about the Lord's holy hill.

b. Circle the four characteristics of the one who may stand in the Lord's holy place.

c. Place parentheses around the two things this person shall receive.

d. Take off your shoes and recite this psalm, asking the Lord to grant you entrance to His holy place.

○ ○ ● ○ ○

After the American Civil War, General Robert E. Lee, who was deeply loved by his soldiers, was riding one day in a district when an old

LEARN ABOUT …

8 Worship God

Worshipping God isn't defined in Scripture—it defies description. Worship literally means to bow or kiss toward. It is not confined to praise; it includes acknowledging God, His nature, attributes, ways, and claims, by pouring out one's heart in praise and thanksgiving. Worship can also include deeds done to acknowledge God's goodness.[57]

9 Holy Place

The tabernacle (and later the temple) contained two divisions: "The veil shall be a divider for you between the holy place and the Most Holy" (Ex. 26:33). The Most Holy place contained the ark of the covenant. At Christ's death the veil was torn in half. Now, we have "boldness to enter the Holiest by the blood of Jesus" (Heb. 10:19).[58]

weather-beaten mountaineer greeted him. "Ain't you General Lee?" the mountaineer asked, grabbing the bridle of the general's horse.

"Yes, sir," the general said.

The old mountaineer asked his former commander to dismount—which he did. The old soldier stood before his commander and said, "I served under you, General. Let me give three rousing cheers for Mast'r Robert." At the first shout Lee saw tears begin to well in the soldier's eyes. The next yell was choked with sobs as the old soldier dropped to his knees hugging Lee's leg. The third hurrah died away as he leaned over and collapsed in tears.[59]

Biblical characters who encountered God in a theophany were dazzled. When Moses met God at the burning bush, he hid his face. When he came down from Mt. Sinai, his face was glowing so that he had to cover it. And when he asked to see God's glory, God hid him in the cleft of the rock so that His glory wouldn't consume a mere human. When Hagar met the angel of the Lord, she understood that God truly saw her, and it changed her life. When Zechariah saw the angel of the Lord under the myrtle tree, he was filled with comfort and hope. Today God has made a way for the living God to be with you wherever you go. Any place you go can be a holy place when Christ dwells in your heart.

LISTEN TO ...

Things that are holy are revealed only to men who are holy.

—Hippocrates

An Earth-Shattering Shout
Joshua 6

Can singing the right note actually shatter glass? Although tricky, it can actually happen! The key lies in matching the sound's frequency to the frequency of the glass. Perhaps a scream could do the trick. But a singer with perfect pitch, sustaining the right note with an incredibly high volume, would be more likely to accomplish the feat.

Every object has a resonant frequency—a natural pitch at which it vibrates. If you run a damp finger along the rim of a glass, you'll hear the hum of its resonant frequency. To shatter that glass, a singer's voice must match the pitch.

However, the singer needs to sing very loudly. A jackhammer operates at about 90 decibels. The human threshold for pain comes at about 120 decibels. To shatter a glass, a singer has to hit a note with an ear-splitting intensity of 135 decibels. And the singer must hold the note for two to three seconds, building up enough vibrations to shatter the glass.

Resonance causes bridges to collapse too. The most famous example of this is the Tacoma Narrows Bridge in Washington State. In 1940, just months after its completion, winds matching the resonant frequency of the bridge caused it to sway uncontrollably. Within hours, the bridge, also known as Galloping Gertie, collapsed.[60]

Is it possible that in one great crescendo the trumpets and voices of the Israelites hit the perfect pitch, causing the walls of Jericho to fall through the law of resonant frequency? Wouldn't you still consider that a miracle? Regardless of *how* the walls fell down, God's unusual battle plan took great faith. The people marched strangely silent for six days. But on the seventh day, an earth-shattering shout of faith was the first signal that the walls would crumble!

Day 1: Joshua 6:1–2   **PERILOUS UNDERTAKING**

Day 2: Joshua 6:2–5   **PROMISE OF VICTORY**

Day 3: Joshua 6:6–16   **POWERFUL SILENCE**

Day 4: Joshua 6:17, 22–25   **PROTECTING A BELIEVER**

Day 5: Joshua 6:20–21; 26–27   **PRONOUNCING A CURSE**

DAY 1
Perilous Undertaking

LIFT UP ...

Lord, You have already made me victorious through Your Son, Jesus. Help me to see how You work on my behalf. Amen.

LOOK AT ...

Today we start to see the conquest of Canaan as the Israelites begin their assault on the fortified city of Jericho. They had not rushed into battle but had paused to reinstate the covenant of circumcision, celebrate the Passover, enjoy the produce of Canaan, and wait for their marching orders.

Once their priorities were in order, the people were ready to mount an offensive against the great walled city. An encounter with the Commander of the Lord's army bolstered the confidence of their new captain, Joshua. However, God's strange battle plan must have made the new leader wonder whether marching silently around Jericho was the right idea. He was challenged to recognize that victory would be theirs only through unity and obedience to God's counterintuitive commands.

Have God's plans for you always appeared reasonable? Or, like Joshua, have you experienced situations that make no earthly sense? Sometimes our friends, families, or neighbors think we're odd people as we walk by faith and not by sight. They just don't "get" us. But the key to the Christian's victory is to trust and obey regardless of what He asks of us or what others might say.

READ JOSHUA 6:1–2.

Now Jericho was securely shut up because of the children of Israel; none went out, and none came in. And the LORD said to Joshua: "See! I have given Jericho into your hand, its king, and the mighty men of valor." Joshua 6:1–2

LEARN ABOUT ...

1 Safety Measures

The walls of stone and the will of men fortified Jericho. Absolutely none of the residents went out or came into the city, revealing an obstinacy neither to surrender nor retreat. Foolishly, they attempted to fortify their hearts against the Almighty: "Why then do you harden your hearts?" (1 Sam. 6:6).

---

3 Believing Is Seeing

God did not say "I will" give Jericho into Joshua's hand as though this were a future event. Instead God insisted that "I have" already given it, as a present reality. Faith believes before it sees: "Now faith is the substance of things hoped for, the evidence of things not seen" (Heb. 11:1).

---

7 Victim Or Victor?

God intended for the Canaanites to be dispossessed of the land. But if the Israelites failed, they instead would be dispossessed. Matthew Henry wrote, "Let us hear this, and fear. If we do not drive sin out, sin will drive us out; if we be not the death of our lusts, our lusts will be the death of our souls."[61]

1. Describe the defensive precautions Jericho had in place.

2. Explain why these safety measures were introduced.

3. Which of the five senses did the Lord ask Joshua to engage?

4. List the three things the Lord had already delivered into Joshua's hand.

5. What was the Lord encouraging Joshua to believe even though it hadn't happened yet?

LOOK AT ...

6. a. Read Numbers 33:50–56. Who was involved in this conversation, and where were they located?

   b. After the people crossed the Jordan, list the six "Ds" God commanded the people to accomplish.

   D_____   D_____
   D_____   D_____
   D_____   D_____

   (Note: If you have a translation other than NKJV, not all of the instructions begin with "d."

7. Describe the consequences of failing to accomplish these tasks.

LIVE OUT ...

8. The inhabitants of Jericho had taken great security measures to keep the Almighty out of their stony city. Have you hardened your heart against the Lord's hand or made it soft to His touch? In the appropriate column, list some attributes that indicate a hard or soft heart. Back them up with Bible references when possible.

HARD HEART   **SOFT HEART**

9. Joshua learned that believing is seeing. God wants us to walk by faith and not by sight.

   a. Read Matthew 20:29–34. Describe the people involved in this passage and where they were located.

   b. Record the condition and request of the two men alongside the road.

   c. Why do you think Jesus paid attention to them and granted their request?

10. In the Christian life we can be either victims or victors. As with Joshua, the victory is already ours. However, we must drive out sin, self, and Satan from controlling our lives or they will drive us away from God's promises.

   Journal about a sin, a selfish attitude, or a satanic lust that you currently face. Next find a biblical promise to counter the enemy. In the space provided rewrite the Scripture into a shout of victory!

LEARN ABOUT ...

8 Hard Heart

Scripture reveals many who hardened their hearts toward God. The Pharaoh witnessed the powerful plagues yet never surrendered. Because Israel hardened her heart, the people were put to the test during the wilderness wanderings. Jesus said that divorce occurs "because of the hardness of your hearts" (Matt. 19:8). God begs, "Do not harden your hearts" (Heb. 4:7).

9 Blinded

There are none so blind as those who will not see. Although they could see, Jesus regarded the Pharisees as blinded. "They are blind leaders of the blind. And if the blind leads the blind, both will fall into a ditch" (Matt. 15:14). Believers can say, "I once was blind but now I see!"

○ ○ ● ○ ○

At a young age, William Sangster found his way into an inner city London mission where a teacher gently asked if he wanted to follow Jesus Christ. "I spluttered out my little prayer," he wrote years later. "It had one merit; I meant it."

By the outbreak of World War II, Sangster had become the senior minister at Westminster Central Hall. The sanctuary, which held three thousand people, was full morning and evening for the sixteen years Sangster preached. He longed to see lukewarm pew-sitters aflame with the oceanic love that bleaches sin's allure and breaks sin's grip, the love that scorches and saves in the same instant.

Toward the end of his life a progressive muscular disease paralyzed his body and vocal chords. On his last Easter, able to move only his fingers, he painfully wrote his daughter a short note: "How terrible to wake up on Easter and have no voice to shout, 'He is risen!' Far worse, to have a voice and not want to shout."[62]

Joshua and the children of Israel were privileged to shout of God's victory at the top of their lungs. Imagine what it must have sounded like to the citizens of Jericho. As Jesus rode triumphally into Jerusalem on the back of a donkey, the people shouted hosannas. The religious leaders couldn't silence the crowd. Jesus warned, "If they kept quiet, the stones along the road would burst into cheers!" (Luke 19:40 NLT).

What about you? Will you let the rocks cry out in your place? Will you allow weakness or sickness to muffle the cries of Christ's victory over death and sin? Today, cheer loudly, proclaiming God's triumph in your life!

LISTEN TO ...

Be an "Amen Christian" but don't shout it any louder than you live.

—Unknown

DAY 2

Promise of Victory

Before David grew into a mighty warrior known for slaying tens of thousands, he was a young shepherd armed with only five smooth stones and a sling to bravely face a giant. God directed one deadly rock, like a guided missile, straight into Goliath's temple. Who would have believed that the promise of victory lay in the hands of a boy?

When King Jehoshaphat of Israel feared attack from the great armies of Moab, Syria, and Ammon, the promise of victory did not come from horses or chariots—but from a choir! As the enemies amassed, Jehoshaphat assembled the nation to fast and pray. God answered by commanding the Levites to lead the charge with praise. They proclaimed, "Praise the LORD, for His mercy endures forever." As they rejoiced, the enemy was routed. They learned, "The battle is not yours, but God's" (2 Chron. 20:15).

As the fledgling nation faced the first battle in the Promised Land, they, too, were promised victory. It was as miraculous as David's encounter with Goliath and Jehoshaphat's confrontation with great armies. They would face their enemies with silence for six days and great shouts on the seventh. As they obeyed, Jericho was obliterated.

Whether shown by slinging, singing, or shouting, the promise of victory comes not by the arm of man but from the hand of God. At one time or another each of us must learn the key spiritual conquest, "'Not by might nor by power, but by My Spirit,' says the LORD of hosts" (Zech. 4:6). So it was for great characters throughout the Bible, and so it is for us today.

LIFT UP ...

Lord, I don't always understand the instructions You give me, but I do know that You have a plan for me. Help me not to question but to obey. I desire to see You do great things in my life. Amen.

LEARN ABOUT ...

1 March On

The word *march* comes from a primitive word that means to surround, border, besiege, or beset. Paul records that Christians "must endure hardship as a good soldier of Jesus Christ" (2 Tim. 2:3). Deborah, the great female general of the Old Testament, sang, "March on, my soul; be strong!" (Judg. 5:21 NIV).

5 Six Days

The Holy Spirit used number patterns in Scripture to instruct us. The universe was created in six days, but on the seventh the Lord rested. Six days the Israelites collected manna, but on the seventh they rested. For six days the Israelites marched silently, but on the seventh they shouted. Seven represents completion.

LOOK AT ...

Today, we see God give Joshua specific instructions for invading a seemingly impenetrable citadel. What we can't see in this battle plan for Jericho is the geography and topography of this portion of the Promised Land. As the children of Israel camped at Gilgal near the Jordan River, they could see the unique situations of the stronghold cities of Jericho and Ai. Theses cities were the key to conquering all of Canaan because they guarded the bluffs leading to the hill country. If the Israelites wanted to capture the heights, they would need to start with these cities to drive a wedge between the northern and southern sections of Canaan. Then neither region would be able to assist the other. Thus, Israel would have a stranglehold on the land's supply routes.

Isn't that true in order to attain victory in our lives? In order to reach the heights, we must conquer the strongholds that impede our ascent. No thing, no one, no other god must be elevated above the Lord in the heart of the Christian. Scripture holds true that "the weapons we fight with are not the weapons of the world. On the contrary, they have divine power to demolish strongholds" (2 Cor. 10:4, NIV).

READ JOSHUA 6:2–5.

And the LORD said to Joshua: "See! I have given Jericho into your hand, its king, and the mighty men of valor. You shall march around the city, all you men of war; you shall go all around the city once. This you shall do six days. And seven priests shall bear seven trumpets of rams' horns before the ark. But the seventh day you shall march around the city seven times, and the priests shall blow the trumpets. It shall come to pass, when they make a long blast with the ram's horn, and when you hear the sound of the trumpet, that all the people shall shout with a great shout; then the wall of the city will fall down flat. And the people shall go up every man straight before him." Joshua 6:2–5

1. By faith, God had already delivered Jericho into Israel's hand. What physical activity did God ask the Israelites to carry out?

2. List the people who would participate in this march.

3. How many days were they required to march one time around the city?

4. Describe the priests' role, including the number of priests and their responsibilities.

5. Contrast the differences between what occurred on the seventh day and what happened the first six days.

6. What did God predict would happen on the seventh day?

7. What were the people instructed to do after that?

LIVE OUT ...

8. Like the children of Israel, believers are called to be soldiers of the Lord. Paul warned, "No one engaged in warfare entangles himself with the affairs of this life, that he may please him who enlisted him as a soldier" (2 Tim. 2:4).

   a. What circumstances have tangled you in the affairs of this life?

   b. How can you disentangle yourself from these things?

   c. According to this verse, what is the result of remaining unencumbered?

LEARN ABOUT ...

7 Fell Flat

Several commentators have supposed that the ground under the foundation of the walls opened and the wall sank into the chasm so that there remained nothing but plain ground for the Israelites to walk over. The literal translation is "the wall of the city shall fall down under itself or from its very foundations."[63]

8 Entangled

Once the Lord has loosed us from the bonds of sin, we must not let them entangle us again. "For if, after they have escaped the pollutions of the world through the knowledge of the Lord and Savior Jesus Christ, they are again entangled in them and overcome, the latter end is worse for them than the beginning" (2 Peter 2:20).

LEARN ABOUT ...

10 Silence Is Golden

Jesus taught us how to handle mockery and abuse: He remained silent. Isaiah prophesied, "He was oppressed and He was afflicted, Yet He opened not His mouth; He was led as a lamb to the slaughter, And as a sheep before its shearers is silent, So He opened not His mouth" (Isa. 53:7).

9. Write the name of someone you know who is serving in the armed forces:

   Think about how you can encourage him or her to keep marching on. This week say a prayer, send a card, or offer support to the family members who are waiting at home.

10. Perhaps as the people marched silently around the walls for six days, the inhabitants of Jericho taunted them. Have you ever been mocked for your obedience to the Lord? If so, how did it feel? How did you respond? Journal about that memory.

○ ○ ● ○ ○

The Commander of the Lord's army gave directions concerning how to besiege Jericho. Strangely the Israelites didn't dig trenches, erect battering rams, or devise weapons of mass destruction.

Instead, the Lord imparted a battle plan that didn't make sense. First, he ordered the army to march silently around Jericho for six days. "Yeah," a skeptic might think, "that will have them shaking in their boots." Second, on the seventh day, he instructed them to march around the city seven times. On the seventh lap, he told the people to shout. "Right," the skeptic would continue, "should they holler, 'Boo'? Or maybe, 'Surprise'?" One more thing, the Commander added, "Have the priests lead the charge!" Exasperated, the cynic may rebuff, "What are you thinking? Priests don't fight battles, privates do!"

What purpose did these unorthodox battle plans serve?

God alone was glorified by the victory: The battle truly belonged to the Lord.

The supernatural victory further caused the Canaanites to fear the one true God.

The Israelites recognized God's presence represented by the ark.

From that time forward they looked on it with reverence as a visual reminder to put God first.

The battle plan elevated the office of the priest over the position of the soldier. Ordinarily priests were excused from war, but this time they led the charge as they carried the ark and sounded the trumpets.

The seven days of marching in silence tested the people's faith and patience. Would they obey an order that seemed foolish or believe a promise that seemed improbable? They proved to themselves and their God that they could patiently endure their enemies' reproach.[64]

At Jericho God promised victory, but He alone would be the victor; He alone received the glory.

LISTEN TO ...

Only by desertion can we be defeated. With Christ and for Christ victory is certain. We can lose the victory by flight but not by death…. But woe to you if by forsaking the battle you forfeit at once both the victory and the crown.

—Bernard of Clairvaux

DAY 3

Powerful Silence

Are you comfortable with silence? If so, you're one of very few people. Not many of us are used to peace and quiet. Most of us wake up in the morning and turn on the coffeepot and the television at the same time to hear the day's news and weather. We turn on the radio while we drive. We're used to a soundtrack playing in the background of our lives—and we're uncomfortable without it. It could be that silence leaves too much room to think about conflicts we're facing, bills that are building, or a future that isn't turning out quite the way we expected.

The mime Marcel Marceau turned silence into an art form. Wearing white face paint, soft shoes, and a battered hat with a red flower, he used silence to speak volumes. He called himself a modern-day Don Quixote, "alone in a fragile world filled with injustice and beauty."[65]

Silence can also be used as a weapon. People use the "silent treatment" to try to settle disputes. It has also been rumored that the military has tested a psychological weapon known as "Silent Sound," an ultrasophisticated mind-altering technology. Supposedly, this electronic technology works on the subliminal level to "speak" directly to the mind of the listener, altering and training the brainwaves, manipulating the brain's electroencephalo-graphic patterns, and artificially implanting feelings of fear, anxiety, despair, and hopelessness.[66]

God enjoined Joshua to use the power of silence against the inhabitants of Jericho. Whether God used divine "Silent Sound" against the fortified city or whether the "silent treatment" got on the people of Jericho's nerves, we'll see that the sound of silence proved to be the right strategic move.

LIFT UP ...

Lord, thank You for being a God Who brings peace to my soul. Give me the strength to be quiet when You ask and to shout when it's time. Amen.

LOOK AT ...

Yesterday we saw God give Joshua final instructions concerning the conquest of Jericho. Now we see Joshua convey the commands to the people and observe their response of patient obedience.

The city of Jericho was one of the oldest occupied cities, perhaps *the* oldest occupied city, in the Promised Land. Jericho was surrounded by a massive earthen embankment held up by a retaining wall twelve to fifteen feet high at the base of the embankment. A six-foot-thick by eight-foot-tall mud brick wall stood atop the retaining wall. The embankment sloped upward toward the city, and at its summit stood another mud brick wall whose base was about forty-six feet above the ground level outside the city.

The total area enclosed by the walls was about nine acres. Archaeologists estimate that Jericho's population was about twelve hundred people. However, people were also living on the embankment between the upper and lower city walls. It's also probable that the Canaanites living in surrounding villages had fled to Jericho for safety. Thus, probably several thousand people were harbored inside the walls when the Israelites came against the city. There is evidence that the inhabitants of Jericho were prepared for a long siege.[67] It would truly take a miracle for the Israelites to take the impregnable city.

As you read this passage, consider what walls you have built separating you from God—walls of disbelief, disobedience, discontent, or distance. Ask God to miraculously tear them down.

READ JOSHUA 6:6–16.

Then Joshua the son of Nun called the priests and said to them, "Take up the ark of the covenant, and let seven priests bear seven trumpets of rams' horns before the ark of the LORD." And he said to the people, "Proceed, and march around the city, and let him who is armed advance before the ark of the LORD." So it was, when Joshua had spoken to the people, that the seven priests bearing the seven trumpets of rams' horns before the LORD advanced and blew the trumpets, and the ark of the covenant of the LORD followed them. The armed men went before the priests who blew the trumpets, and the rear guard came after the ark, while the priests continued blowing the trumpets. Now Joshua had commanded the people, saying,

Learn about ...

2 Church and State

Israel was established as a theocracy, where God's rule was supreme. His laws were the statutes of the kingdom. The priests and prophets were to interpret these laws. Moses and then Joshua were Jehovah's agents and appointees. Later the judges took on this role. In early Israel, there was no separation of church and state.[68]

4 Trumpet Sound

The trumpet or *shophar* was the greatest of Jewish ritual instruments. It was used for warlike purposes: to call to arms; to warn of an approaching enemy; to encourage during battle; and to recall troops. Also used for religious purposes, it marked the proclamation of the law, inaugurated the Year of Jubilee, heralded the ark's approach, and hailed new kings.[69]

5 Atypical Tactics

The conduct of this army was extremely atypical. Usually, to take a fortified city the army would have laid siege against it, built ramps to try to climb over the walls, or used battering rams to tear down the walls. The Jews trusted God to give them victory. The inhabitants of Jericho must have wondered if they possessed a secret weapon.

"You shall not shout or make any noise with your voice, nor shall a word proceed out of your mouth, until the day I say to you, 'Shout!' Then you shall shout." So he had the ark of the LORD circle the city, going around it once. Then they came into the camp and lodged in the camp. And Joshua rose early in the morning, and the priests took up the ark of the LORD. Then seven priests bearing seven trumpets of rams' horns before the ark of the LORD went on continually and blew with the trumpets. And the armed men went before them. But the rear guard came after the ark of the LORD, while the priests continued blowing the trumpets. And the second day they marched around the city once and returned to the camp. So they did six days. But it came to pass on the seventh day that they rose early, about the dawning of the day, and marched around the city seven times in the same manner. On that day only they marched around the city seven times. And the seventh time it happened, when the priests blew the trumpets, that Joshua said to the people: "Shout, for the LORD has given you the city!" Joshua 6:6–16

1. Recount the specific instructions Joshua gave to the priests.

2. Describe the order in which the people were to march around Jericho. What does this tell you about the nation's hierarchy?

3. a. "Joshua had commanded the people" to refrain from doing what and for how long?

   b. What would it be like for you to do this? Why?

4. What was the only sound made during the procession's first six days, and who made this sound?

5. a. Describe what the people were to do after circling "the city, going around it once."

b. How might they have felt about this going on for six days?

6. Recount what "came to pass on the seventh day."

7. Why did Joshua finally tell the people to shout?

LIVE OUT ...

8. a. Quietness is a spiritual discipline that God greatly values. Fill in the following table to discover some of the benefits of a quiet life.

SCRIPTURE	BENEFITS OF QUIET LIFE
Isaiah 30:15	
1 Thessalonians 4:11–12	
1 Timothy 2:1–4	
1 Peter 3:3–4	

b. Which of these passages spoke to you personally and why?

c. How can you seek more quiet in your life? (For example, try turning off radio, TV, and other media for a week, and talk to the Lord about thoughts and feelings that come up in the quiet. Or take five minutes each day to be alone, quiet, not reading, just being with yourself and God. What goes on in your head when you do that?)

9. If silence was a test of self-discipline, following in rank for six days without fighting was a test of obedience, fighting the war in God's way. Read 2 Corinthians 10:3–6.

a. What kinds of wars do believers fight? What does Paul mean by "strongholds"?

LEARN ABOUT ...

7 Victory Shout

The word *shout* means to split the ears with sound, to make a joyful noise, to sound an alarm or triumph.[70] The Israelites could shout in triumph because God would reward their patience and conquer the seemingly unconquerable city: "Let them shout for joy and be glad, Who favor my righteous cause" (Ps. 35:27).

8 Quiet Heart

To be quiet means to have a spirit of tranquility both without and within. It denotes peace even in the midst of a storm. Despite outward and inward conflicts, the believer can have a quiet heart, trusting that God is in control of all things. A quiet heart imitates "those who through faith and patience inherit the promises" (Heb. 6:12).

9 Stronghold

A stronghold is a fortified city with walls, towers, gates, and bars. The Amorites and Canaanites built many such cities. Figuratively speaking, we may put up walls against feeling certain emotions or devise a gateway to faith in God. But God promises to be "a stronghold in the day of trouble. (Nah. 1:7).

b. What weapons do we use?

c. Use the active verbs in the text to describe the specific actions we as believers are called to take (such as "pulling down strongholds").

d. How does a person go about taking thoughts into captivity?

e. What lets you know that you are capable of winning these battles (see v. 4)?

f. Journal about a stronghold you're facing—anything that is exalting itself above God or a disobedient habit that is standing in your way like a tall fortress. Ask God to tear it down so you can move forward in faith. What would it look like in your life for you to use the weapons and take the actions described in this passage?

○ ○ ● ○ ○

What do President George W. Bush, President Dwight D. Eisenhower, Jimmy Stewart, Kirk Douglas, Meryl Streep, and Raquel Welch have in common? The answer might surprise you: They were all cheerleaders.

The cheerleader's goal is to generate energy and enthusiasm during a game. Today there are an estimated 3.5 million cheerleaders in America. Surprisingly, cheerleading began with a man from Minnesota named Johnny Campbell, who didn't like sitting in the bleachers but wanted to be in front, urging his team on to victory. In 1898, Johnny Campbell, an undergraduate at the University of Minnesota, led the crowd in a famous chant: "Rah, Rah, Rah! Sku-u-mar, Hoo-Rah! Hoo-Rah! Varsity! Varsity! Varsity, Minn-e-So-Tah!" The Minnesota student publication *Ariel* said: "The following were nominated to lead the Yelling today: Jack Campbell, F.G. Kotlaba, M.J. Luby, Albert Armstrong of the Academics; Wickersham of the Laws; and Litzenverg of the Medics. These men would see to it that everybody leaves the park today breathless and voiceless, as this is the last game here, it ought to be a revelation to the people of Minnesota in regard to University enthusiasm."[71]

Perhaps Joshua, not Johnny Campbell, was the first "Yell Leader" who led the Israelites in a great shout so the walls of Jericho would come tumbling down. You don't need uniforms or acrobatics to generate enthusiasm. You can encourage those you love by acknowledging what God is doing in their lives and coming alongside them with words of encouragement. Don't sit idly in the bleachers—cheer others on to spiritual victory and let the walls come down!

LISTEN TO ...

Trumpets, though one were to sound for ten thousand years, cannot throw down walls; but faith can do all these things.

—*John Chrysostom*

DAY 4

Protecting a Believer

An Associated Press story about the Witness Protection Program gives some disturbing insight into this secretive system:

> An old mobster once gave Joseph Paonessa some advice that, if a bit chilling, has served him well during his many years working in the Federal Witness Protection Program. He said, "Kid, three people can keep a secret when two of them are dead," said Paonessa, a senior official in the U.S. Marshals Service.
>
> When managing a program that has relocated and provided new identities to 18,000 people, keeping a tight lid on information is more than a fond wish.... One important rule: "Don't find a counterfeiter a job in a printing plant," said Gerald Shur.... "When obtaining a legal name change for someone with a new identity, ask a judge to do it in secret and dispense with the requirement that the new name be published in a newspaper's legal notices. Remember that spouses and children are often part of the deal. One teenager asked his father, a protected witness, for a new car. When the father refused," Shur said, the teenager replied, "I'm going to go out and tell everybody who you are."[72]

Apparently, protecting witnesses is not for the faint of heart!

Rahab protected the Israeli spies, proving her faith in the Hebrew God. In return, she asked the spies to protect her and her family. In essence, the spies promised to put Rahab and her family under Witness Protection to save the family from God's judgment on Jericho. Would Rahab and her family maintain their part of the deal? And would the witnesses be protected? We'll see that God makes sure all who believe are saved.

LIFT UP ...

Lord, thank You for protecting me from the death penalty I deserve. I'm so grateful You came to save people of all races, ages, and genders. You are truly a merciful God. Amen.

LOOK AT ...

We've seen the Israelites exhibit the patience, obedience, and self-control to walk silently around the city of Jericho for six days before hearing Joshua give the okay to shout for victory. Now we see that while the city was destroyed, the promise to protect Rahab the harlot was miraculously preserved.

According to the scriptural record, Rahab's inn was located on the very walls that were doomed for destruction. The spies instructed her to hang a scarlet cord from her home and bring her family inside to save them from the coming onslaught. But if the walls fell, how was Rahab spared? Again, we look to the archaeological record. Digs at the site of old Jericho show that only one portion of the city walls endured. Bryant Wood wrote,

> The German excavation of 1907–1909 found that on the north a short stretch of the lower city wall did not fall as everywhere else. A portion of that mudbrick wall was still standing to a height of over two meters [eight feet]. What is more, there were houses built against the wall! It is quite possible that this is where Rahab's house was. Since the city wall formed the back wall of the houses, the spies could have readily escaped. From this location on the north side of the city it was only a short distance to the hills of the Judean wilderness where the spies hid for three days. Real estate values must have been low here, since the houses were positioned on the embankment between the upper and lower city walls. Not the best place to live in time of war! This area was no doubt the overflow from the upper city and the poor part of town, perhaps even a slum district.[73]

God kept the spies' promise to Rahab to protect her home and her family despite a disaster of epic proportions. Don't ever doubt that He is able to protect you and those you love.

READ JOSHUA 6:17.

"Now the city shall be doomed by the LORD to destruction, it and all who are in it. Only

Rahab the harlot shall live, she and all who are with her in the house, because she hid the messengers that we sent." Joshua 6:17

1. Following the great shout, describe what would happen to the city.

2. Explain who would live and why.

LOOK AT ...

As we continue with Rahab's story, we gain insight into how she was spared from the destruction of her hometown and became integrated into the Israelite community. Please turn your attention now to Joshua 6:22–25.

> *But Joshua had said to the two men who had spied out the country, "Go into the harlot's house, and from there bring out the woman and all that she has, as you swore to her." And the young men who had been spies went in and brought out Rahab, her father, her mother, her brothers, and all that she had. So they brought out all her relatives and left them outside the camp of Israel. But they burned the city and all that was in it with fire. Only the silver and gold, and the vessels of bronze and iron, they put into the treasury of the house of the LORD. And Joshua spared Rahab the harlot, her father's household, and all that she had. So she dwells in Israel to this day, because she hid the messengers whom Joshua sent to spy out Jericho.* Joshua 6:22–25

3. Recount what Joshua told the two spies.

4. Describe the action they took toward Rahab's family.

5. Explain what happened to the city and to the precious metals.

6. According to this account, what happened to Rahab and why?

7. Review Matthew 1:1–6 and describe how Rahab was ultimately honored.

LIVE OUT ...

8. In Jericho, Rahab's house was literally built into the wall. The spies came to her house and ultimately brought salvation to her and the people in her home.

   a. Talk about the people who brought the message of the gospel to you and how you received salvation into your heart.

   b. Now imagine your heart as the home built into the wall of the sinful city. Journal a prayer, thanking God for saving you from destruction through your Joshua, Jesus.[75]

9. We saw that Rahab and her family were sent outside the camp until they could be drawn inside by obedience to the laws. With this in mind, read Hebrews 13:12–16.

   a. Why was Jesus crucified "outside the gate" of Jerusalem? What did this signify?

   b. What do you think it means for us to go "outside the camp"?

   c. Why should we do this?

   d. Since Jesus offered the sacrifice of Himself outside the gate, what sacrifices can we offer (see verses 15–16)? How can you offer these today?

LEARN ABOUT ...

4 Outside the Camp

According to the Levitical laws, anything that was unclean was to be put "outside the camp." Since Rahab and her family were considered unclean Gentiles, that is where they were initially sent. Once the men were circumcised and the family began submitting to the law of Moses, they could become insiders.

5 Firstfruits

The first town the Israelites conquered and all that was within it were considered "firstfruits" of the victories. Warren Wiersbe said, "Ordinarily the soldiers shared the spoils of war (Deut. 20:14), but not at Jericho, for everything there belonged to the Lord and was put into His treasury (Deut. 13:16)."[74]

8 Gospel Message

The gospel is the joyous good news of salvation in Jesus Christ. The Greek word translated "gospel" simply means good news. The gospel is the saving work of God in His Son Jesus Christ and is a call to faith in Him (see Rom. 1:16–17). Jesus is more than a messenger of the gospel; He *is* the gospel.[76]

10. a. Today we saw the Israelites celebrate the offering of firstfruits. Read the verses below and draw a line to the verse that best describes the verse you are reading.

Leviticus 2:14	The Spirit
Deuteronomy 18:4	Your increase
Proverbs 3:9	Those who have fallen asleep
Romans 8:23	Offer firstfruits of grain, new wine, oil, fleece
1 Corinthians 15:20	Grain burnt on the altar

b. Which of these offerings have you participated in? Talk about which are relevant today and why.

o o ● o o

Imagine marrying into a culture where you don't know the language, rituals, or ways of the people. The people in your new family look at you as an outsider at best or an enemy at worst. You're a war bride and you feel that the war came with you.

During the Korean Conflict, marriage to Asian women from Japan and Korea was strongly discouraged for servicemen. The soldiers faced daunting obstacles if they chose to marry. Retired Naval Aid to the Far East Command Ralph Lucas recalls mounds of paperwork for an interracial marriage at least an inch and a half thick. The would-be bridegroom was asked to supply health information, family background information, and criminal background search results, among other things. According to Lucas, it took about eighteen months for the paperwork to be completed and processed. "Every 'T' had to be crossed and every 'I' had to be dotted before the paperwork was approved," he recalled. Apparently, military officials felt that some of the women were not "choice" women.[77]

Rahab was a war bride. Most would have said she was not a "choice" woman since she was a pagan, a prostitute, and an enemy of the Israelites. Yet she integrated into the Hebrew culture, marrying and embracing Hebrew faith. Some commentators believe that her future husband was Salmon, one of the spies and a member of the tribe of Judah. Her inclusion in the messianic line is a portrait of how God can take a war bride and offer her a peace treaty. Through her, the Prince of Peace was born, bringing salvation to all who would believe.

LISTEN TO ...

Be assured, if you walk with Him, and look to Him, and expect help from Him, He will never fail you.

—*George Muller*

DAY 5

Pronouncing a Curse

In today's culture, curses are more apt to define movie ratings than summon divine wrath. Mothers teach their children not to say curse words. But the concept of a curse does not carry the weight that curses did in ancient times. In fact, we even pay to see curses. Think about it. Movies like *Pirates of the Caribbean: The Curse of the Black Pearl* rake in millions of dollars. We stand in line to see exhibits of King Tut's artifacts and talk about the legends surrounding those who were cursed because they entered his tomb. If you're a baseball fan, you might talk about Bambino's curse on the Red Sox, who didn't win the World Series until 2004 because Babe Ruth was traded to the Yankees. One computer technician even programmed a Bible curse generator that would come up with multiple phrases to curse people using biblical words.

But these are not what we read about when we encounter curses in Scripture. In the Bible, a curse is a prophecy made by a holy man. Curses are not prompted by feelings of revenge but are predictions of the future. A biblical curse carries with it the power to bring about the result foretold—it's the real deal, not some Hollywood fantasy.

God Himself cursed the Serpent in the garden of Eden. And He cursed Cain, condemning him to be a vagabond for murdering his brother Abel. God promised Abraham to curse those who cursed him. And now we see Joshua pronounce a curse on the city of Jericho.

LIFT UP ...

Lord, thank You that You are able to balance mercy with judgment. If You were only merciful, You would not be just. If you were only just, You would not be merciful. Thank You for showing grace to me by blessing me. Amen.

LOOK AT ...

Over the past few days we've seen the people obediently walk in silence around the walls of Jericho, waiting for Joshua to give the command to shout on the seventh day.

We've also seen God's plan to wage a rescue mission even as He judged the people of Jericho. Now we see the walls fall and the utter destruction of the seemingly impregnable city.

This invasion fulfilled God's command to completely destroy the inhabitants of the Canaanite cities. This was not Joshua's war—this was God's war on the sin of the pagan nations of Canaan. He had given them over four hundred years to repent, but only Rahab and her family turned in faith to the living God.

Many people question why a God of love could allow such devastation. But God is also a God of justice. His mercy must be balanced with judgment or He would not be a righteous God. The psalmist wrote, "The LORD is righteous, He loves righteousness" (Ps. 11:7). As people living in the age of grace, too often we forget that God will one day come to judge the earth in righteousness. Let's remember to walk in holy fear of the Lord, desiring to please Him and point others toward His merciful love so that they never have to face His righteous judgment.

READ JOSHUA 6:20–21.

So the people shouted when the priests blew the trumpets. And it happened when the people heard the sound of the trumpet, and the people shouted with a great shout, that the wall fell down flat. Then the people went up into the city, every man straight before him, and they took the city. And they utterly destroyed all that was in the city, both man and woman, young and old, ox and sheep and donkey, with the edge of the sword. Joshua 6:20–21

1. Use the following transition words to recount the series of events. (Put them into your own words.)

   So:

   And:

   And:

   That:

   Then:

   And:

LEARN ABOUT ...

2 Utter Destruction

God ordered utter destruction to protect His people: "Of the cities of these peoples which the LORD your God gives you as an inheritance, you shall let nothing that breathes remain alive, but you shall utterly destroy them ... lest they teach you to do according to all their abominations which they have done for their gods, and you sin against the LORD your God" (Deut. 20:16–18).

4 Curse on Jericho

Joshua's curse represented a desire that nothing be disturbed at the site. It emphasized the completeness of the divine judgment against the city as well as offering the city to God as the first city conquered in the land. It would be devoted to God by complete destruction.

5 Famous

Joshua's fame grew because God was faithful. The queen of Sheba heard of Solomon's fame concerning the name of the LORD (see I Kings 10:1); Mordecai grew famous in Persia when he saved the Jews from destruction; Jesus grew famous in Galilee for His ability to heal the sick.

2. What was destroyed in the city?

3. Describe what happened to the human beings and animals.

LOOK AT ...

Following the destruction of the city, Joshua moved forward by addressing the people and pronouncing the future of Jericho. Let's look at Joshua 6:26–27 to see what happened next.

Then Joshua charged them at that time, saying, "Cursed be the man before the LORD who rises up and builds this city Jericho; he shall lay its foundation with his firstborn, and with his youngest he shall set up its gates." So the LORD was with Joshua, and his fame spread throughout all the country. Joshua 6:26–27

4. Explain the curse against anyone rebuilding the city.

5. Describe who was with Joshua and how this affected his reputation.

6. What impression of God do you get from Joshua 6?

LIVE OUT ...

7. Just as Joshua commanded the Israelites to kill everything in Jericho to protect them from the sinfulness there, there are times when we must be protected from our own sinfulness. It may feel like God is punishing us when in fact He is protecting us. Check the boxes below to indicate some things you have needed protection from:

❏ my ways—doing things I shouldn't do (see Ps. 39)

❏ my mouth—saying things I shouldn't say (see Ps. 141:3)

❏ my will—doing things in haste (see Isa. 52:12)

❏ my heart and mind—thinking ungodly thoughts (see Phil. 4:7)

❏ my intellect—thinking I know better (see 1 Tim. 6:20)

Now journal a prayer asking God to put to death anything that is not of Him. Ask Him to protect you from those things that are dangerous to your spiritual well-being.

8. a. We saw that Joshua cursed the city of Jericho. Read 1 Kings 16: 30–34 and describe how this curse was fulfilled.

b. What do you learn about God's character from this?

9. a. Joshua's fame spread throughout the country. Talk about some of the people who are famous in our country. What makes them famous and why?

b. Now talk about why Joshua became famous. How would our nation change if this were the standard today?

LEARN ABOUT …

7 Protection

Many of us put up a guard, even from God, thinking we can do things in our own strength. But the truth is we need protection from the world, the flesh, and the Devil. When we turn to the Lord, He "is faithful, who will establish you and guard you from the evil one" (2 Thess. 3:3).

---

9 Fleeting Fame

Fame is fleeting unless the focus is the fame of the Lord. True servants of the Lord are more concerned with God's reputation than their own. The psalmist wrote, "Your name, O LORD, endures forever, Your fame, O LORD, throughout all generations" (Ps. 135:13). Spread God's fame—it lasts forever.

○ ○ ● ○ ○

The Great Bambino, legendary baseball player Babe Ruth, said, "Most of the people who have really counted in my life were not famous. Few ever heard of them, except those who knew and loved them." He went on to speak of his clergyman:

I knew an old minister once whose hair was white and whose face shone. I have written my name on thousands and thousands of baseballs in my life; he wrote his name on just a few simple hearts. How I envy him! He was not trying to please himself and win the plaudits of the world. So fame never came to him. I am listed as a famous homerun hitter. Yet, beside that humble, obscure minister, who was so good and wise, I never got to first base![78]

Ultimately, like Joshua, the only things that really matter are those things we do for God. Are we helping to write God's name on the hearts and minds of those we love? Are we helping to tear down strongholds that separate us from a deeper walk of faith? Are we walking in obedience to God's commands, bringing blessing to those around us? When we become more concerned with God's fame than with our own creature comforts or our own reputations, then the walls that separate us from God will truly tumble down.

LISTEN TO ...

It is better to be faithful than famous.

—Theodore Roosevelt

Something Is Rotten in the State of Israel

Joshua 7—8

One of Shakespeare's most famous plays is *Hamlet,* the story of the anguished prince of Denmark. In act 1, scene IV, the ghost of the murdered king of Denmark appears to guards watching over the castle at Elsinore. The following night, the ghost appears again, seeming to beckon Hamlet to come away from the others, clearly desiring to speak to his son in private. The officers warn Hamlet not to follow, but he refuses to obey. As Hamlet goes after his father's ghost, the officer Marcellus utters one of the most famous lines from the play, "Something is rotten in the state of Denmark." This turns out to be a prophetic statement, predicting the evil lurking in the heart of the new king who is greedy for power and will stop at nothing to attain what he seeks. The play finds Hamlet struggling to retain his personal integrity and fight the corruption within his kingdom.

Following the great victory at Jericho, the Israelites presumed they would move onward to victory. But something was rotten in the State of Israel. Despite outward appearances, inward corruption was lurking in the heart of one man and his family. This threatened to destroy the integrity of the nation and temporarily stalled its military progress. Joshua was forced to deal with the disappointment of defeat because of one family's disobedience. Let's learn from the mistakes at Ai so we can move forward in faith.

Day 1 Joshua 7:1–12   NATIONAL TRAGEDY

Day 2 Joshua 7:13–26   PERSONAL MALADY

Day 3 Joshua 8:1–9   COMMUNAL REMEDY

Day 4 Joshua 8:10–29   TRIBAL VICTORY

Day 5 Joshua 8:30–35   SPIRITUAL SOLIDARITY

DAY 1
National Tragedy

LIFT UP ...

Lord, I know nothing is hidden from You. I don't want to live a life hiding sin from You because it affects everyone around me. Please bring it to light so I may ask for forgiveness. Amen.

LOOK AT ...

The Israelites experienced the supernatural conquest of Jericho when they saw the walls fall and their enemies conquered. God was truly with them as they followed His commands to take the fortified city. Now Joshua turned his attention to the next city in the Promised Land: Ai.

Ai was a place of reckoning, where the Israelites would face defeat before they would taste victory again. Ai was located east of Bethel. Joshua may have chosen this as a strategic route to secure the hill country and stand between Jerusalem and Bethel. Sadly, the Israelites would march up to Ai but would be brought down by their own sin and by their enemies.

Many years before, Abraham pitched his tent between Bethel and Ai before journeying down to Egypt. We, too, are between places at times. The Israelites were between a victory and a defeat, yet they did not know it. Defeat loomed, yet they failed to look first to the One who could show them the way. Are you moving toward Ai without asking for the proper guidance? Don't look for wisdom from the world or the people around you. Stop and ask God for direction before trying to rally the troops and take Ai.

READ JOSHUA 7:1–5.

But the children of Israel committed a trespass regarding the accursed things, for Achan the son of Carmi, the son of Zabdi, the son of Zerah, of the tribe of Judah, took of the accursed things; so the anger of the LORD burned against the children of Israel. Now Joshua sent men from Jericho to Ai, which is beside Beth Aven, on the east side of Bethel, and spoke to them, saying, "Go up and spy out the country." So the men went up and spied out Ai. And they returned to Joshua and said to him, "Do not let all the people go up, but let about two or three thousand men go up and attack Ai. Do not weary all the people there, for the people of Ai are few." So about three thousand men went up there from the people, but they fled before the men of Ai. And the men of Ai struck down about thirty-six men, for they chased them from before the gate as far as Shebarim, and struck them down on the descent; therefore the hearts of the people melted and became like water. Joshua 7:1–5

1. a. This chapter opens with the cautionary word *But*. In your own words explain "But" what happened.

   b. How did the Lord feel about it? Why?

2. "Now" describe the reconnaissance sent for the next city and the report Joshua received.

3. Do you think Joshua knew about the trespass at this time? What gives you that impression?

4. Describe the initial attack on Ai and the resulting losses, both emotional and physical.

LOOK AT ...

The Israelites suffered their first defeat in the Promised Land. Direct your attention to Joshua 7:6–12 to see Joshua's response and the Lord's reply.

Then Joshua tore his clothes, and fell to the earth on his face before the ark of the LORD until evening, he and the elders of Israel; and they put

LEARN ABOUT ...

1 Trespass

The word *trespass* means a violation of law. The Hebrew word translated as trespass means "a stepping aside from the [correct path."[79] In this case, Achan trespassed by taking some of the plunder from Jericho. It was supposed to be devoted for God's use or destroyed, not to be used for a man's greed.

3 Presumption

Joshua had specific instructions from the Lord of Hosts concerning how to march on Jericho. He hadn't yet received instructions concerning Ai. It was wise to send the spies but foolish to follow their advice. A good rule is to do the last thing God told you or wait for His next command: "Keep back Your servant also from presumptuous sins" (Ps. 19:13).

LEARN ABOUT ...

6 Corporate Sin

God considered the Israelites a unit—the sin of one affected all. In God's eyes, though only Achan sinned, all of Israel was infected and required cleansing. But God had made provision for unintentional sin saying, "The priest shall make atonement for the whole congregation of the children of Israel, and it shall be forgiven them" (Num. 15:25).

dust on their heads. And Joshua said, "Alas, Lord GOD, why have You brought this people over the Jordan at all—to deliver us into the hand of the Amorites, to destroy us? Oh, that we had been content, and dwelt on the other side of the Jordan! O Lord, what shall I say when Israel turns its back before its enemies? For the Canaanites and all the inhabitants of the land will hear it, and surround us, and cut off our name from the earth. Then what will You do for Your great name?" So the LORD said to Joshua: "Get up! Why do you lie thus on your face? Israel has sinned, and they have also transgressed My covenant which I commanded them. For they have even taken some of the accursed things, and have both stolen and deceived; and they have also put it among their own stuff. Therefore the children of Israel could not stand before their enemies, but turned their backs before their enemies, because they have become doomed to destruction. Neither will I be with you anymore, unless you destroy the accursed from among you." Joshua 7:6–12

5. a. Joshua and the elders mourned their loss. Describe the physical attitude Joshua and the elders displayed. What do you think this meant?

   b. What was the first question Joshua asked the Lord? Who did he blame for their loss?

   c. What was the second question Joshua asked? Who was he most concerned about?

   d. Recount the third question. Who was Joshua concerned about?

6. a. Note how the Lord responded to Joshua's cries. What was the true reason for Israel's defeat?

   b. What would be the remedy for this sin?

LIVE OUT ...

7. a. Today we saw God's anger burn against Achan for taking forbidden things. With this in mind, fill in the following chart to discover other things that make God burn with anger.

SCRIPTURE	WHAT MAKES GOD ANGRY
Exodus 4:10–17	
Numbers 11:1–3	
Judges 2:11–12	
2 Chronicles 33:1–6	

   b. Have you ever made God angry, perhaps in one of the ways mentioned above? If so, journal about it. What feelings or questions do you have when you think God is angry?

8. Joshua asked three questions, two of them self-absorbed and one of them God-centered. Think about your life circumstances and ask the questions Joshua asked, reaching the ultimate question about God's reputation.

   a. "Alas, Lord, why have You brought me

   _____?"

   b. "Lord, what will I say when

   _____?"

   c. "Lord, what will You do for Your great name in this circumstance

   _____?"

9. a. God didn't allow Joshua to wallow in self-pity over the loss at Ai. He told him, "Get up," and deal with the concealed sin. According to 1 John 1:9, describe the remedy for sin.

   b. When was the last time you did this? How did it make you feel?

LEARN ABOUT ...

7 Divine Anger

God's anger is unlike human anger. His anger is absolutely righteous, perfectly holy, and completely just. The word *anger* speaks of a fierce, hot displeasure. God's wrath is in no way vindictive or malicious—It is holy indignation—His anger is directed against sin.[80] "God is a just judge, and God is angry with the wicked every day" (Ps. 7:11).

9 Kneel Down

The best way to get up from our sins is to kneel down and confess them to the Lord. Though God burns with anger over sin, He burns with love for the sinner and is quick to forgive. The psalmist wrote, "'I will confess my transgressions to the LORD,' and You forgave the iniquity of my sin" (Ps. 32:5).

○ ○ ● ○ ○

We've all heard that "one bad apple spoils the barrel." The phrase came from one of Chaucer's *Canterbury Tales*, but Chaucer put it a bit differently: "Better is one rotten apple out of hoard, than that it should rot all the remnant."

We began to wonder, does one rotten apple really spoil the barrel? It turns out that it does. Scientists say that ethylene is involved in the ripening process of fruits known as "climacteric" fruits, which include apples, bananas, avocados, tomatoes, and others. These fruits produce a burst of ethylene as they ripen, which is followed by increased respiration and accelerated ripening. Exogenous ethylene stimulates ripening in these fruits. This is why one rotten apple does indeed spoil the whole barrel. One overripe apple produces ethylene, which diffuses to the others and accelerates their ripening.[81]

The same is true in both the physical and spiritual realms. When we humans come in contact with a person infected with a virus, we are in danger of being contaminated with the virus and passing it on to those around us. Spiritually, sin is a virus that is just as contagious as a cold or the flu. Achan had been contaminated with greed, and it had already cost the Israelites a great deal. The only way to deal with this deadly danger was to isolate the source and destroy it before it infected the rest of the people. Achan was a bad apple who could have spoiled the whole nation.

LISTEN TO ...

There is more evil in a drop of sin, than in a sea of affliction.

—*Thomas Watson*

DAY 2

Personal Malady

I'll never forget the time I (Penny) took my sweet three-year-old daughter, Ryan, to the Bible bookstore. As I bought the latest Christian novel, I chatted with Marc, the owner of the store, who was a family friend. Unbeknownst to me, Ryan had grabbed two pencils that said, "Jesus Loves Me." As I said good-bye to Marc, I grabbed Ryan's hand and headed out the door, unaware that I was headed for a showdown.

When we reached the car, I opened the door then picked up Ryan to put her in the car seat. That's when I saw the pencils in her hand. I said, "Ryan, where did you get those pencils?"

She said, "They're mine."

I replied, "I didn't pay for those pencils. You took something that isn't yours. That's stealing. God says it's a sin to steal."

Ryan just looked at me and said, "NO, they're mine!"

I said in my "firm mommy" voice, "Ryan Rose, we are going to tell Mr. Marc that you took those pencils and you are asking him to forgive you."

She looked at me and said, "No."

I knew I had to win this battle of the wills. I said, "Ryan, we'll stand here until you decide to go in and return those pencils and ask Mr. Marc to forgive you." Then I prayed, "Dear Lord, please help Ryan to understand that stealing is wrong. Help her to have the courage to admit it."

She tugged my arm and said, "Mommy, I'm ready to go talk to Mr. Marc."

Greed is never pretty. Though it is difficult to deal with, it is better to deal with it quickly than let it affect those around us.

Lift up ...

Lord, I know my sin affects so many people around me. Please cleanse me of all my unrighteousness that I may be truly clean. Amen.

LOOK AT ...

Yesterday we saw the disastrous effects of moving forward without awaiting God's direction. We also saw that Joshua was unaware of the spiritual condition of the people in the congregation. Today we see God direct Joshua to sanctify the people and to punish those who defied His commands by taking the accursed things at Jericho.

The investigation and trial of Achan and his family must have been a fearful and solemn reminder that the personal malady of sin is contagious. Perhaps they thought of the accursed things they had taken. Maybe they thought of the times they had laughed, fellowshipped, and worshipped with Achan and his family. For us this is a solemn reminder that nothing is hidden from the Lord. Jeremiah said, "The heart is deceitful above all things, And desperately wicked; Who can know it? I, the LORD, search the heart, I test the mind, Even to give every man according to his ways, According to the fruit of his doings" (Jer. 17:9–10). We may think we're hiding a secret sin, but we can hide nothing from God.

READ JOSHUA 7:13–21.

"Get up, sanctify the people, and say, 'Sanctify yourselves for tomorrow, because thus says the LORD God of Israel: "There is an accursed thing in your midst, O Israel; you cannot stand before your enemies until you take away the accursed thing from among you." In the morning therefore you shall be brought according to your tribes. And it shall be that the tribe which the LORD takes shall come according to families; and the family which the LORD takes shall come by households; and the household which the LORD takes shall come man by man. Then it shall be that he who is taken with the accursed thing shall be burned with fire, he and all that he has, because he has transgressed the covenant of the LORD, and because he has done a disgraceful thing in Israel.'" So Joshua rose early in the morning and brought Israel by their tribes, and the tribe of Judah was taken. He brought the clan of Judah, and he took the family of the Zarhites; and he brought the family of the Zarhites man by man, and Zabdi was taken. Then he brought his household man by man, and Achan the son of Carmi, the son of Zabdi, the son of Zerah, of the tribe of Judah, was taken. Now Joshua said to Achan, "My son, I beg you, give glory to the LORD God of Israel, and make confession to Him, and tell me now what you have done; do not hide it from

me." And Achan answered Joshua and said, "Indeed I have sinned against the LORD God of Israel, and this is what I have done: When I saw among the spoils a beautiful Babylonian garment, two hundred shekels of silver, and a wedge of gold weighing fifty shekels, I coveted them and took them. And there they are, hidden in the earth in the midst of my tent, with the silver under it." Joshua 7:13–21

1. Recount the instructions Joshua was to get up and give to the people.

2. Describe how God said He would narrow down the suspects "in the morning."

3. What punishment did God decree for him "who is taken with the accursed thing" and why?

4. List the names of those who were taken after "Joshua rose early" the next morning.

5. a. Recount what Joshua said to Achan.

   b. What tone do you think Joshua was speaking in and why?

6. a. In your own words note how Achan answered Joshua.

   b. Describe the items that were found in Achan's tent.

LOOK AT ...

We've seen how Achan confessed his sin of covetousness before the entire congregation. Now let's move ahead to Joshua 7:22–26 to see the consequences of personal sin on public society.

LEARN ABOUT ...

I Sanctify

To sanctify means to make something sacred or set apart; to make it ceremonially clean or purified and dedicated to the Lord. The dominant idea of sanctification, therefore, is separation from the secular and sinful and the setting apart for a sacred purpose. In the Old Testament, this could include ceremonial cleansing, the offering of sacrifices, and other Levitical rites.[82]

---

6 Covetousness

To covet means to fix a desire upon, to lust after, to passionately yearn to possess something that does not belong to you. One of the Ten Commandments specifically prohibited this attitude. Covetousness springs from feelings of greed and self-centeredness: "You shall not covet" (Ex. 20:17).

Learn about ...

7 Troubled

Achan's name sounds like the Hebrew for *trouble*. Here, Joshua is using his name as a double entendre to pronounce his punishment: The troubler would be troubled. The Valley of Achor was probably named after this incident, because Achor means trouble.

9 Holiness

God is utterly holy, set apart from what is common for us. Because of the fall, humans are naturally unholy and sinful. Only through God's work of salvation do we become holy, set apart for Him. As we walk with God, we work in tandem with the Holy Spirit and strive to become more holy: "Be holy in all your conduct" (1 Peter 1:15).

So Joshua sent messengers, and they ran to the tent; and there it was, hidden in his tent, with the silver under it. And they took them from the midst of the tent, brought them to Joshua and to all the children of Israel, and laid them out before the LORD. Then Joshua, and all Israel with him, took Achan the son of Zerah, the silver, the garment, the wedge of gold, his sons, his daughters, his oxen, his donkeys, his sheep, his tent, and all that he had, and they brought them to the Valley of Achor. And Joshua said, "Why have you troubled us? The LORD will trouble you this day." So all Israel stoned him with stones; and they burned them with fire after they had stoned them with stones. Then they raised over him a great heap of stones, still there to this day. So the LORD turned from the fierceness of His anger. Therefore the name of that place has been called the Valley of Achor to this day. Joshua 7:22–26

7. a. Describe what happened in the Valley of Achor to Achan, his family, and his possessions.

   b. Why do you think Achan's family was punished with him?

8. How did the Lord respond to this action?

Live out ...

9. a. What do you learn about God from this incident with Achan?

   b. What emotions and questions does this story raise for you? Can you think of other passages of Scripture that address your questions?

10. a. Today's passage revealed the path toward covetousness. Have you ever been greedy? If you have, then beside each phrase

of Achan's confession, describe a time when you acted greedily:

I saw:

I coveted:

I took:

b. Now reword Hebrews 13:5 into a personal prayer asking God to take away any covetousness and make you truly content: "Let your conduct be without covetousness; be content with such things as you have."

11. Achan and his family received the death penalty in the Valley of Achor (The Valley of Trouble). Read the following verses and describe what will happen in this valley in the future.

Isaiah 65:10

Hosea 2:15

LEARN ABOUT ...

II Hope
God can transform the Valley of Trouble into the Valley of Hope. When we bring our troubles to the Messiah, He offers us the hope of supernatural strength, a new song in our hearts, and a place of spiritual rest: "Be of good courage, And He shall strengthen your heart, All you who hope in the LORD" (Ps. 31:24).

○ ○ ● ○ ○

The story is told of a man and an angel who went on a walk together. The man was complaining about his neighbors. "What a horrible group of people!" he moaned. "The townsfolk are the greediest group of people I've ever encountered. Not to mention the fact that among them there are many thieves who would steal the shirt off your back."

The angel looked at the man and asked, "Is that true? Do you have proof?"

The complaining man said, "Well, just look at that man walking toward us. His eyes are set so close together. He has a furrowed brow. And his gaze is shifty. And just look at that large overcoat—it's perfect for holding the goods he's stolen. Why I wouldn't trust that man within an inch of my life."

The angel replied, "I think you're a very good judge of character. But there's one thing you've failed to notice. You're looking into a mirror."[83]

It's not pretty to look into the mirror of covetousness. We may not be guilty of stealing people's property, but most of us have looked at another person's possessions and said in our hearts, "I want that!" Sadly, this attitude can kill the joy we have in possessing those things God has given us. Let's learn the lesson from Achan. Rather than being greedy, let's become generous. The prophet Isaiah wrote, "Generous people plan to do what is generous, and they stand firm in their generosity" (Isa. 32:8 NLT).

LISTEN TO ...

O greedy men, what will satisfy you if God himself will not?

—*Blaise Pascal*

DAY 3

Communal Remedy

Intrigue and adventure abound in *The Three Musketeers* by Alexander Dumas. Hollywood, recognizing it as the quintessential "swashbuckling" novel, has created countless films from its pages. Ask any school-age boy if he knows the trio's famous proclamation and he'll shout, "All for one and one for all!"

Athos, Porthos, and Aramis, known as "the three inseparables" from among the king's guard, are the main characters. When a young, ambitious d'Artagnan arrives on the scene, he somehow offends all three comrades in one day. Each demands a duel. In the midst of d'Artagnan's sword-wielding encounter with the trio, the soldiers of the shifty Cardinal Richelieu arrive to arrest the musketeers. Displaying bravery and brilliant fencing skills, d'Artagnan defends the musketeers and finds himself accepted into their confidence. Eventually he becomes known as the unofficial "fourth musketeer."

The traitor Cardinal Richelieu appears seemingly omnipresent and omniscient—a dangerous combination. He skillfully enacts legislation that forces the king's guard to stand down. Afterward, the cardinal commands his troops to stage a coup against reigning King Louis. However, the loyal intervention of "the four musketeers" saves the kingdom from destruction.

Joshua's reign as commander has been challenged by the disobedience of Achan. His disloyalty to God and nation causes Israel's first defeat. But as Joshua rallies the nation to stand, "One for all and all for one," the tide turns. They discover a communal remedy to a personal malady.

LIFT UP ...

Lord, I want You to draw out those areas in my life that interfere with our relationship. I don't want anything standing between me and the victory You have planned. Help me in my efforts to be obedient to You. Amen.

LOOK AT ...

The sin of Achan brought national consequences as the children of Israel mounted an offensive against Ai. Defeat found the leader, Joshua, on his knees asking God for wisdom and deliverance. God demanded sanctification, purging the nation of the sin as well as the sinner. Drastic times called for drastic measures as Achan and his entire household were taken to the Valley of Achor to be stoned to death and then burned.

Now God reaffirms His assistance and assures victory in a second offensive against Ai. Staying true to form, God works all things together for the good of His people. He alone can turn defeat into victory. Because Joshua's armies fled previously, God instructs them to feign retreat once again. He knows the men of Ai will foolishly follow, leaving the city vulnerable.

If God can transform cowardice into conquest for an entire nation, imagine what He can do with the failures in your own life. What shameful situation do you face? Have you asked God for His counsel? Perhaps by losing you can win. Or through poverty you'll be made rich. Maybe foolishness will once again confound the wise. All things are possible with Him. He is the God of second chances.

READ JOSHUA 8:1–9.

Now the LORD said to Joshua: "Do not be afraid, nor be dismayed; take all the people of war with you, and arise, go up to Ai. See, I have given into your hand the king of Ai, his people, his city, and his land. And you shall do to Ai and its king as you did to Jericho and its king. Only its spoil and its cattle you shall take as booty for yourselves. Lay an ambush for the city behind it." So Joshua arose, and all the people of war, to go up against Ai; and Joshua chose thirty thousand mighty men of valor and sent them away by night. And he commanded them, saying: "Behold, you shall lie in ambush against the city, behind the city. Do not go very far from the city, but all of you be ready. Then I and all the people who are with me will approach the city; and it will come about, when they come out against us as at the first, that we shall flee before them. For they will come out after us till we have drawn them from the city, for they will say, 'They are fleeing before us as at the first.' Therefore we will flee before them. Then you shall rise from the ambush and seize the city, for the LORD your God will

deliver it into your hand. And it will be, when you have taken the city,
that you shall set the city on fire. According to the commandment of the
LORD you shall do. See, I have commanded you." Joshua therefore sent
them out; and they went to lie in ambush, and stayed between Bethel and
Ai, on the west side of Ai; but Joshua lodged that night among the people.
Joshua 8:1–9

1. How did the Lord comfort Joshua after the incident with Achan?

2. This time, what were they allowed to do with Ai's "spoil and its cattle"?

3. What did Joshua instruct the chosen "thirty thousand mighty men of valor" to do?

4. What was Joshua planning to do once he approached the city and drew out the people of Ai?

5. Why was success guaranteed once they rose from the ambush and seized the city?

6. What were they commanded to do after they had taken the city?

7. Where was Joshua while the men prepared to lie in ambush? Who were the "people" he spent the night with?

LIVE OUT ...

8. For Achan, covetousness led to compromise. Struggles on the inside often lead to battles on the outside. In the columns below list some of the ways the two fronts may intersect.

LEARN ABOUT ...

1 Personal Assurance

Achan's sin has likely discouraged Joshua. So God again encourages him not to fear. Churches are weakened more by corruptions within than oppositions from without. God assures Joshua that His power to keep Israel from ruin by their enemies can also keep them from ruining themselves. He conquers sin and sinners!

4 Proposed Ambush

Ambush means to lurk or to lie in wait. This is the first time the word *ambush* or the concept of lying in wait appears in Scripture. Apparently this was a new strategy for God's people. The Lord instructs us to be wise as serpents. They lie still before striking their prey.

7 Present Among Them

Normally kings and generals don't join the front lines. When they do, it's to boost morale. Likely, the army was gun shy from their previous defeat. With Joshua present among them, they'd be inspired to unity and victory. God promises us: "Fear not, for I am with you; Be not dismayed, for I am your God. I will strengthen you" (Isa. 41:10).

LEARN ABOUT ...

8 Perpetuating Angst

Achan's sin had secondary ramifications. If one comrade betrayed the people, perhaps others would follow. Unfortunately, we begin to mistrust others who may be completely trustworthy: "It is better to trust in the LORD Than to put confidence in man" (Ps. 118:8). A good rule of thumb is to trust those who trust Him.

---

9 Prevailing Anyway

Our enemies may appear well armed and skillfully prepared. But God promises, "'No weapon forged against you will prevail, and you will refute every tongue that accuses you. This is the heritage of the servants of the LORD, and this is their vindication from me,' declares the LORD" (Isa. 54:17 NIV).

	INWARD BATTLES	**OUTWARD BATTLES**
	(Lust after reading romance novels.)	(Flirt with a friend instead of your spouse.)

9. God instructed Joshua how to lay an ambush against his enemies. God promised David that our enemies won't be able to ambush us. Rewrite Psalm 56:6–9, 11 into a personal prayer for deliverance from your enemies from within or without.

10. Joshua became the nation's fearless leader as he joined the army on the battlefront. Knowing that you're not alone engenders courage. What is a situation in which you need to know God is present with you? How can you be confident that He is there? What other comrades can you rely on?

○ ○ ● ○ ○

Swimmy was the only black fish in a large school of tiny red fish that lived happily in a corner of the sea. One day a huge hungry fish appeared and swallowed all the little red fish in one gulp. Only Swimmy escaped, swimming all alone through the big deep sea. He swam and he swam until he spotted a school of little fish, just like his own, hidden in the dark shade of rocks and weeds.

"Let's go and swim and play and *see* things!" he said happily.

"We can't," the little red fish said. "The big fish will eat us all."

"But you can't just lie there," Swimmy said. "We must think of something." Swimmy thought and thought. Then suddenly he said, "I have it! We are going to swim all together like the biggest fish in the sea!"

He taught them to swim close together; each in his own place, and when they had learned to swim like one giant fish, he said, "I'll be the eye." So they swam in the cool morning water, then through the midday sun, and chased the big fish away.[84]

Much like Swimmy's first family, the battalion in the initial attack on Ai died in the battle. This left Joshua distraught and confused. Those who escaped returned to their leader for advice. Unlike Swimmy who thought and thought, Joshua prayed and prayed. And then the Lord spoke words of wisdom to him, "United we stand!" If the Israelites would come out in full force, with some setting an ambush from behind while the others created a decoy from ahead, the enemy would be chased away.

LISTEN TO ...

Be united with other Christians. A wall with loose bricks is not good. The bricks must be cemented together.

—*Corrie ten Boom*

DAY 4
Tribal Victory

Solomon, the wisest man who ever lived, said, "Go to the ant…! Consider her ways and be wise" (Prov. 6:6). Perhaps that is just what God did when He decided the tactics for Joshua's attack on Ai.

A crafty species of ant sets up an ambush to attack other insects. They swarm together to capture their victim. Scientists report that such incredible cooperation among ants has never before been described.

The ants called *Allomerus decemarticulatus*, live in trees in the Amazon. They make their trap out of natural plant hairs, regurgitated goo, and a binding fungus that the ants appear to farm. This trap makes it possible for the ants to catch meals of large flying insects that they couldn't get on their own. An insect lands on what seems to be part of the tree, but is actually the trap. Ants quickly appear from dozens of holes, grab the bug's legs, then stretch them out to immobilize the prey. Then worker ants arrive and sting the bug to death. Before long, the insect is carved up and carted away.[85]

Organized ambushes occur in ant colonies and human society. Many military strategies rely on concealment and surprise. Tribal societies as well as world powers have used ambush with great success. Typically the operation gets under way when warriors take up concealed positions and wait for the signal. To pull off an ambush, you must have two things: patience and planning. Joshua had both.

LIFT UP …

Lord, thank You for going before me and protecting me during the battles I face. I trust You to help me conquer my enemies. Amen.

LOOK AT …

We've seen God promise Joshua victory over the city of Ai and instruct him explicitly in achieving the victory. Today we see that when Joshua followed God's commands to the letter, the tribes again gained victory over the enemy.

It's important to note that God does not work in the same way every time He moves in our lives. He proves that in this encounter at Ai. It was decidedly different from the battle at Jericho. The battle at Jericho was fought in broad daylight, but the battle at Ai was fought at night. At Jericho the troops marched openly, while at Ai the men lay in ambush. At Jericho, God's supernatural hand brought the walls down, while at Ai the Israelites laid a trap for the army by pretending to be beaten. In addition, at Ai the Israelites took two towns at once: both Bethel and Ai.

Many times we grow into a spiritual rut, thinking God will do things as He always has done them. Let's learn the lesson of the battle of Ai. Look for God to work in new and unique ways in your life—He may just allow you to conquer double the territory!

REVIEW JOSHUA 8:10–17.

Then Joshua rose up early in the morning and mustered the people, and went up, he and the elders of Israel, before the people to Ai. And all the people of war who were with him went up and drew near; and they came before the city and camped on the north side of Ai. Now a valley lay between them and Ai. So he took about five thousand men and set them in ambush between Bethel and Ai, on the west side of the city. And when they had set the people, all the army that was on the north of the city, and its rear guard on the west of the city, Joshua went that night into the midst of the valley. Now it happened, when the king of Ai saw it, that the men of the city hurried and rose early and went out against Israel to battle, he and all his people, at an appointed place before the plain. But he did not know that there was an ambush against him behind the city. And Joshua and all Israel made as if they were beaten before them, and fled by the way of the wilderness. So all the people who were in Ai were called together to pursue them. And they pursued Joshua and were drawn away from the city. There was not a man left in Ai or Bethel who did not go out after Israel. So they left the city open and pursued Israel. Joshua 8:10–17

1. a. Describe who Joshua mustered to fight against Ai, when they went, and where they camped.

LEARN ABOUT ...

1 Early Riser

Joshua set a good example by rising early. Perhaps he wanted to perform his own reconnaissance on the city of Ai; perhaps he wanted to make sure everything was as it should be in his own camp; most likely, he arose early to pray and spend time with the Lord: "O God, You are my God; Early will I seek You" (Ps. 63:1).

5 Spear

The spear was common to all nations of antiquity. A spear was used as a thrusting and a throwing weapon. When David faced Goliath, he brought stones, not a spear, saying, "This assembly shall know that the LORD does not save with sword and spear; for the battle is the LORD's" (1 Sam. 17:47).

b. How was this different from the first time they went against Ai?

2. Describe Joshua's placement of soldiers to the west, to the north, and in the midst of the valley.

3. Recount what the king of Ai saw and did. What did he not know?

4. Explain how Joshua's ruse worked.

LOOK AT ...

The stage was set for Joshua to be victorious. The king of Ai had left his city defenseless as he chased after Joshua. Now let's see how God orchestrated the perfect ambush by examining Joshua 8:18–23.

Then the LORD said to Joshua, "Stretch out the spear that is in your hand toward Ai, for I will give it into your hand." And Joshua stretched out the spear that was in his hand toward the city. So those in ambush arose quickly out of their place; they ran as soon as he had stretched out his hand, and they entered the city and took it, and hurried to set the city on fire. And when the men of Ai looked behind them, they saw, and behold, the smoke of the city ascended to heaven. So they had no power to flee this way or that way, and the people who had fled to the wilderness turned back on the pursuers. Now when Joshua and all Israel saw that the ambush had taken the city and that the smoke of the city ascended, they turned back and struck down the men of Ai. Then the others came out of the city against them; so they were caught in the midst of Israel, some on this side and some on that side. And they struck them down, so that they let none of them remain or escape. But the king of Ai they took alive, and brought him to Joshua. Joshua 8:18–23

5. What happened when Joshua signaled his men with his spear?

6. What happened to the men of Ai?

LOOK AT ...

Joshua and the troops set in ambush developed signals to communicate to one another during the battle. For Joshua, it was a raised spear. Those hiding in ambush used a smoke signal, setting the city on fire to indicate that the city had fallen. Let's see how the battle progressed as we focus on Joshua 8:24–29.

———————

And it came to pass when Israel had made an end of slaying all the inhabitants of Ai in the field, in the wilderness where they pursued them, and when they all had fallen by the edge of the sword until they were consumed, that all the Israelites returned to Ai and struck it with the edge of the sword. So it was that all who fell that day, both men and women, were twelve thousand—all the people of Ai. For Joshua did not draw back his hand, with which he stretched out the spear, until he had utterly destroyed all the inhabitants of Ai. Only the livestock and the spoil of that city Israel took as booty for themselves, according to the word of the LORD which He had commanded Joshua. So Joshua burned Ai and made it a heap forever, a desolation to this day. And the king of Ai he hanged on a tree until evening. And as soon as the sun was down, Joshua commanded that they should take his corpse down from the tree, cast it at the entrance of the gate of the city, and raise over it a great heap of stones that remains to this day. Joshua 8:24–29

7. a. Describe in detail what happened to the inhabitants of Ai.

   b. Why did God want this?

8. What did the Lord allow the Israelites to keep?

LEARN ABOUT ...

8 Booty

Booty refers to the spoils of war. It includes anything a soldier or army could capture and carry off the battlefield. Unlike everything at Jericho, which was devoted to God as firstfruits, at Ai the soldiers were allowed to take booty. Had Achan been patient, he would have gained riches during the conquest.

LEARN ABOUT ...

10 Prayer's Security

Seeking God in prayer is the place of greatest security. Scripture speaks of several types of prayer: 1) *deesis*, praying for special benefits; 2) *proseuche*, general prayer; 3) *enteuxis*, prayer concerning personal needs; 4) *euche*, making a vow to God. Whether praying for the day or preparing for battle, prayer is always the right thing to do.

---

11 Salvation's Weapons

The Messiah will one day come to completely destroy evil. Habakkuk describes a future day when the Anointed casts down the sun and moon with arrows and a sword. In Revelation, John foresaw Jesus coming on a white horse, and "out of His mouth goes a sharp sword, that with it He should strike the nations" (Rev. 19:15).

9. What two things did the people of Israel make into a "heap"?

LIVE OUT ...

10. a. We saw that Joshua arose early to muster the people and prepare for the day. Fill in the chart below to learn about other people who rose early and why they did.

SCRIPTURE	WHO AND WHY THEY ROSE EARLY
Genesis 19:27	
Genesis 22:3–5	
Genesis 28:16–22	
Mark 16:1–7	
John 8:1–2	

   b. Most of the early risers put God first in their days. When you rise, what's the first thing on your mind? Journal a prayer asking God to help you put Him in first place.

11. a. Just as Joshua held forth the spear to conquer Ai, the Messiah will one day wield a spear to overcome all evil. Read Habakkuk 3:11–13. What will cause the sun and moon to stand still (v. 11)?

   b. What will happen to the land and the nations, and why (v. 13)?

   c. How do you feel about the Messiah's coming?

   d. How should you prepare for His return, given that nobody knows how soon it will happen?

○ ○ ● ○ ○

"If only" is one of the saddest phrases in human experience. "If only I had listened." "If only I'd been wiser." Surely Joshua was plagued with "if onlys" after his first encounter with the warriors at Ai. "If only I hadn't listened to the spies' report." "If only I'd prayed more." "If only I'd waited for God to tell me what to do." "If only I'd watched Achan more closely." "If only I'd been a better leader."

"If only" thoughts plague us with what might have been. We focus on the past rather than moving toward the future. Thankfully, God wants His people to put the past behind them and move forward. Through the prophet Jeremiah, God reminds us, "For I know the thoughts that I think toward you, says the LORD, thoughts of peace and not of evil, to give you a future and a hope. Then you will call upon Me and go and pray to Me, and I will listen to you. And you will seek Me and find Me, when you search for Me with all your heart" (Jer. 29:11–13).

God allows us to move past our failures and learn from defeat when we turn to Him in prayer. The road back may be fraught with difficulty, but when we call upon the Lord, we wind up victorious. When you are stuck in the mind-set of saying, "If only I hadn't …" replace that thinking with, "But God can give me a future and a hope."

LISTEN TO …

The kingdom of God is a kingdom of paradox, where through the ugly defeat of a cross, a holy God is utterly glorified. Victory comes through defeat; healing through brokenness; finding self through losing self.

—*Charles Colson*

DAY 5

Spiritual Solidarity

In July 1942, seven months following the United States' entrance into World War II, magazine publishers began their own campaign. It was not a military campaign but a campaign for unity and support among the American populace. They joined together to feature the American flag on their covers and adopted the slogan "United We Stand." Altogether some five hundred publications waved the Stars and Stripes on the covers of their magazines.

For the publishers, displaying the flag was a way to prove their loyalty for the war effort. For the U.S. government, the campaign was an opportunity to sell bonds and boost morale. The magazines brought home a message of patriotism and ideals worth fighting for.

Patriotism is a noble calling. But there is something much more important than national pride and loyalty. Spiritual solidarity—devotion to God—must come first. Proper priorities dictate God and country, not the other way around. That's why the Pledge of Allegiance proclaims that the United States is "one nation under God"!

Perhaps those who put "under God" into the pledge learned a thing or two from Joshua. He understood that continued victory over his enemies was tied to the nation's ongoing allegiance to God. Rather than forging ahead to greater wars on different battle-fields, Joshua decided to unite the nation around worshipping God and obeying His commands. Blessings or curses would follow, depending upon whether or not they adhered to God's Word.

LIFT UP ...

Lord, You are worth celebrating and honoring. You are worthy of all praise. We are reminded of Your justice, mercy, and grace when we read Your Word. Help us to hide it in our hearts so that we will never depart from You. Amen.

LOOK AT ...

Again the Bible surprises us with the response of the fledgling nation. Prior to this, instead of attacking hard and fast at Jericho, the children of Israel paused to renew the ritual of circumcision. Doing so temporarily disabled their entire army. And now, after the defeat of Ai and Bethel, logic might have dictated that the Israelites take advantage of their momentum by pushing on toward victory in other cities. Perhaps they could have marched into the heart of the pagan land, because they now controlled the border towns. However, Joshua kept the main thing the main thing—worshipping God first. Matthew Henry notes, "The camp of Israel is drawn out into the field, not to engage the enemy, but to offer sacrifice, to hear the law read, and to say Amen to the blessings and the curses."[86]

When you break through to personal victory, how do you respond? Perhaps you gloat, glorying in your own prowess, or greedily desire more. But do you take time to thank God, remembering that He makes victory possible? Don't be like nine of the ten lepers who, after being healed, failed to thank the very One who had cleansed them. Luke records that only "one of them, when he saw that he was healed, returned, and with a loud voice glorified God, and fell down on his face at His feet, giving Him thanks. And he was a Samaritan" (Luke 17:15–16).

READ JOSHUA 8:30–35.

Now Joshua built an altar to the LORD God of Israel in Mount Ebal, as Moses the servant of the LORD had commanded the children of Israel, as it is written in the Book of the Law of Moses: "an altar of whole stones over which no man has wielded an iron tool." And they offered on it burnt offerings to the LORD, and sacrificed peace offerings. And there, in the presence of the children of Israel, he wrote on the stones a copy of the law of Moses, which he had written. Then all Israel, with their elders and officers and judges, stood on either side of the ark before the priests, the Levites, who bore the ark of the covenant of the LORD, the stranger as well as he who was born among them. Half of them were in front of Mount Gerizim and half of them in front of Mount Ebal, as Moses the servant of the LORD had commanded before, that they should bless the people of Israel. And afterward he read all the words of the law, the blessings and the cursings, according to all that is written in the

LEARN ABOUT ...

1 Before Conquering

Even though Israel had conquered Ai, they had not conquered Shechem, the city situated the closest to Mounts Ebal and Gerizim. This opened them up to danger. When we are obedient to God's duties, we are under His special protection. God watches over those who worship Him. "He who keeps his command will experience nothing harmful" (Eccl. 8:5).

3 Written Word

Joshua follows the example of his leader Moses by writing his own copy of God's law in stone. Perhaps chiseling the commands on rock denoted their permanence more than penning them on paper. "Moses wrote all the words of the LORD" (Ex. 24:4). Have you permanently carved God's Word into your life?

5 Spoken Word

Joshua wrote God's Word in stone as an enduring memorial to the next generation. He also spoke it audibly for the entire congregation to hear. Imagine the impact on your children if you kept this same discipline. "These words which I command you today shall be in your heart. You shall teach them diligently to your children" (Deut. 6:6–7).

Book of the Law. There was not a word of all that Moses had commanded which Joshua did not read before all the assembly of Israel, with the women, the little ones, and the strangers who were living among them. Joshua 8:30–35

1. After conquering Ai, how did Joshua honor the Lord?

2. After offering sacrifices, what did Joshua do next "in the presence of the children of Israel"?

3. Why do you think he did this?

4. Make a list of all the people who "stood on either side of the ark before the priests."

5. a. What did Joshua read "afterward"?

   b. Why do you think he did this?

6. What phrase indicates that Joshua did a thorough reading before everyone that day?

LIVE OUT ...

7. Like Moses, Joshua wrote a personal copy of God's commands. In Deuteronomy 17, God stipulated that each new Israelite king must also write his own copy of God's law. Read Deuteronomy 17:14–20.

   a. From what background must a king be selected?

   b. Why do you think this was so?

c. List the two things the nation's ruler was forbidden to perform.

d. What reasoning might be behind these restrictions?

e. Once "he sits on the throne of his kingdom," describe in detail what the king was required to do. How do you think this would have influenced his reign?

8. Joshua wrote a personal copy of God's commands. List the Ten Commandments "you shall" keep (see Ex. 20:1–17).

1)	6)
2)	7)
3)	8)
4)	9)
5)	10)

9. a. Joshua not only wrote the law of the Lord, he also proclaimed it verbally to the children of Israel. Write the name of a person, or persons, who you will recite the Ten Commandments to this week.

b. Journal a prayer asking God to help you perform, as well as proclaim, His Word.

○ ○ ● ○ ○

A rabbi and a New England minister were getting to know one another. Proudly, the minister exclaimed, "One of my ancestors signed the Declaration of Independence."

"I understand your pride," the rabbi responded. "One of my ancestors signed the Ten Commandments."[88]

Who could boast in knowing the signatory of the Ten

LEARN ABOUT ...

7 King's Commands

Perhaps the king could have obtained his predecessors' copy of the law. But hopefully it was worn out from constant use. Instead the king had to start with a fresh copy and carefully apply it to himself. God's Word had to be more important to him than many horses, wives, or riches.

_____

8 Ten Commandments

Jesus elevated the Ten Commandments to a higher plane by requiring us to keep not only the legal, but also the spiritual, aspects of the law. Placing His eternal approval of them, He declared, "Do not think that I came to destroy the Law or the Prophets. I did not come to destroy but to fulfill" (Matt. 5:17).[87]

Commandments? John tells us that "as many as received Him, to them He gave the right to become children of God, to those who believe in His name" (John 1:12). You might say that Christians can boast, "My Father authored the Ten Commandments."

After the Lord inscribed the original document, Moses, Joshua, and the kings of Israel all wrote personal copies. But rather than taking pride in copying the Ten Commandments, we must strive to obey them. Sadly, the generation that followed Joshua "forgot the LORD their God" (Judg. 3:7).

Just as the nation of Israel was founded upon the Ten Commandments, the United States was birthed by biblical underpinnings. Yet we, too, have gone astray. *Readers Digest* quotes Ted Turner, creator of Cable News Network, as saying, "The rules we're living under is the Ten Commandments, and I bet nobody here even pays much attention to 'em, because they are too old. Nobody around likes to be commanded. Commandments are out."[89]

God warned the nation of Israel that they would experience blessings or cursings based upon their adherence to God's law. Woe to us if we fail to keep God's law! How can we expect God to bless America when America does not bless God?

LISTEN TO ...

The commands of God are all designed to make us more happy than we can possibly be without them.

—Thomas Wilson

LESSON SEVEN

Nothing up My Sleeve

Joshua 9

Every Saturday morning two cartoon characters amused their TV audience with the art of illusion. "And now, for my next trick …" Bullwinkle J. Moose would announce to the camera.

He would then turn to his furry friend and say, "Hey, Rocky, watch me pull a rabbit out of my hat."

"That trick never works," Rocky Q. Squirrel would groan.

Undaunted, Bullwinkle would continue, "Nothing up my sleeve." The squirrel would watch Bullwinkle as he tore the fur off his arm as if it were a shirtsleeve.

Reaching into the inverted top hat, Bullwinkle waved his wand and conjured the magic word, "Presto."

"Rrrrrroar!" Out would pop a ferocious lion, to the shock of all.

The befuddled moose confessed, "Must be the wrong hat." Children of all ages were delighted with the trick of "Nothing Up My Sleeve."

In Joshua 9, we witness the nation of Gibeon engaged in an elaborate hoax. They had more than something up their sleeves. Their entourage dressed in ragged clothing and worn-out shoes. Instead of a top hat planted with a bunny rabbit or vicious lion, their saddlebags were packed with dry, moldy bread. This deceit was cleverly orchestrated with one thing in mind—to make an alliance with Israel. Sadly, Joshua was duped by the ploy. And we learn an important lesson—for tricksters, the hand is quicker than the eye. The leaders of Israel should have consulted God before making an alliance with people from another land. He cannot be fooled by those who try to deceive: "For the eyes of the LORD run to and fro throughout the whole earth" (2 Chron. 16:9).

Day 1: Joshua 9:1–6   THE ART OF ILLUSION

Day 2: Joshua 9:7–13   SMOKE AND MIRRORS

Day 3: Joshua 9:14–17   THE VANISHING ACT

Day 4: Joshua 9:18–21   PRESTO CHANGO

Day 5: Joshua 9:22–27   ESCAPE ARTISTS

DAY 1
The Art of Illusion

LIFT UP ...

Lord, this world is full of deception. Give me wisdom to detect the schemes of the enemy so I don't fall prey to him. I desire to take counsel from You and not from men. Help me to bring everything to You in prayer. Amen.

LOOK AT ...

The sin of Achan brought Israel's first defeat in the Promised Land. But after his treachery was exposed and corrected, the Lord turned His anger away from the wounded nation. At the Lord's encouragement, Joshua instructed his army in two new military ploys: lying in ambush and playing decoy in retreat. These new strategies brought great victory.

Up to this point, the Canaanites had acted defensively as the Israelites mounted their offensive against Jericho and Ai. Now, Israel's enemies decided to rally. The surrounding kings formed a coalition, combining their armies in order to attack the Hebrew invaders.

Donald K. Campbell writes, "When righteousness becomes aggressive, it has a way of uniting the forces of good—and also evil." The same occurred when Jesus walked the earth. Before He claimed to be the Messiah, the Pharisees, Sadducees, and Herodians were fractured and fighting among themselves. But our Lord's righteous claims caused them to unite together and seek His demise.

READ JOSHUA 9:1–6.

And it came to pass when all the kings who were on this side of the Jordan, in the hills and in the lowland and in all the coasts of the Great Sea toward Lebanon—the Hittite, the Amorite, the Canaanite, the Perizzite, the Hivite, and the Jebusite—heard about it, that they gathered together to fight with Joshua and Israel with one accord. But when the inhabitants

Learn about ...

2 Gathering

Israel's victory roused the surrounding nations to war. They rallied themselves in three geographical areas: the hill country, the valleys, and the costal plains. Some of them formed a formidable alliance to fight Israel "with one accord." The previously factious nations united around a common enemy.

---

3 Gibeon

Gibeon was about twenty-five miles from Israel's camp at Gilgal. (See the map on page 389.) It was the head of four Hivite cities, and the Hivites were on God's list for destruction. Archeologists believe Gibeon existed from the time of the exodus until the fall of Jerusalem. They also believe that winemaking was one of its major industries.

---

6 Guarantee

The Gibeonites requested a covenant with Israel. A covenant is a binding agreement between two parties. It can include a promise, a pledge, or a contract to perform some agreement. Jesus offers us a covenant: "For this is My blood of the new covenant, which is shed for many for the remission of sins" (Matt. 26:28).

of Gibeon heard what Joshua had done to Jericho and Ai, they worked craftily, and went and pretended to be ambassadors. And they took old sacks on their donkeys, old wineskins torn and mended, old and patched sandals on their feet, and old garments on themselves; and all the bread of their provision was dry and moldy. And they went to Joshua, to the camp at Gilgal, and said to him and to the men of Israel, "We have come from a far country; now therefore, make a covenant with us." Joshua 9:1–6

1. Read Deuteronomy 20:16–18. How did God want his people to deal with the six nations listed there? Why?

2. Joshua 9:1 lists those same six nations. How did they plan to deal with the danger the Israelites posed?

3. a. The Gibeonites took a different approach. Who did they pretend to be?

   b. Read Deuteronomy 20:10–15. What light does it shed on the intent of the Gibeonites' ruse?

4. Describe how they disguised themselves to deceive Joshua.

5. What kind of impression was this disguise intended to make?

6. Why did the Gibeonites want to make a covenant with the Israelites?

7. Why shouldn't Joshua have made a covenant with them?

Live out ...

8. a. The city-states that had once been at odds with one another

now formed a coalition to attack Joshua's army. Have you ever felt like people, circumstances, or even your own issues were ganging up on you? If so, journal about how you typically respond when that happens.

b. How do you think God would like you to respond? What helps you do that?

9. a. Today we see that Israel's greatest danger was not a confederation of armies from Canaan, but a group of deceitful men from Gibeon. Satan is also the master of deception. Fill in the following chart to discover some of his famous façades.

Scripture	Enemy's Facade
Matthew 16:21–24	
2 Corinthians 11:14	
1 Peter 5:8	
Revelation 12:9	

b. What is one way Satan tries to deceive you?

10. The Gibeonites went to great lengths to obtain a covenant of peace with the Israelites. Although we were enemies of God, Jesus offered us a peace treaty. Rewrite Ephesians 2:17–19 into a personal prayer, accepting God's covenant of peace with you:

He came and preached peace to you who were afar off and to those who were near. For through Him we both have access by one Spirit to the Father. Now, therefore, you are no longer strangers and foreigners, but fellow citizens with the saints and members of the household of God. (Eph. 2:17–19)

LEARN ABOUT …

9 Deceit

To deceive means to make another accept as true or valid that which is false. This can be achieved by giving a false impression or by leading another astray, either intentionally or unintentionally. The Lord warns that, "He who works deceit shall not dwell within my house; He who tells lies shall not continue in my presence" (Ps. 101:7).

10 Decisions

The Gibeonites employed questionable tactics with noble motives. They desired peace with Israel, because they had seen God's power at work on behalf of His people. However, the remaining Canaanite kings declared war. The gospel is a great divider: "To those who are perishing, we are a dreadful smell of death and doom. But to those who are being saved, we are a life-giving perfume" (2 Cor. 2:16 NLT).

○ ○ ● ○ ○

The curtain went up in Heller's Wonder Theatre on Broadway to reveal a blindfolded lady comfortably seated center stage. As a volunteer from the audience, she was asked to "pick a card, any card!" She did, thinking all along that it was her free choice. But it wasn't. Robert Heller, the premier American magician of the mid-nineteenth century, was highly skilled at "forcing" a card. "Forcing" a card is a tactic used by skilled illusionists; they induce susceptible volunteers to select the precise card they had planted in advance.

Heller became fascinated with magic at fourteen years old. His career as an illusionist began in New York City in 1858. In an attempt to copy the style of another illusionist, Jean Eugène Robert-Houdin, Heller wore a dark wig and spoke in a French accent when he performed. Eventually Heller abandoned the accent and costume and focused on well-orchestrated illusions. His tour spanned from 1869 to 1875, and he became a success throughout much of the United States, Great Britain, Europe, and Asia.

The Gibeonites were also master illusionists. They dressed in clever disguises, transforming themselves into foreigners who had traveled a great distance to negotiate with the children of Israel. Like Heller, they seemed to have the ability to force a hand. The unsuspecting Israelites were duped by their ploy. It would be too late when the scam was discovered. Jesus cautioned His followers, "Behold, I send you out as sheep in the midst of wolves. Therefore be wise as serpents and harmless as doves" (Matt. 10:16). Let's not learn the hard way that looks can be very deceiving.

LISTEN TO ...

Illusion is the dust the devil throws in the eyes of the foolish.

—*Minna Antrim*

DAY 2
Smoke and Mirrors

Have you ever been to a house of mirrors at a fair or carnival? They're made up of cleverly designed glass labyrinths with dim lights and smoke-filled rooms. In one mirror you appear tall and skinny; in the next you're altered into a shorter, stubbier version of yourself. Around a sharp corner you encounter multiple images of yourself, as if you're seeing yourself through a diamond. Before you leave the dark, hazy maze, you're dazed and confused. But what if you actually believed that the mirror's reflection was reality?

Although I (Lenya) wouldn't want to live in a house of mirrors, I wouldn't mind owning one of those tall, thin mirrors. Even on the days when my skinny jeans don't fit, I could look at my magic reflection and feel ten pounds thinner. Recently I was shopping with a friend, and everything I tried on looked flattering. Suddenly she exclaimed, "Hey, that mirror looks warped. I bet it would make everyone look skinny." That shop owner was clever. She almost sold me a bill of goods.

Just as smoke and mirrors can distort reality, the Gibeonites disguised themselves as foreigners from a distant land to distort the truth of their identity. However, the Israelites were not convinced that these travelers were really from far, far away. So under interrogation, the imposters employed another trick: flattery. They elevated the children of Israel and their God by humbling themselves to the place of servitude. The Bible says, "Smooth words and flattering speech deceive the hearts of the simple" (Rom. 16:18). A tall, skinny mirror might manipulate you into buying a new outfit, just as the Gibeonites' smooth, flattering words could finagle a peace treaty.

LIFT UP ...

Lord, I make decisions every day and don't always ask for Your guidance. Forgive me for moving forward when I should follow Your leading. Please give me discernment to choose wisely who I should associate with and who I should distance myself from. Amen.

LOOK AT ...

The Israelites indicated they were suspicious of the intruders. And the Gibeonites embellished the truth by indicating they were from "a *very* far country." This tells us that they knew something of the Hebrew laws. Perhaps some from among them had spied on the Jews as they proclaimed God's Word at Mt. Ebal and Mt. Gerizim. Moses had made it clear that when the children of Israel entered the Promised Land they were to utterly wipe out the Canaanite nations nearby. However, they were permitted to make a peace treaty with the people from distant lands (see Deuteronomy 20).

The Gibeonites cleverly used God's commands to their advantage. Isn't it reminiscent of Satan, who actually quoted Scripture to Jesus when testing Him in the wilderness? It also reminds us of the time the Serpent questioned Eve, "Has God indeed said, 'You shall not eat of every tree of the garden'?" (Gen. 3:1). Satan used God's Word but twisted it ever so slightly. Beware! Just because someone quotes a Bible verse does not mean they adhere to God's precepts. What about you? Have you ever twisted the Bible to suit your situation?

READ JOSHUA 9:7–13.

Then the men of Israel said to the Hivites, "Perhaps you dwell among us; so how can we make a covenant with you?" But they said to Joshua, "We are your servants." And Joshua said to them, "Who are you, and where do you come from?" So they said to him: "From a very far country your servants have come, because of the name of the LORD your God; for we have heard of His fame, and all that He did in Egypt, and all that He did to the two kings of the Amorites who were beyond the Jordan—to Sihon king of Heshbon, and Og king of Bashan, who was at Ashtaroth. Therefore our elders and all the inhabitants of our country spoke to us, saying, 'Take provisions with you for the journey, and go to meet them, and say to them, "We are your servants; now therefore, make a covenant with us."' This bread of ours we took hot for our provision from our houses on the day we departed to come to you. But now look, it is dry and moldy. And these wineskins which we filled were new, and see, they are torn; and these our garments and our sandals have become old because of the very long journey." Joshua 9:7–13

1. Based on yesterday's homework, recount the other name by which these Hivites were known.

2. Suspicious of the Gibeonites' intentions, the men of Israel asked what two-pronged question?

3. How did the Gibeonites respond to this question?

4. a. What God-fearing reason did they cite for coming from a "very far country"?

   b. Why do you suppose they chose this way to make their case?

5. Explain what the "elders and all the inhabitants" of their country supposedly instructed these travelers to do.

6. List the four pieces of evidence the Gibeonites offered as proof of how far they had come.

LIVE OUT ...

7. Try to put yourself and your family into the thoughts and feelings of the Gibeonites. If you lived in those hills and heard about Joshua's mighty God and great victories, you'd have a choice to make too. Would you fight? Would you run? Or would you try to negotiate peace? Explain your reasoning.

8. Now try to imagine Joshua's predicament. Examining a caravan of people offering to submit to his people as slaves, he's in a quandary too. Should he massacre them all, because they might be people God has told him to massacre? Should he chase them away? Should he try to find a peaceable

LEARN ABOUT ...

1 Shut Out

God's commands warned against making a covenant with the Hivites: "When the LORD your God brings you into the land which you go to possess, and has cast out … the Hivites … you shall conquer them and utterly destroy them. You shall make no covenant with them nor show mercy to them" (Deut. 7:1–2).[90]

3 Servitude

According to the Near Eastern diplomatic relations of that day, the Gibeonites entered into a political treaty by willingly offering themselves as subordinates bound to an overlord. They understood and accepted that Israel had the power to be the upper hand in this agreement.

6 Show and Tell

Unwisely, the Israelites were set on passing judgment based on first impressions. But God's Word warns: "Trust in the LORD with all your heart, And lean not on your own understanding; In all your ways acknowledge Him, And He shall direct your paths. Do not be wise in your own eyes" (Prov. 3:5–7).

LEARN ABOUT ...

7 So Close

Like Rahab, the Gibeonites had heard about these strange people and their God. But unlike Rahab, they did not have an open heart to worship Him. The Gibeonites didn't display honesty and transparency to seek God and come to personal faith in Him. Instead, they tried to save themselves through deceptive tactics.

---

9 Fresh Life

God commanded the Israelites to cleanse the land of idolatrous people so that His people could have a fresh start in the Land of Promise. Yet His people continually broke God's laws and sinned against Him. Jesus willingly paid the death penalty for sin so that everyone everywhere can have a fresh start: "For the letter kills, but the Spirit gives life" (2 Cor. 3:6).

solution and have a bit less blood on his hands? Write your thoughts.

9. a. It appears that the Gibeonites knew something of the law of Moses and they were looking for loopholes. Read Deuteronomy 20:16–18 again. What reason did God give for inflicting genocide on these groups?

b. This is the only situation in the Bible in which God commands or even condones genocide. Jesus gives Christians an entirely different task: "But I say to you, love your enemies, bless those who curse you, do good to those who hate you, and pray for those who spitefully use you and persecute you" (Matt. 5:44). If somebody said it was God's will today to wipe out a whole group of people, including women and children, because they're like the Canaanites, what would you say?

○ ○ ● ○ ○

The famous English art critic Duveen took his young daughter on an outing to visit the ocean. While he was splashing merrily in the water, he tried to persuade the little girl to join him. She stubbornly refused, protesting that the water was too cold. Undaunted, Duveen built a fire, heated a tea kettle, and with much fanfare poured the boiling liquid into the sea. Without another thought the child ran gleefully into the water.

This father's trick illustrates how deception often works. Just mix a small amount of truth into an ocean of falsehood, and people wade in, not realizing how they have been fooled.[91]

Unfortunately, human beings are gullible. What makes us so vulnerable is when we trust our natural understanding. You've heard it said, "You can't judge a book by its cover," or, "Look before you leap." Too often, we make decisions based on what we see, hear, touch, or smell. Sadly, our senses are easily fooled, just as the Israelites who saw old wineskins and moldy bread and believed that the people had traveled from a distant land.

What is true in the physical world is also true in the spiritual realm. We face an enemy who is powerful, cunning, and cruel. Our physical senses fall short of the ability to sniff him out. Alan Redpath wrote, "Never, *never*, NEVER trust your own judgment in anything. When common sense says that a course is right, lift your heart to God, for the path of faith and the path of blessing may be in a direction completely opposite to that which you call common sense."[92]

LISTEN TO ...

The difference between appreciation and flattery? That is simple. One is sincere and the other insincere. One comes from the heart out; the other from the teeth out. One is unselfish; the other selfish. One is universally admired; the other is universally condemned.

—Dale Carnegie

DAY 3
The Vanishing Act

According to naturalists, certain butterflies of the Kallima family have the ability to pull off a vanishing act. Also known as "dead-leaf butterflies," these insects have brilliant colors on the outside of their wings. But their undersides strangely lack color. Underneath they bear the lines and markings of an old, dead leaf.

Therefore, in flight the obvious flash of bright colors can be easily spotted by both friend and foe. But when this winged wonder settles upon a branch, something magical happens. The colors disappear as its detailed camouflage transforms it into a "dead leaf." Cleverly the butterfly positions itself down stem similar to a leaf and then begins to sway gently in the breeze. Observers say it is almost impossible to detect these little creatures since the leaf-vein appearance on the wings includes other markings that mimic holes, tears, and fungal growths.

Magicians might call this trick "The Vanishing Act." Like the "dead-leaf butterfly," the Gibeonites had pulled off an incredible vanishing act. However, their camouflage was effective for only a short period of time. At the end of three days their true colors were revealed and the jig was up. In a sense, the Gibeonites revealed their craftiness by succeeding in the escapade. As the butterfly lives to fly another day, the Gibeonites would live to serve another day.

LIFT UP ...

Lord, I know my life would be filled with confusion instead of peace without Your counsel. I don't want to be confused about what You want for my life. Please lead me in all I do. Amen.

LOOK AT ...

You have to give the Israelites credit. They did question the tricksters and ask for concrete evidence. The Gibeonite hoax was an elaborate one complete with old, crusty bread and worn-out clothing. However, eventually the imposters fell prey to the Israelites.

Evidence that the trick worked can be seen when the Israelites partook of the food of the Gibeonites. Some commentators believe that this meal was part of the covenant ceremony signifying that the treaty had been ratified. They suggest that a better translation of "The men of Israel took some of their provision" might be "The Israelites ate some of their provisions as a sign of fellowship" or "As a sign that they had agreed to the treaty they took the food."

Partaking of a shared meal or breaking bread was very significant in ancient times. It was believed that as each party digested the same bread they were becoming one. Therefore, the act of breaking bread (even moldy bread) was sacred and ceremonial. The Gibeonites got what they asked for—they became servants of God's people.

LEARN ABOUT ...

2 Urim and Thummim

In the Old Testament the method for inquiring of the Lord's will was through gems and stones called the Urim and Thummim carried by the high priest. No one knows exactly what the process entailed. "The governor said to them that they should not eat of the most holy things till a priest could consult with the Urim and Thummim" (Ezra 2:63).

READ JOSHUA 9:14–17.

Then the men of Israel took some of their provisions; but they did not ask counsel of the LORD. So Joshua made peace with them, and made a covenant with them to let them live; and the rulers of the congregation swore to them. And it happened at the end of three days, after they had made a covenant with them, that they heard that they were their neighbors who dwelt near them. Then the children of Israel journeyed and came to their cities on the third day. Now their cities were Gibeon, Chephirah, Beeroth, and Kirjath Jearim. Joshua 9:14–17

1. What did the men of Israel take from the Gibeonites? What did this signify?

2. What grave mistake did the men of Israel make?

3. How did Joshua respond to the Gibeonites' earlier request for a covenant?

4. Who else among the Israelites ratified this alliance?

LEARN ABOUT ...

4 Presumption

The Israelites were guilty of the sin of presumption, believing that they knew better than the Lord, and did not need His counsel. "Keep back Your servant also from presumptuous sins; Let them not have dominion over me. Then I shall be blameless, And I shall be innocent of great transgression" (Ps. 19:13).

---

5 Neighbors?

The term neighbor can mean either "one close at hand" or "friend." God had commanded that the Jews not make friends with their neighbors in the land of Canaan. Now the Jews were obligated not to lie to the liars: "You shall not bear false witness against your neighbor" (Deut. 5:20).

---

8 Broken Bread

Breaking bread was significant to ancient Middle Easterners, denoting intimacy. It was even more meaningful than inviting someone to your home for dinner in our culture. David grieved when his companions, with whom he'd dined, betrayed him: "Even my own familiar friend in whom I trusted, Who ate my bread, Has lifted up his heel against me" (Ps. 41:9).

5. What fact surfaced three days after making the covenant?

6. How long did it take Israel to reach the neighboring cities?

7. List the names of the cities from which the travelers had come.

LIVE OUT ...

8. a. Bread holds great significance in the Bible. Fill in the following chart to discover what else bread symbolizes in Scripture.

SCRIPTURE	SYMBOLISM OF BREAD
Psalm 80:5	
Proverbs 4:17	
Matthew 4:4	
John 6:48–5	

   b. What type of bread have you eaten recently? Journal a prayer asking the Bread of Life to sustain and strengthen you.

9. Joshua and the rulers of the congregation were guilty of the sin of presumption. How would you define presumption in your own words?

10. a. The greatest mistake the leaders made was in failing to seek counsel of the Lord. So often we are guilty of the very same thing. Describe a time in your life when you neglected to ask for God's advice before making a decision. What was the result?

    b. Read sidebar 10 concerning God's guidance. How do you know when God is providing guidance for you? What do you do if you're unsure about His will in a particular circumstance?

○ ○ ● ○ ○

An accomplished magician was headlining the entertainment on a cruise ship. Every night as he performed a trick, a heckler in the audience would yell, "It's a hoax. He's a phony. That's not magic."

One evening while the magician was performing a dramatic disappearing act, a horrendous storm sank the ship. Somehow the heckler and the magician ended up in the same lifeboat. For several hours they sat glaring at each other, neither willing to utter a word. Finally the heckler said, "All right, smarty, enough of your stupid tricks. What did you do with the ship?"

Trickery, whether funny or foolhardy, may work temporarily—but not permanently. If you search for the people throughout Scripture who employed deception, you'll discover they ended with tragic results.

Jacob and his mother, Rebekah, tricked Isaac into giving him the birthright due to Esau, the firstborn. Fast-forward several years. Jacob himself was victimized by the treachery of his father-in-law, Laban, who forced him to work seven extra years for his beloved wife, Rachel, after he had tricked Jacob into marrying Leah.

David thought he might get away with adultery, murder, and a cover-up. However, the prophet Nathan trapped the king with a clever story and a poignant message "You are the man" who sinned. As a result, David and his wife, Bathsheba, lost their firstborn son because of their immorality.

Ananias and Sapphira thought that they could trick people in the first-century church into thinking they were big-time donors. They told the disciples they had offered everything they owned to the Lord. But the Holy Spirit knew differently and God's judgment fell upon them. Both refused to tell the truth and died for their deception.

How many of us have been just as foolish, thinking we can get away with moral deception? Perhaps you thought you could get away with cheating on your spouse or your taxes. But over the years your conscience

LEARN ABOUT ...

10 God's Guidance

Wouldn't it be nice if we could roll the dice to discern what God wanted us to do? Or hear His voice audibly? But God doesn't speak that way today. His guidance is more subtle. We can sense His guiding hand through His written Word, providential circumstances, the wise counsel of others, and the still small voice of His Holy Spirit.

was plagued and your faith compromised. Wouldn't it be better to admit the truth and live a life transparent before God and men? As Job said, "With Him are strength and prudence. The deceived and the deceiver are His" (Job 12:16). Imagine what your life would be like if you never succumbed to deception and trickery again and put yourself wholly in His hands.

LISTEN TO ...

O what may a man within him hide, Though angel on the outward side!

—*William Shakespeare*

Presto Chango

Some of the most difficult magic tricks are known as "close-up" tricks. These tricks are performed right before the audience's eyes. In close-up tricks an unspoken agreement exists between the magician and the audience. The audience willingly suspends their disbelief—they go along for the ride. In return, the performer presents a gimmick so clever that the audience cannot figure out how it was done. The magician uses such techniques as sleight of hand, misdirection, deception, collusion with an audience member, special equipment, or other trickery. The sense of bafflement is part of the entertainment. One of the most famous close-up tricks is Presto Chango, where the magician puts a person in a box onstage and says, "Presto Chango!" The magician opens the box and the person inside has "magically" disappeared or been replaced by an empty box or another person. Then, after the magician again says the magic words, "Presto Chango!" the original person reappears inside the magic box. This trick involves both special equipment and audience participation.

The Gibeonites were a close-up tribe who pretended to be from far away. The Israelites unwittingly agreed to go along for the ride, willingly believing the visitors were not neighbors but guests from a distance. The trick worked and the Hebrew rulers were put into a compromised position. They were forced into a covenant with an enemy. Thankfully, God is able to say the words, "Presto Chango," and turn enemies into friends. In this case, He turned the people of Gibeon into servants of the Lord's house. When you meet a person you think is against you or against God, remember that God can change foes into friends. Remember that you "who once were far off have been brought near by the blood of Christ" (Eph. 2:13).

LIFT UP ...

Lord, alliances made through deception end up in bondage. I don't want to be anyone's servant except Yours. May my service be pleasing to You. Amen.

LEARN ABOUT ...

I Swear Words

The phrase *to swear* occurs more than 180 times in the Hebrew Bible. It literally means to strongly affirm a promise. The root for *to swear* and *seven* are the same in Hebrew. Since the number seven is the perfect number, some conjecture that to swear is to somehow "seven oneself," or bind oneself with seven things, like Samson.[93]

---

3 Lord God of Israel

The title "The LORD God of Israel" is used 111 times in Scripture. It is used only once in the New Testament, in the book of Luke. The leaders invoked God's name as part of their oath, reminding the people that if they did not keep their word they would be taking the Lord's name in vain.

LOOK AT ...

We've seen how the Israelites failed to consult God and entered into a covenant with the Gibeonites. Today we see that, when they realized their mistake, they kept their word and honored their covenant.

God had made it clear that the Israelites were forbidden to make covenants with the people living in the cities of the Promised Land. Yet once they did, the rulers were honor bound to keep their promise. Scripture makes it clear that we should "not be unequally yoked together with unbelievers" (2 Cor. 6:14). However, once the Israelites made a mistake, they turned it into a work for God's glory. The lesson is clear: When we make mistakes (and we all will), God can use them for good.

READ JOSHUA 9:18–21.

But the children of Israel did not attack them, because the rulers of the congregation had sworn to them by the LORD God of Israel. And all the congregation complained against the rulers. Then all the rulers said to all the congregation, "We have sworn to them by the LORD God of Israel; now therefore, we may not touch them. This we will do to them: We will let them live, lest wrath be upon us because of the oath which we swore to them." And the rulers said to them, "Let them live, but let them be woodcutters and water carriers for all the congregation, as the rulers had promised them." Joshua 9:18–21

1. Explain why the children of Israel did not attack the people from Gibeon.

2. Describe who had a meeting and why.

3. What religious reason did the rulers give for making their decision?

4. What did the rulers fear would happen if they broke their oath to the Gibeonites?

5. In exchange for their lives, what tasks would the Gibeonites perform for the Israelites?

6. According to Deuteronomy 29:11, what did God consider those who cut wood and drew water?

LIVE OUT ...

7. Like the children of Israel in the wilderness, the people began to complain against their rulers.

   a. According to Exodus 16:8, when the people complained against Moses and Aaron, who was their complaint really against?

   b. Describe a time when you complained against someone in spiritual authority over you. How does it make you feel to know you were really criticizing God?

   c. Describe some specific ways you will offer your support to those who lead you.

8. a. The rulers of Israel made a covenant with the pagan peoples. Read 2 Corinthians 6:14–16 and give some reasons why we as believers should not become tied to unbelievers.

   b. Have you ever been "unequally yoked" (marriage, business, friendship, etc.)? If so, how did God work it out for your good and His glory?

LEARN ABOUT ...

6 Strangers

In the Old Testament, strangers were not merely foreigners, they were clients or outsiders who became permanent residents. For some reason they were people who sought a new place to dwell. The Gibeonites presented an interesting case: They became strangers in their own land, willingly accepting refuge from the Hebrew people.[94]

7 Authority

Ruler literally means a sheik, a prince, or an exalted one. Most commentators believe the rulers or authorities in this passage were the leaders of the twelve tribes. The rulers in Christ's day were the Pharisees and Sadducees. Today, they are the church leaders: "Be subject to rulers and authorities" (Titus 3:1).

8 Edifying Unbelievers

Believers, like the Israelites, should keep their word. If you are married to an unbeliever, the Bible is clear: "The unbelieving husband is sanctified by the wife. … [H]ow do you know, O wife, whether you will save your husband?" (1 Cor. 7:14, 16). "Your godly lives will speak to them without any words" (1 Peter 3:1 NLT).

9. The rulers reasoned with the people and restored unity among them. Read
   Psalm 133.

> Behold, how good and how pleasant it is
> For brethren to dwell together in unity!
> It is like the precious oil upon the head,
> Running down on the beard,
> The beard of Aaron,
> Running down on the edge of his garments.
> It is like the dew of Hermon,
> Descending upon the mountains of Zion;
> For there the LORD commanded the blessing—
> Life forevermore.

a. Underline the benefits of brethren dwelling together in unity.

b. Put parentheses around the psalmist's symbolism of unity toward the priesthood.

c. Circle the psalmist's metaphor connecting unity and water.

d. Unity among believers promises what blessing?

○ ○ ● ○ ○

An old legend tells about a herd of mules that were attacked every night by a pack of wolves from a nearby forest. When the wolves came, the mules would begin kicking viciously in all directions. Sometimes the mules would maim and injure one another while the wily wolves escaped unharmed. Finally, a wise old mule called all of the mules together for a conference and suggested a plan. All of the mules saw the wisdom and agreed to follow through with the proposal. That night the wolves lunged in from the forest as usual and circled the vulnerable mules. But rather than kicking, the mules all ran and put their heads together in a circle. Then they began to kick their strong legs outward. The mules did not harm one another, but the wolves felt the intense pain of the mules' strong leg thrusts and ran off howling into the woods.

When the rulers and the people of Israel put their heads together, they reached a good conclusion: It was best to keep their promise lest they face God's wrath. Warren Wiersbe said, "That wasn't the end of the story. Joshua and his associates teach us an important lesson: If you make a mistake, admit it: *and then make your mistake work for you!*"[95] We can be stubborn as mules and refuse to admit our mistakes, or we can be wise enough to admit our mistakes and ask God to help us turn our mistakes into blessings.

LISTEN TO ...

Anyone may make a mistake; none but a fool will persist in it.

—Cicero

DAY 5

Escape Artists

Harry Houdini, the famous escape artist, challenged his audiences with the promise that he could be locked up in any jail cell and free himself within an hour. He always met the challenge. But one time something went terribly wrong.

Houdini was ushered into a cell and the steel door clanged shut behind him. He was wearing street clothes, but concealed inside his belt was a strong, flexible piece of metal. He took the instrument out and went to work on the lock. After thirty minutes he had made no progress. An hour passed, but the door remained shut. Sweat poured off his forehead and the great Houdini was getting frustrated. Finally, after two hours of unsuccessful lock picking, he collapsed to the floor and leaned against the door. At that moment, the door swung open. It hadn't been locked at all! His assumption that the door was locked had kept him from walking free.

The people of Gibeon willingly entered servitude to save themselves from death. The historical record shows that they never fought the Israelites and faithfully carried out their duties. As believers, we, too, are slaves. Paul tells us in Romans 6:22 that we are "slaves of God." He bought us at the price of Christ's death. But Christ's death set us free. Some of us, like the great Houdini, are unaware that we are free to live an abundant life in Christ: "If the Son makes you free, you shall be free indeed" (John 8:36).

LIFT UP ...

Lord, I am grateful that You are on my side. I don't have to earn Your love or attempt to deceive You in order to gain Your favor. You know everything about me and You still love me. Thank You for Your grace. Amen.

LOOK AT ...

We've seen that the covenant between the Gibeonites and Israelites was ratified. The deception caused tension between the rulers and people of Israel, but once they held a conference, they all agreed to keep their word and allow the Gibeonites to become workers in the temple. Today we see Joshua address the Gibeonites and finalize this agreement—there would be no escape from their deception, but they would escape the death penalty.

The Israelites began to call the Gibeonites the Nethinim. They performed menial tasks in the temple and lived in the Levitical cities. They were even carried into captivity when the Babylonians conquered Israel. There is no record that they ever turned against the Israelites. In fact, some Nethinim returned to Jerusalem with Ezra following the captivity out of loyalty to the Jews to serve in the temple.

LEARN ABOUT ...

I Deceived

Joshua used the word *deceived*, which means to beguile or betray. Paul tells us that the Serpent deceived Eve by his craftiness (see 2 Cor. 11:3). To deceive speaks of enticing to sin through false reasoning or baiting a trap.

REVIEW JOSHUA 9:22–27.

Then Joshua called for them, and he spoke to them, saying, "Why have you deceived us, saying, 'We are very far from you,' when you dwell near us? Now therefore, you are cursed, and none of you shall be freed from being slaves—woodcutters and water carriers for the house of my God." So they answered Joshua and said, "Because your servants were clearly told that the LORD your God commanded His servant Moses to give you all the land, and to destroy all the inhabitants of the land from before you; therefore we were very much afraid for our lives because of you, and have done this thing. And now, here we are, in your hands; do with us as it seems good and right to do to us." So he did to them, and delivered them out of the hand of the children of Israel, so that they did not kill them. And that day Joshua made them woodcutters and water carriers for the congregation and for the altar of the LORD, in the place which He would choose, even to this day. Joshua 9:22–27

1. What did Joshua ask the Gibeonites? Describe the tone of voice you think he was using and how you think the Gibeonites were feeling.

LEARN ABOUT ...

3 Servants

In speaking to Joshua, the Gibeonites referred to themselves as "servants" on a par with Moses, the servant of God. This term speaks of a person in royal service as opposed to a bondservant or slave. This is the same word used of Joshua as a servant of Moses. They were clearly overstating their position.

---

4 Slaves

Joshua saved the enemies of Israel by turning them into slaves. In the same way, God saved us when we were His enemies by turning us into His slaves. "When we were enemies we were reconciled to God through the death of His Son" (Rom. 5:10). Jesus exhorted us, "Whoever desires to be first among you, let him be your slave" (Matt. 20:27).

---

6 Truth

It's been said that the greatest remedy for falsehood is truth. The light of truth exposes the darkness of deception. Satan is a charlatan who only wants to lie, steal, and destroy. But Christ offers truth, spiritual riches, and abundant life. Jesus said, "I am the way, the truth, and the life. No one comes to the Father except through Me" (John 14:6).

2. What curse did he place upon them because of the deception?

3. The Gibeonites foreshadow sinners coming to Christ (here typified by Joshua). Write the phrases from their response that reveal the elements for spiritual conversion:

   Hear and believe God's promises:

   Fear His judgment:

   Frankly admit sin:

   Cast themselves on His mercy:

4. Describe how Joshua delivered the Gibeonites and why.

5. Describe what job Joshua gave to them and how long it lasted.

LIVE OUT ...

6. Today we saw how the Gibeonites tried to deceive Joshua about their nationality and residence. There are many spiritual deceivers trying to trick people into walking away from the one true God today. Name an infamous deceiver and describe his or her deceptive ploys. What truths from Scripture could you use to expose the deception?

7. We saw the Gibeonites foreshadow the road to salvation. Journal through the steps they took and tell about your own faith journey. (If you've never accepted Christ as Savior, now is the perfect time!)

   I heard and believed God's promises:

   I feared His judgment:

   I frankly admitted sin:

   I cast myself on His mercy:

8. Though we become God's slaves at salvation, He allows us the privilege of being called His friends.

   a. Describe some of the things you like to do with your best friends.

   b. Now list some ways you could be a better friend to God.

○ ○ ● ○ ○

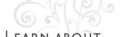

LEARN ABOUT ...

8 God's Friend

A friend is a term of endearment that literally means one who walks beside, one who is near, one who is beloved, or those who belong to one another. As God made man, Jesus had every right to expect those He died for to serve Him as slaves, yet He chose to consider us His friends: "No longer do I call you servants, for a servant does not know what his master is doing; but I have called you friends" (John 15:15).

In the 1800s, an evangelical Christian named William Wilberforce wrote one of the most widely read devotionals of his time: *Practical Christianity*. To Wilberforce, one part of being a Christian was the concept that all people should be treated with equality. Thus, he began to lobby British parliament to abolish the slave trade. In 1807, slavery was abolished in the colonies. In 1833, the Abolition of Slavery Act was passed. Wilberforce heard of this on his deathbed and died a happy man.

Unfortunately, the slave trade was still practiced in some parts of the world, and slave traders from Britain were doing a booming business. One day a strong, handsome man was put up on the auction blocks for sale. The bids kept rising. Finally, an Englishman won the bidding. The young slave began to mock him, "Ha! You buy a slave when slavery has been abolished in England." The purchaser kindly replied, "You mistake me. I have bought you to set you free." The young slave was overcome with emotion. He fell at the man's feet and said, "Then sir, I will be your willing slave forever."[96]

Jesus abolished slavery to sin forever with His death on the cross. The only reasonable response is to fall at His feet and offer to be His willing slave forever. He would never force allegiance upon us—He is a true gentleman. But the moment we ask Him into our hearts, He becomes our lifelong friend.

LISTEN TO ...

The man who surrenders to Christ exchanges a cruel slave driver for a kind and gentle Master whose yoke is easy and whose burden is light.

—A. W. Tozer

The Day the Sun Stood Still

Joshua 10

Who doesn't like a good science-fiction film? Sci-fi buffs are notorious for their knowledge of the characters in the stories, their ability to blend fantasy with reality, and to loyally follow a series for decades. Trekkies (*Star Trek* fans) travel great distances to conventions just to catch a glimpse of Captain Kirk or Dr. Spock. They know what they're seeing isn't real, but they buy into the unreality. One classic science-fiction film is *The Day the Earth Stood Still*. The movie poster showed an alien from outer space shooting a laser beam from his eyes. He was carrying a blond beauty who had fainted from shock. Behind them a large robotic hand held the earth in its grasp, while tanks and other weapons of war were lined up, ready to fight for survival. The tag line on the poster proclaimed: "FROM OUT OF SPACE … A WARNING AND AN ULTIMATUM!"

Fans of the film know that the alien, Klaatu, came to Earth to warn the planet against violence. He told the president that he was on a mission of peace. His message to Earth was that his colleagues in outer space would destroy them if they continued to commit acts of aggression. They must change their ways or be eliminated. To show the world he meant business, Klaatu demonstrated his power: He made the earth stand still by suppressing electrical power all over the world. In retaliation, the military authorities shot Klaatu. His robotic companion, Gort, revived Klaatu long enough for Klaatu to give one final warning: Abandon warfare or be destroyed. Yes, it was a mixed message, but it was good science fiction.

It is fantastical to believe that the earth could stand still, but in the book of Joshua we encounter an equally fantastic event—the day the sun stood still. This was not science fiction but a true miracle from the hand of God. A coalition of rulers made war against the Israelites, so Joshua called upon God's power to finish the war and give God the glory.

Day 1: Joshua 10:1–5   WHEN WORLDS COLLIDE

Day 2: Joshua 10:6–15   STAR WARS

Day 3: Joshua 10:16–27   THE CAVE

Day 4: Joshua 10:28–39   WAR OF THE WORLDS

Day 5: Joshua 10:40–43   SUPERMAN

DAY 1
When Worlds Collide

LIFT UP ...

Lord, Thank You that You hear me when I cry out and that You come to my rescue. Thank You for being a God who saves. Amen.

LOOK AT ...

Last week we learned how the Israelites were deceived into entering into covenant with the Gibeonites. Though God had instructed the Israelites to destroy them, they instead made an alliance and were then honor bound to keep it. Now we see that the Gibeonites were in trouble because of the treaty.

When the kings in the land heard about the alliance, they formed a coalition and sought to destroy the Gibeonites. Rather than turning to the Israelites for mercy, the kings decided to wage war against the people they once called friends. Joshua and his army had successfully made a thrust to control the center of the land and could now engage the north and south separately. While they had won Gibeon without any bloodshed, they were now faced with taking on five kingdoms at one time. The Israelites learned that by allying themselves with enemies, they had no choice but to defend them. Let's learn the lesson: Those you choose to partner with, you must also protect.

READ JOSHUA 10:1–5.

Now it came to pass when Adoni-Zedek king of Jerusalem heard how Joshua had taken Ai and had utterly destroyed it—as he had done to Jericho and its king, so he had done to Ai and its king—and how the inhabitants of Gibeon had made peace with Israel and were among them, that they feared greatly, because Gibeon was a great city, like one of the royal cities, and because it was greater than Ai, and all its men were mighty.

LEARN ABOUT ...

1 Adoni-Zedek

Adoni-Zedek's name is literally translated "the lord is righteousness." However, he made an unrighteous alliance against God's people. Rather than battling God and His people, Adoni-Zedek could have followed in the footsteps of Melchizedek, an earlier king of Salem (Jerusalem), whose name meant "king of righteousness." Melchizedek worshipped God and praised Him for Abraham's victory in battle.

---

2 Gibeon

Gibeon was one of the key cities in Canaan, located ten miles northwest of Jerusalem. Archaeologists have found a wall five feet thick and more than half a mile in circumference around the sixteen-acre town. Since Gibeon made a pact with Israel, Jerusalem was next in line for attack. No doubt the Amorite kings considered the Gibeonites traitors.

---

5 Amorite

The Amorites descended from Canaan: "Canaan begot Sidon his firstborn, and Heth; the Jebusite, the Amorite, and the Girgashite" (Gen. 10:15–16). *Amorite* probably means "western highlanders." When Israel first invaded Canaan, they first fought against the Amorite kings Sihon and Og east of the Jordan River.

Therefore Adoni-Zedek king of Jerusalem sent to Hoham king of Hebron, Piram king of Jarmuth, Japhia king of Lachish, and Debir king of Eglon, saying, "Come up to me and help me, that we may attack Gibeon, for it has made peace with Joshua and with the children of Israel." Therefore the five kings of the Amorites, the king of Jerusalem, the king of Hebron, the king of Jarmuth, the king of Lachish, and the king of Eglon, gathered together and went up, they and all their armies, and camped before Gibeon and made war against it. Joshua 10:1–5

1. Describe what Adoni-Zedek had heard about Ai and Jericho.

2. Describe what Adoni-Zedek had heard about the inhabitants of Gibeon. What additional information do you learn about Gibeon here?

3. List the four kings Adoni-Zedek sent a message to.

4. In your own words recount what he asked of these kings.

5. How did the Amorite kings respond?

LIVE OUT ...

6. Adoni-Zedek formed an unholy alliance to oppose the Israelites. Throughout history, people have had an intense hatred for the people of Israel. Talk about some of the persecutions of which you are aware. Why do you think the hatred is so intense? Use Scripture to back up your answers.

7. By aligning themselves with the Israelites, the Gibeonites were given shelter not only by the Israelites, but also by their God.

With this in mind, rewrite Psalm 61:3–4 into a personal prayer asking God to be your shelter and strong tower in this world: "You have been a shelter for me, A strong tower from the enemy. I will abide in Your tabernacle forever; I will trust in the shelter of Your wings."

8. There are times when the only way to make peace is to wage war. At other times, peace is wrought by not pursuing war.

   a. Fill in the following chart to discover some things the Bible says about war.

SCRIPTURE	LESSONS ON WAR
1 Samuel 23:1–2	
2 Samuel 22:35–36	
Ecclesiastes 3:8	
Luke 14:31–32	
Revelation 19:11	

9. Have you ever felt under attack for your spiritual values? Maybe those you once were close to, even your own friends and family, turned on you when you came to faith. Talk about how you felt and who you turned to for help in those times.

○ ○ ● ○ ○

In the movie *When Worlds Collide*, life on Earth was threatened by impending impact with a star. The only hope for humanity's survival was for a few people to board a spacecraft and populate a new planet. The movie revealed man's inhumanity when people showed their willingness to kill one another to save their own lives.

Perhaps it's human nature to fend for ourselves when trouble comes.

LEARN ABOUT …

6 Unholy Trinity
The book of Revelation prophesies that in the future an unholy trinity will set itself up against Israel. Satan, the Antichrist, and the false prophet will seize power before the second coming of Christ and establish a false worship system. Those who do not worship the Antichrist will be persecuted. Christ's return will end their reign of terror.

---

8 Just War
Through the ages, noted scholars have struggled to determine when war is necessary and just. Today many governments adhere to a "just war" theory containing seven key principles: 1) a just cause; 2) a just intention; 3) as a last resort; 4) a formal declaration; 5) with limited objectives; 6) using proportional means; 7) noncombatant immunity.

But it's godly to be self-sacrificing in desperate times. For instance, during World War II a Jewish woman was fleeing the German Gestapo in France; she realized they were closing in, and she wanted to give up. She went to a widow's home to rest. The widow encouraged her to flee the country. The fugitive said, "It's no use, they'll find me."

The Christian widow said, "They will find someone here." Pointing to other people getting ready to flee she said, "Go with these people—I will take your identification and wait here."

The hunted lady then understood the plan; the Gestapo would come and find the Christian widow and think she was the fleeing Jew. The Jewish lady woman, "Why are you doing this?"

The widow responded, "You came to me for shelter and I know I have eternal shelter in Christ."

The widow helped her friend to escape but was caught and imprisoned. Within six months she died in a concentration camp. The Jewish woman never forgot the sacrifice. She, too, became a follower of Jesus Christ and lived her life serving others.

LISTEN TO ...

Christ made it clear that His coming, far from meaning peace, meant war. His message was a fire that would set society ablaze with division and strife.

—*Billy Graham*

DAY 2
Star Wars

Star Wars is one of the most popular science-fantasy series ever made. It is made up of six films by George Lucas, and the first movie is set nineteen years after the formation of the evil Galactic Empire, when a Death Star is built. This weapon is able to destroy an entire planet. The movie introduces us to Princess Leia, the leader of the Rebel Alliance. We also meet young Luke Skywalker, who will be trained by the wise Obi-Wan Kenobi as a Jedi knight in the ways of the Force. We meet Han Solo, the dashing pilot of the Millennium Falcon, and his hairy friend, Chewbacca. And of course, we meet the film's archvillain: the creepy man in black, Darth Vader. And who could forget the opening crawl as the screen rolls out the words, "A long time ago in a galaxy far, far away …"

When the film was released in 1977, we saw things we had never seen before: light saber duels, tractor beams, Stormtroopers, and the amazing firefight when Luke used the Force to fly into the Death Star's trenches and send a torpedo into the tiny hole of the ventilation port. It took a lot of filmmaking magic to make the special effects work in *Star Wars* so that we could be carried away to that galaxy far, far away.

But a long time ago in a land across the ocean, God created some amazing effects that really did happen. He used a daring man named Joshua, and the mighty men of valor, to win a war against all odds. And God used miraculous means to accomplish His purposes. You might even say He let the stars go to war for Him.

LIFT UP …

Lord, I know that You are still in the miracle business. Thank You for being a mighty God who works wonders on behalf of His children. Would You please work miracles in my life so that Your name will be glorified? Amen.

LOOK AT …

We've seen that the Amorite kings formed a coalition to fight against Gibeon because of their alliance with Israel. Today we see that Gibeon turned to Israel for help against the five kings.

The Gibeonites had made some new and powerful enemies. They had probably reached the conclusion that the "the enemy of my enemy is my friend." Therefore they called on their new friend, Israel, to protect them against their foes. Israel was once again faced with the consequences of disobedience. Rather than methodically and strategically taking on one kingdom at a time, the soldiers were forced to fight five kingdoms at once. The odds were stacked against them. But God works best against the odds. When you feel backed into a corner or that you're facing overwhelming odds, remember that God is the One who is always in control. If you are His friend, then your enemies are His enemies.

READ JOSHUA 10:6–11.

And the men of Gibeon sent to Joshua at the camp at Gilgal, saying, "Do not forsake your servants; come up to us quickly, save us and help us, for all the kings of the Amorites who dwell in the mountains have gathered together against us." So Joshua ascended from Gilgal, he and all the people of war with him, and all the mighty men of valor. And the LORD said to Joshua, "Do not fear them, for I have delivered them into your hand; not a man of them shall stand before you." Joshua therefore came upon them suddenly, having marched all night from Gilgal. So the LORD routed them before Israel, killed them with a great slaughter at Gibeon, chased them along the road that goes to Beth Horon, and struck them down as far as Azekah and Makkedah. And it happened, as they fled before Israel and were on the descent of Beth Horon, that the LORD cast down large hailstones from heaven on them as far as Azekah, and they died. There were more who died from the hailstones than the children of Israel killed with the sword. Joshua 10:6–11

1. a. Recount what the men of Gibeon asked Joshua to do once they learned of the Amorites' alliance.

   b. How did Joshua respond?

2. What two reasons did the Lord give Joshua for not fearing the Amorite kings?

3. Using the following verbs, describe the initial phases of the battle:

Routed _____

Killed _____

Chased _____

Struck _____

4. Describe what happened to those fleeing on the descent of Beth Horon and the significance of this occurrence.

LOOK AT …

God supernaturally intervened with hailstones from heaven, killing more Amorites than the Israelites had killed. But that's not the only miraculous part of the hailstones. God's aim was so precise that *only* Amorites were killed; none of the Israelites were harmed by the hail from heaven. Now let's see the next phase in the amazing battle as we examine verses 12–15.

Then Joshua spoke to the LORD in the day when the LORD delivered up the Amorites before the children of Israel, and he said in the sight of Israel: "Sun, stand still over Gibeon; And Moon, in the Valley of Aijalon." So the sun stood still, And the moon stopped, Till the people had revenge Upon their enemies. Is this not written in the Book of Jasher? So the sun stood still in the midst of heaven, and did not hasten to go down for about a whole day. And there has been no day like that, before it or after it, that the LORD heeded the voice of a man; for the LORD fought for Israel. Then Joshua returned, and all Israel with him, to the camp at Gilgal. Joshua 10:12–15

5. What did Joshua ask God to do on that day?

6. Describe in detail how God answered Joshua's prayer.

LEARN ABOUT …

1 Forsaken

To *forsake* means to abandon or leave behind. One nuance of forsake is "to leave in the lurch." A different nuance means to "let someone alone with a problem." The Gibeonites may have thought Joshua would be fickle and forsake them in their time of need. God had promised Joshua that He would not forsake nor destroy His people (see Deut. 4:31).

4 Heavenly Hailstones

In the Middle East, hail usually falls in the spring or summer and usually in the daytime. Hailstones are made up of alternate layers of ice and snow, and sometimes reach considerable size. If they fall before harvest, they damage grain and fruit, injure property, and endanger life.[97]

5 Still Sun, Motionless Moon

Joshua asked for the sun to stand still so they could continue the fight against innumerable enemies. While miracles cannot be explained by human reasoning, one author suggests three ways God could have caused this to happen: 1) refraction of the sun and moon's light, 2) precession of the earth's axis, 3) slowing of the earth's rotation.[98]

LEARN ABOUT ...

9 Suddenly

Life can change in an instant. A car can crash into us and take the life of a loved one. We can look across the room and see the person we'll live with for the rest of our lives. The woman with an issue of blood "suddenly" touched the hem of Christ's garment and was healed instantly. Jesus said, "Be of good cheer, daughter; your faith has made you well" (Matt. 9:22).

---

10 Heavens

"The heavens" refers to three areas of space. The first heaven is the atmosphere above us where the clouds float and the birds fly. The second heaven is outer space where the planets orbit and the stars shine. The third heaven is the spiritual realm no one can see, the place where God dwells.

7. How do you know this was a unique day in history?

LIVE OUT ...

8. a. We know that Joshua is a picture or foreshadowing of Jesus. Based on Hebrews 13:5–6, how might we be like the Gibeonites?

   b. How is Jesus like Joshua in dispensing his favor?

   c. How does this comfort you?

9. Just as Joshua attacked the Amorites suddenly, many things in life occur suddenly. Describe a time in your life when something either wonderful or horrible suddenly happened. How was your life changed in an instant? How did God use it in your life?

10. Today we learned that God answered Joshua's prayer for the sun and moon to stand still. When Jesus was born, a star miraculously stood over the stable in Bethlehem. Read Psalm 19:1–4 and discover more about the miraculous messages from the heavens.

> The heavens declare the glory of God;
> And the firmament shows His handiwork.
> Day unto day utters speech,
> And night unto night reveals knowledge.
> There is no speech nor language
> Where their voice is not heard.
> Their line has gone out through all the earth,
> And their words to the end of the world.

   a. Draw a star beside the two messages the heavens proclaim.

b. Draw a sun and moon beside the way the heavens communicate.

c. Circle the lines that show how far-reaching the celestial message is.

d. What do you learn from this psalm about God's ability to communicate?

○ ○ ● ○ ○

On Christmas Eve 1968, three astronauts, Frank Borman, Jim Lovell, and Bill Anders, flew the *Apollo 8* spacecraft on a bold mission around the back of the moon to test navigation and communication systems. Circling the dark side of the moon, they captured pictures of the first "Earth rise," photographs that have become iconic in American space history. The sight of the lunar sunrise casting its glow upon the blue and white earth over the horizon of the moon was nothing short of spectacular. The space cowboys who were trained in technological advances didn't try to relate what was happening in scientific lingo. They didn't try to describe the exact position of the earth, sun, and moon. Instead, they proclaimed this message to Mission Control:

> 086:06:40 ANDERS: "We are now approaching lunar sunrise, and for all the people back on Earth, the crew of *Apollo 8* has a message that we would like to send to you.

> "'In the beginning, God created the Heaven and the Earth. And the Earth was without form and void, and darkness was upon the face of the deep. And the spirit of God moved upon the face of the waters, and God said, "Let there be light." And there was light. And God saw the light, that it was good, and God divided the light from the darkness.'"

> 086:07:29 LOVELL: "'And God called the light Day, and the darkness he called Night. And the evening and the morning were the first day. And God said, "Let there be a firmament in the midst of the waters. And let it divide the waters

from the waters." And God made the firmament and divided the waters which were under the firmament from the waters which were above the firmament. And it was so. And God called the firmament Heaven. And the evening and the morning were the second day.'"

086:08:07 BORMAN: "'And God said, "Let the waters under the Heavens be gathered together into one place. And let the dry land appear." And it was so. And God called the dry land Earth. And the gathering together of the waters He called seas. And God saw that it was good.'

"And from the crew of *Apollo 8*, we close with good night, good luck, a Merry Christmas and God bless all of you—all of you on the good Earth."

Some have said if you can believe Genesis 1:1, then everything else in the Bible is easy to believe. God can make the sun and moon stand still just as easily as He can conquer any enemies you face on earth.

LISTEN TO ...

The extravagant gesture is the very stuff of creation. After the one extravagant gesture of creation in the first place, the universe has continued to deal exclusively in extravagances, flinging intricacies and colossi down aeons of emptiness, heaping profusions on profligacies with ever fresh vigor. The whole show has been on fire from the word go!

—*Annie Dillard*

The Cave

Spelunkers are those who explore caves as a recreational hobby. The depth of challenge depends on the cave, whether it includes pitches, squeezes, and the presence of water. Crawling, climbing, and rope rapelling are some of the skills a spelunker must master.

The Cave is a 2005 science-fiction thriller in which a team of European scientists requires the help of some expert American spelunkers. An expedition results after the discovery of a giant underground cave system in a Romanian forest, beneath a thirteenth-century abbey. Dr. Nicolai and his associate Dr. Bacovia believe the caverns contain an undiscovered ecosystem.

Jack and Tyler, brothers and thrill-seeking professional cavers, lead a team of top divers into the abyss. They soon discover bizarre creatures as well as a group of explorers from three decades ago, who are no longer quite human. The scientists conclude that these beings sprang from a parasite that infects its host (the human) enabling them to survive in the cave system. Several crew members become infected and could expose the whole world.

Joshua 10 introduces us to a group of royal spelunkers. They have retreated to a cave system in Makeddah. Before they can escape to infect their armies with hatred, rallying them to a second attack on Israel, Joshua rolls a stone in front of the cave opening. He will find a way to deal with these ungodly creatures. Those dwelling in darkness will be brought to light and justice.

LIFT UP …

Thank you, Lord, that You are greater than my greatest foe. I know that with You by my side no enemy will be able to prevail against me. May I witness the powers of darkness flee as I submit to You. Amen.

LEARN ABOUT ...

1 Stuck In

In ancient times caves were used for habitations, refuge, and prison. Makkedah, "a place of shepherds," was a royal Canaanite city in the low country of a region that was ultimately assigned to the tribe of Judah. Some archeologists identify this place with el-Mughar, "the caves," located southwest of Ekron.[99]

---

4 Stopped Up

God stopped the advance of the soldiers as well as the mouths of its citizens. Similarly, God silenced the Egyptians: "But against none of the children of Israel shall a dog move its tongue, against man or beast, that you may know that the LORD does make a difference between the Egyptians and Israel" (Ex. 11:7).

LOOK AT ...

The mighty Amorite kings put on a brave, bold appearance as they came out to attack Gibeon. However, the Gibeonites had help from God's chosen people. Joshua routed the armies as God rained down hailstones from heaven and caused the earth to stand still.

Joshua may have thought that his work was done, that he could go back to camp with his army for refreshment. So they returned to Gilgal, perhaps to receive new orders from God. Soon they discovered there was much more to be done. They had to continue the victory they'd begun and conquer the kings hiding in a cave.

Like the physical enemies and literal battles of Joshua, the Christian faces spiritual foes and fights. The land full of blessing is enjoyed through intensive warfare. We must learn to conquer and possess all that is ours in Christ Jesus our Lord.

READ JOSHUA 10:16–21.

But these five kings had fled and hidden themselves in a cave at Makkedah. And it was told Joshua, saying, "The five kings have been found hidden in the cave at Makkedah." So Joshua said, "Roll large stones against the mouth of the cave, and set men by it to guard them. And do not stay there yourselves, but pursue your enemies, and attack their rear guard. Do not allow them to enter their cities, for the LORD your God has delivered them into your hand." Then it happened, while Joshua and the children of Israel made an end of slaying them with a very great slaughter, till they had finished, that those who escaped entered fortified cities. And all the people returned to the camp, to Joshua at Makkedah, in peace. No one moved his tongue against any of the children of Israel. Joshua 10:16–21

1. Note where the five kings hid and how Joshua heard about it. What action did Joshua take to ensure they would not flee?

2. Explain the two things Joshua told the warriors not to do and why.

3. Describe how long they fought and how intense the battle was.

4. What was the end result?

Look at ...

Joshua and his warriors fought a long and hard battle against the Amorites, killing most of the people. Only a few escaped into the fortified cities. Those who did were stunned into silence at the power of the Israelites. Now let's look at Joshua 10:22–27 to see how Joshua dealt with the kings trapped in the cave at Makkedah.

Then Joshua said, "Open the mouth of the cave, and bring out those five kings to me from the cave." And they did so, and brought out those five kings to him from the cave: the king of Jerusalem, the king of Hebron, the king of Jarmuth, the king of Lachish, and the king of Eglon. So it was, when they brought out those kings to Joshua, that Joshua called for all the men of Israel, and said to the captains of the men of war who went with him, "Come near, put your feet on the necks of these kings." And they drew near and put their feet on their necks. Then Joshua said to them, "Do not be afraid, nor be dismayed; be strong and of good courage, for thus the LORD will do to all your enemies against whom you fight." And afterward Joshua struck them and killed them, and hanged them on five trees; and they were hanging on the trees until evening. So it was at the time of the going down of the sun that Joshua commanded, and they took them down from the trees, cast them into the cave where they had been hidden, and laid large stones against the cave's mouth, which remain until this very day. Joshua 10:22–27

5. Explain Joshua's orders concerning the five kings and how this order was obeyed.

6. a. Who did Joshua gather together?

   b. What did he order the captains to do to the kings?

LEARN ABOUT ...

6 Stamped Out

To put your feet upon someone's neck symbolized complete defeat and suppression. Often this act is pictured on the monuments of the kings of Egypt and Assyria. God had promised Moses, "Your enemies shall submit to you, And you shall tread down their high places" (Deut. 33:29).

---

9 Crushed

Israel's enemies were crushed under their feet as a symbol of defeat and demoralization. Our enemy Satan will one day be dashed beneath our feet: "The God of peace will crush Satan under your feet shortly. The grace of our Lord Jesus Christ be with you" (Rom. 16:20).

---

10 Quieted

You don't need to have your mouth shut up by God if you choose to silence it yourself. Like David, you can exercise self-control. "You have tested my heart; You have visited me in the night; You have tried me and have found nothing; I have purposed that my mouth shall not transgress" (Ps. 17:3).

c. What was Joshua's purpose here?

7. Recount Joshua's words of encouragement to his men.

8. Look at what happened to the kings. Why did Joshua do all this?

LIVE OUT ...

9. Imagine God telling you to put your foot on the neck of an enemy. Who or what might that enemy be? Why does God want to impress on you the need for courage and confidence in that situation? Journal a prayer to Him about this.

10. Because of God's great hand of deliverance, the children of Israel enjoyed a gossip-free season. Not one bad word was said against them. Fill in the following chart to see other mouths that God promises to stop.

SCRIPTURE	THOSE GOD SILENCES
Psalm 63:11	
Daniel 6:22	
Titus 1:10–11	

11. The kings thought they could hide in a cave, but the Israelites discovered and exposed them. Jesus said, "For there is nothing covered that will not be revealed, and hidden that will not be known" (Matt. 10:26).

    Journal about a situation when you thought you could hide from the Lord. How did He uncover what you thought was hidden?

○ ○ ● ○ ○

Shoichi Yokoi, a Japanese soldier, lived in a cave on the island of Guam. Fearing for his life, he fled there in 1944, when the tides of war began to change. He stayed hidden for twenty-eight years, only venturing out at night. During this self-imposed exile, he lived on frogs, rats, nuts, and mangoes. Even when he realized that the war had ended, he was afraid to come out for fear of execution. Unlike the five kings who found judgment when they left their cave, Shoichi was found by two hunters, who escorted him to liberty.[100] He had stayed hidden because he was afraid to face his sins. If he had come out sooner, he would have experienced forgiveness and freedom.

Doctors believe that patients get sick physically and emotionally because they are not facing their sins. Dr. John S. Bonnell, in his book *Pastoral Psychiatry*, shares four case studies. 1) A university student experienced drumming noises in his head, blurred vision, and dizziness. 2) A woman suffered from neuritis. 3) A medical student struggled with mental disorders. 4) A patient lived with persistent indigestion. Relief came when each patient broke down and confessed their hidden sins.

Sometimes all of us would like to "cave up," to hide from the consequences of our actions. But hiding never brings healing. John wrote, "But if we walk in the light as He is in the light, we have fellowship with one another, and the blood of Jesus Christ His Son cleanses us from all sin" (1 John 1:7). Today hear God calling, "Come out, come out, wherever you are!"

LISTEN TO ...

A guilty conscience is a hidden enemy.

—*Indian Proverb*

DAY 4

War of the Worlds

In 1938, Orson Welles adapted H. G. Wells' book *War of the Worlds* into a lifelike radio broadcast from New York City. Although the program began with a brief disclaimer, it cleverly wove ordinary music segments with sensational news flashes about a Martian rocket capsule landing in New Jersey. The news reports grew more frequent and increasingly ominous as Americans were told how the Martians were incinerating curious onlookers with "Heat-rays."

The result was sheer panic among many radio listeners who, when later surveyed, indicated they never heard the disclaimer before contacting neighbors to warn them of the earth's demise at the hands of creatures from Mars.

The plot crescendoed as Martian ships supposedly wreaked havoc throughout the United States, destroying bridges and railroads while spraying poisonous gas in the air. The hoax included interviews with the secretary of Interior and someone who sounded just like President Franklin Delano Roosevelt. The story ended, as does the novel, with the Martians falling victim to earthly germs and bacteria.

After the play ended, Welles broke character to remind listeners that the broadcast was only a Halloween concoction. However, contemporary newspapers reported that panic had ensued, with people fleeing the area and others thinking they could smell the poison gas or could see the flashes of the lightning in the distance.

The Canaanites witnessed the war of their worlds as Joshua's armies invaded their cities. They could do nothing to stop these aliens from a distant land. Panic must have gripped the citizens as news that their enemies were advancing spread throughout the land.

LIFT UP ...

God, I know that You are a detailed and thorough God. That which You begin, You also complete. Not one of Your promises goes unfulfilled. Thank You that You are the author and finisher of my faith! Amen.

LOOK AT ...

Israel's first few battles, including Ai and Jericho, are recorded with great detail in the book of Joshua. However, in chapter 10 the pace quickens with an impressive sweep of southern Canaan. Joshua took advantage of his army's momentum by conquering seven kings and guarding the southern highlands. Years into the future, Sennacherib and Nebuchadnezzar copied Joshua's strategy when they attacked Israel.

Joshua's leadership style revealed his strict obedience to God's command to utterly destroy the inhabitants of Canaan. As a result, the Lord delivered the great southern cities into his hands. "So Israel made a vow to the LORD, and said, 'If You will indeed deliver this people into my hand, then I will utterly destroy their cities'" (Num. 21:2). Similarly, when we completely obey God, we discover incredible results. Cooperation with the divine will spells victory for all of God's children. God views partial obedience as disobedience. Be sure that you follow all that God's Word commands.

READ JOSHUA 10:28–39.

On that day Joshua took Makkedah, and struck it and its king with the edge of the sword. He utterly destroyed them—all the people who were in it. He let none remain. He also did to the king of Makkedah as he had done to the king of Jericho. Then Joshua passed from Makkedah, and all Israel with him, to Libnah; and they fought against Libnah. And the LORD also delivered it and its king into the hand of Israel; he struck it and all the people who were in it with the edge of the sword. He let none remain in it, but did to its king as he had done to the king of Jericho. Then Joshua passed from Libnah, and all Israel with him, to Lachish; and they encamped against it and fought against it. And the LORD delivered Lachish into the hand of Israel, who took it on the second day, and struck it and all the people who were in it with the edge of the sword, according to all that he had done to Libnah. Then Horam king of Gezer came up to help Lachish; and Joshua struck him and his people, until he left him none remaining. From Lachish Joshua passed to Eglon, and all Israel with him; and they encamped against it and fought against it. They took it on that day and struck it with the edge of the sword; all the people who were in it he utterly destroyed that day, according to all that he had done to Lachish. So Joshua went up from Eglon, and all Israel with him, to Hebron; and they

LEARN ABOUT ...

1 Jericho's King

Two rulers from southern cities met the same fate as "the king of Jericho." Joshua 8:2, 29 reveal that the kings of Jericho and Ai were hanged from trees, thrown at their city gates, then covered with heaps of stones as signs of judgment.

---

3 Lord's Deliverance

God displayed His love to His nation by delivering so many people to them in exchange for their lives. Matthew Henry writes that as a result the Israelites would "forever spend their lives to the glory of that God who had sacrificed so many of the lives of his creatures to their interest."[101]

---

6 Sword's Edge

Nothing explains this military execution except that the Israelites did as the God of Israel commanded (see Josh. 10:40). They revealed God's hatred for the idolatries and abominations that the Canaanites had engaged in for centuries, such as child sacrifice and prostitution in the worship of their pagan gods.

fought against it. And they took it and struck it with the edge of the sword — its king, all its cities, and all the people who were in it; he left none remaining, according to all that he had done to Eglon, but utterly destroyed it and all the people who were in it. Then Joshua returned, and all Israel with him, to Debir; and they fought against it. And he took it and its king and all its cities; they struck them with the edge of the sword and utterly destroyed all the people who were in it. He left none remaining; as he had done to Hebron, so he did to Debir and its king, as he had done also to Libnah and its king. Joshua 10:28–39

1. Summarize what Joshua did to the king of Makkedah. Who did the writer compare this king to?

2. After Makkedah, the Israelites turned their attention to Libnah. Describe this battle and what it was compared to.

3. After Libnah came Lacish. Describe this battle and how it differed from the other battles.

4. After Lacish came Eglon. Describe this battle. What strategy did Joshua use in this battle, and what battle was it compared to?

5. From Eglon Joshua went to Hebron. Describe this battle and how it was fought.

6. From Hebron the warriors went to Debir. How was this battle fought? What was destroyed in it?

7. a. Reread this passage in Joshua while underlining the phrases "utterly destroyed" and "none remained." How many times do they occur?

   b. Circle the names of cities that met this fate.

LIVE OUT ...

8. The Jews hanged the Canaanite kings as a symbol of divine judgment for their sins. Jesus, the King of Kings, also hanged from a tree—the cross—in order to pay the price for divine judgment upon your sins.

   a. Read John 10:17–18. Who ordained that Christ die on the cross? How did Jesus feel about it?

   b. Read Acts 5:30–32. What were the results of Christ's death "on a tree"?

   c. Read Acts 10:39–43. How was the world affected by this ignoble death?

9. The Israelites' enemies were the Canaanites. Fill in the following chart to discover some of the Christian's enemies.

Scripture	Our Enemies
Matthew 10:36–37	
1 Corinthians 15:26	
Colossians 3:5	
James 4:4	
1 Peter 5:8	

10. The weapon of choice for the Israelite army was a sword. As Christians, Paul says that we have the "sword of the spirit" and God's Word that is "sharper than any two-edged sword." How will you use these heavenly weapons to slay your spiritual enemies?

    Journal a prayer of spiritual warfare with the greatest enemy you are currently facing.

LEARN ABOUT ...

8 Hanging

Biblically, a curse is connected to anyone hanging from a tree. Even the apostles connected Jesus' hanging on a tree with a curse (see Acts 5:30; Gal. 3:13). However, Jesus transformed this dishonorable form of death into a beautiful picture of God's sacrificial and redeeming love.[102]

9 None Remaining

The Jews were thorough in eliminating their enemies. They did "not let one remain." The Christian faces the enemies of sin, self, and Satan. Paul is emphatic about utterly destroying our sinful flesh: "Put on the Lord Jesus Christ, and make no provision for the flesh, to fulfill its lusts" (Rom. 13:14).

○ ○ ● ○ ○

Like Joshua, the Christian encounters many enemies. You, too, are armed and equipped for whatever battle lies ahead. With the Lord as the Commander of God's armies you are enlisted as "a good soldier of Jesus Christ" (2 Tim. 2:3). You have been given spiritual armor that protects you from head to toe (see Eph. 6:10–17). You are also supplied with an amazing arsenal that is "mighty in God for pulling down strongholds" (2 Cor. 10:4). And the Bible promises that "we are more than conquerors through Him who loved us" (Rom. 8:37).

John Dorsey poetically described the mighty battle between the believer and his ultimate enemy, the Devil:

> I had a battle fierce today within my place of prayer;
> I went to meet and talk with God, but I found Satan there.
> He whispered, "You can't really pray, you lost out long ago;
> You might say words while on your knees, but you can't pray, you know."
> So then I pulled my helmet down, way down upon my ears,
> And found it helped to still his voice and helped allay my fears.
> I checked my other armor o'er; my feet in peace were shod;
> My loins with truth were girded 'round; my sword the Word of God.
> My righteous breastplate still was on, my heart's love to protect.
> My shield of faith was all intact—his fiery darts bounced back.
> I called on God in Jesus' name; I pled the precious blood;
> While Satan sneaked away in shame, I met and talked with God![103]

LISTEN TO …

The Bible is the only thing that can combat the devil. Quote the Scriptures and the devil will run … use the Scriptures like a sword and you'll drive temptation away.

—Billy Graham

DAY 5

Superman

Who is "faster than a speeding bullet, more powerful than a locomotive, and able to leap tall buildings in a single bound"? SUPERMAN! Wouldn't it be nice if there were such a person as Superman? He used his powers for good against all of the evils in the world. Superman was created by Jerry Siegel and Joe Shuster, who were both of Jewish descent. Over the years there has been speculation that the authors of Superman were greatly influenced by Moses and other Hebrew stories. For instance, Superman's name on Krypton was Kal-El, which resembles the Hebrew phrase "vessel of God" or "all that is God." Some people believe that Superman is a representative of a Golem. Golems are mythical Jewish creatures supposedly created to protect and serve persecuted Jews. People have even seen Superman as an allegory for Jesus, the One who saved the world from sin.

The fascination with the Superman legend speaks of humanity's longing for an all-powerful being to come to our rescue in a time of need. Don't you sometimes wish someone would look up into the sky and say, "It's a bird! It's a plane! It's Superman!" Sadly, Superman is just a comic book hero who has been turned into countless television and movie incarnations

But real-life heroes *do* exist. There really was a Moses who God empowered to set His people free from Egypt's tyranny. And there really was a Joshua who was able to pray to the all-powerful God and cause the sun and moon to stop so the fighting could continue. And there really is a Jesus who died on a cross and who will one day come to earth in the clouds. We will look in the sky and proclaim, "It's the Savior!"

LIFT UP ...

Lord God, You are my hero. Thank You for being stronger than any human, stronger than any supernatural foe. Thank You for conquering the greatest enemy—death! Amen.

LEARN ABOUT ...

I Hill and Dale

The chapter ends with a description of the lands that Joshua conquered. It includes four regions: 1) the hill country, 2) the Negev, 3) the western foothills, and 4) the mountain slopes. However, Jerusalem was bypassed and later brought grief to the nation.

LOOK AT ...

We've seen Joshua and the troops exert a near superhuman effort as they conquered the five kings and the people within the kingdoms. The devastation must have been extraordinary. But more than exterminating the people, God was exterminating idolatry.

For more than four hundred years, God had given the people in Canaan time to turn from their ways. During this time the children of Israel had lived in slavery. Now the iniquity of the Amorites was full (see Gen. 15:16) and God used Joshua and the Israelites as instruments of divine judgment. In addition, by clearing out the idolaters, they were laying claim to the land for the true worshippers of God. The psalmist wrote: "You have brought a vine out of Egypt; You have cast out the nations, and planted it. You prepared room for it, And caused it to take deep root, And it filled the land" (Ps. 80:8–9). God was fulfilling His covenant promise to Israel in the hope that they would keep their covenant promise to Him. This is a solemn warning to all of us. For now God is extending His hand of grace. But one day He will come in judgment. Are you ready?

READ JOSHUA 10:40–43.

So Joshua conquered all the land: the mountain country and the South and the lowland and the wilderness slopes, and all their kings; he left none remaining, but utterly destroyed all that breathed, as the LORD God of Israel had commanded. And Joshua conquered them from Kadesh Barnea as far as Gaza, and all the country of Goshen, even as far as Gibeon. All these kings and their land Joshua took at one time, because the LORD God of Israel fought for Israel. Then Joshua returned, and all Israel with him, to the camp at Gilgal. Joshua 10:40–43

1. Describe how much of the land Joshua conquered.

2. How many of the kings did he kill?

3. What two key phrases, highlighted in yesterday's lesson, are repeated in this text? What additional phrase was added for impact?

4. List the land he took for Israel.

5. According to this passage, how was Joshua able to overcome these kings and take their land in one fell swoop?

6. After this battle, what did Joshua and the people do?

7. Scan through Joshua 10 looking for all citations of "Gilgal." How often does it occur? List each time it is recorded throughout this part of the war.

LIVE OUT ...

8. Reread Joshua 10 looking for all the instances where "Jerusalem" is recorded.

   a. Who was the king of Jerusalem? Describe his fate.

   b. Read ahead to Joshua 15:1–8. Who eventually inherited Jerusalem?

   c. Read ahead to Joshua 15:63. Describe the struggle between the Jews and the inhabitants of Jerusalem.

   d. Read Judges 1:4–8. Explain the fate Jerusalem eventually met.

LEARN ABOUT ...

3 Written Word

God breathed the breath of life into man (see Gen. 2:7). Eventually God judged the corruption of man with a flood, extinguishing all who breathed. "Behold, I Myself am bringing floodwaters on the earth, to destroy from under heaven all flesh in which is the breath of life; everything that is on the earth shall die" (Gen. 6:17).

---

7 Headquarters

Gilgal was the base of military operations and the line of communication for Israel's army. Joshua amassed his attack against southern Canaan from there. He retreated to it halfway through the battle to regroup. After victory he returned once again. Later in the Old Testament, King Samuel's coronation and Absalom's revolt both occurred at Gilgal.

---

8 Jerusalem

Jerusalem, whose name means "possession of peace," was the well-known capital of Palestine during Bible times. It appears for the first time during the struggle of Joshua and the Israelites to take the land of Canaan (see Josh. 10:1–4). However, they were unsuccessful in their efforts to take the city until the time of the judges.[104]

9. God can give or take away the very breath of life within us. As long as you are breathing, God requires your worship: "Let everything that has breath praise the Lord. Praise the Lord!" (Ps. 150:6).

Journal your own psalm of praise. Worship Him with every breath He imparts.

10. a. The Jews were to utterly destroy all of their foes. However, they left Jerusalem unconquered. Read the following text, and then circle the foes we are admonished to put to death. Underline which enemies you have not defeated.

Therefore put to death your members which are on the earth: fornication, uncleanness, passion, evil desire, and covetousness, which is idolatry. Because of these things the wrath of God is coming upon the sons of disobedience, in which you yourselves once walked when you lived in them. But now you yourselves are to put off all these: anger, wrath, malice, blasphemy, filthy language out of your mouth. Do not lie to one another, since you have put off the old man with his deeds (Col. 3:5–9).

b. Explain how you will "put off the old man with his deeds."

o o ● o o

On October 18, 1931, something stranger than science fiction took place; Thomas Edison died with a rack of eight empty test tubes close to his bedside. His son Charles recounted that his father had a real love for chemistry; therefore, it wasn't strange that the symbolic tubes were close to him at the end. What is weird is that Charles had the tubes sealed with paraffin by the attending physician. Later he gave one of them to

Henry Ford, a longtime friend and admirer of Edison. That glass container is now on display at the Henry Ford Museum in Detroit, Michigan, labeled "Edison's Last Breath," memorializing the automaker's hero.

Henry Ford believed that the human soul exited the body with its last breath. He was also interested in reincarnation, and some believe he was collecting the essence of Edison. Others assert that he simply wanted a souvenir of his departed buddy. There are even reports that he hung the vial from his rearview mirror. Sounds like the stuff of Hollywood, doesn't it?

In truth, you breathe 23,040 breaths per day. And someday, just like Edison and the enemies of Israel, you'll breathe your last breath. And when you do, you will certainly not be reincarnated and may not be recorded in the history books or memorialized in a museum. However, if you are a believer, Paul promises your first breath in heaven will follow your last breath on earth. "We are confident, yes, well pleased rather to be absent from the body and to be present with the Lord" (2 Cor. 5:8).

LISTEN TO ...

Let each man think himself an act of God, his mind a thought of God, his life a breath of God.

—*Philip James Bailey*

The Divine Developer
Joshua 11—13 & 16—19

Did you know that in 1889 many people considered Oklahoma "the Promised Land"? People could attain 160 acres of land just by staking a claim. Those who improved the claim for five years would receive title to their land.

Although Oklahoma had been withheld as Indian Territory, President Benjamin Harrison opened two million acres to settlement. Farmers, tradesmen, professionals, and laborers all looked to Oklahoma to make their fortune. The *New York Herald* wrote, "It is an astonishing thing that men will fight harder for $500 worth of land than they will for $10,000 in money."

The "boomers" camped in tents until the day of the land run. They eagerly stood in line until the trumpet sounded, then rushed to the plot of ground they desired and planted their stakes. The "sooners" crept onto the property early and hid out until high noon, the time set for the race to start. Many fistfights and courtroom battles ensued between the boomers and the sooners over the legal division of the land. But today, the boomers and the sooners have come together as one great state. The University of Oklahoma's fight song proudly proclaims: "Boomer Sooner! Boomer Sooner! I'm a Sooner born and bred!"[105]

The Hebrew nation had long looked to Israel as the Promised Land. After four hundred years in captivity, they had crossed the Jordan River to make their own land run. The division of the land was not nearly as capricious or chaotic as the land run of 1889. God made sure the chosen people received the portion properly allotted to them through His divine development plan.

Day 1: Joshua 11   **COSTLY LAND**

Day 2: Joshua 12   **CONSTRUCTIVE EVICTION**

Day 3: Joshua 13   **CHAIN OF TITLE**

Day 4: Joshua 16—17   **COUNTEROFFER**

Day 5: Joshua 18—19   **COVENANTS, CONDITIONS, AND RESTRICTIONS**

DAY 1

Costly Land

LIFT UP ...

Lord, You are a comfort and strength when I am in the middle of the battle. Thank You for continuing to deliver me from my enemies. Please give me victory over all areas that threaten to overcome me. Amen.

LOOK AT ...

We know that the southern kings plotted against Joshua and failed miserably. Why would anyone else plot against him? Reason would hold that they would surrender as the Gibeonites had and become vassals of Joshua, the conquering commander. But the northern kings failed to learn the lesson and followed the same tactics as the rulers to the south, forming a coalition to fight against Joshua and his army.

We learn early in this chapter that Jabin, a strong king, "heard these things" about Israel's triumph in conquering the kings to the south. Surely they heard about God's hand in the victory. They must have heard about the hail coming from the sky to strike the Amorites. Word must have spread about the sun standing still. The northerners should have been struck with the fear of the Lord, but instead they hardened their hearts and determined to fight harder. Scripture tells us that "faith comes by hearing, and hearing by the word of God" (Rom. 10:17). Clearly, hearing about what God has done it is not enough. We must also believe the warnings and turn to Him for forgiveness. If you have been listening to God's Word for years, don't harden your heart as the kings in Canaan. Become like the psalmist who said, "I have trusted in Your mercy; My heart shall rejoice in Your salvation" (Ps. 13:5).

LEARN ABOUT ...

1 Chariots

Chariots quickly brought power to the heart of the battle. A chariot usually carried two soldiers: a driver controlling the reins and a warrior wielding his weapon. Commentators believe that God forbade the use of chariots by prohibiting multiplying horses: "Some trust in chariots, and some in horses; But we will remember the name of the LORD" (Ps. 20:7).

2 Hamstrung Horses

In essence, hamstringing the horses would cripple them and put the Israeli foot soldiers on even ground with their opponents. God had prepared them beforehand: "When you go out to battle against your enemies, and see horses and chariots and people more numerous than you, do not be afraid of them; for the LORD your God is with you" (Deut. 20:1).

READ JOSHUA 11:1–11.

And it came to pass, when Jabin king of Hazor heard these things, that he sent to Jobab king of Madon, to the king of Shimron, to the king of Achshaph, and to the kings who were from the north, in the mountains, in the plain south of Chinneroth, in the lowland, and in the heights of Dor on the west, to the Canaanites in the east and in the west, the Amorite, the Hittite, the Perizzite, the Jebusite in the mountains, and the Hivite below Hermon in the land of Mizpah. So they went out, they and all their armies with them, as many people as the sand that is on the seashore in multitude, with very many horses and chariots. And when all these kings had met together, they came and camped together at the waters of Merom to fight against Israel. But the LORD said to Joshua, "Do not be afraid because of them, for tomorrow about this time I will deliver all of them slain before Israel. You shall hamstring their horses and burn their chariots with fire." So Joshua and all the people of war with him came against them suddenly by the waters of Merom, and they attacked them. And the LORD delivered them into the hand of Israel, who defeated them and chased them to Greater Sidon, to the Brook Misrephoth, and to the Valley of Mizpah eastward; they attacked them until they left none of them remaining. So Joshua did to them as the LORD had told him: he hamstrung their horses and burned their chariots with fire. Joshua turned back at that time and took Hazor, and struck its king with the sword; for Hazor was formerly the head of all those kingdoms. And they struck all the people who were in it with the edge of the sword, utterly destroying them. There was none left breathing. Then he burned Hazor with fire. Joshua 11:1–11

1. "It came to pass" that a new coalition of kings rose against Joshua and the Israelites.

   a. List the kings involved in this coalition.

b. What poetic phrase is used to describe the number of people who went out to fight the Israelites?

c. What form of transportation and weaponry did they use against the Israelites?

2. Recount God's words of comfort as well as His instructions to Joshua.

3. Describe how the attack was carried out and what happened to Hazor, the people, and the king.

LOOK AT ...

Despite their enemy's more sophisticated weaponry, the Israelite soldiers fought off the northern alliance's attack. They were utterly victorious against Hazor and that city's confederates. Joshua's swift actions and obedience to God's commands again served him well. He was close to completing the first part of his commission: to wage war on the people in Canaan. Let's take a moment to remember Joshua's accomplishments by examining Joshua 11:12–20.

So all the cities of those kings, and all their kings, Joshua took and struck with the edge of the sword. He utterly destroyed them, as Moses the servant of the LORD had commanded. But as for the cities that stood on their mounds, Israel burned none of them, except Hazor only, which Joshua burned. And all the spoil of these cities and the livestock, the children of Israel took as booty for themselves; but they struck every man with the edge of the sword until they had destroyed them, and they left none breathing. As the LORD had commanded Moses his servant, so Moses commanded Joshua, and so Joshua did. He left nothing undone of all that the LORD had commanded Moses. Thus Joshua took all this land: the mountain country, all the South, all the land of Goshen, the lowland, and the Jordan plain—the mountains of Israel and its lowlands, from Mount Halak and the ascent to Seir, even as far as Baal Gad in the Valley of Lebanon below Mount Hermon. He captured all their kings, and struck them down and killed them. Joshua made war a long time with all those kings. There was not a city that made peace with the children of Israel, except the Hivites, the inhabitants of Gibeon. All the

others they took in battle. For it was of the LORD to harden their hearts, that they should come against Israel in battle, that He might utterly destroy them, and that they might receive no mercy, but that He might destroy them, as the LORD had commanded Moses. Joshua 11:12–20

4. a. Describe how many kings and their cities were taken by Joshua.

   b. What happened to them? What exception did he make for Hazor?

5. a. What did the children of Israel do with the spoil of the remaining conquered cities?

   b. What happened to the people?

6. Describe how Joshua had learned what to do and then list his accomplishments.

7. Why did these people harden their hearts and come against Israel in battle?

LOOK AT ...

In every war there are cleanup operations. This war was no different. Let's look at Joshua 11:21–23 to see the final battles Joshua fought before moving on to divide the land.

And at that time Joshua came and cut off the Anakim from the mountains: from Hebron, from Debir, from Anab, from all the mountains of Judah, and from all the mountains of Israel; Joshua utterly destroyed them with their cities. None of the Anakim were left in the land of the children of Israel; they remained only in Gaza, in Gath, and in Ashdod. So

Joshua took the whole land, according to all that the LORD had said to Moses; and Joshua gave it as an inheritance to Israel according to their divisions by their tribes. Then the land rested from war. Joshua 11:21–23

8. After seeing many battles and being divided among the Israelites, what did the land finally enjoy?

LIVE OUT ...

9. a. The northern enemies came against the Israelites with fearful weapons. With this in mind, read Isaiah 54:17. What does God promise about the weapons of the world?

   b. What comfort do you take about the sharpest weapon of all—the tongue?

   c. Who does God make these promises to? How do you know you will receive these promises?

10. Today's passage had a remarkable phrase, "He left nothing undone of all that the LORD had commanded Moses" (Josh. 11:15). We all have daily "To Do" lists, but what about spiritual "To Do" lists? Write a list of the things the Lord has commanded you to do. Then spend some time asking God to help reprioritize your life so you will obey.

   MY "TO DO" LIST FOR GOD

11. Joshua conquered the kings and rested from war. Using the acronym REST, list some characteristics of God that you can rest in this week. Spend time praising God that He alone can give you rest.

R

E

S

T

○ ○ ● ○ ○

General Norman Schwarzkopf was a born leader. During his years of service he commanded army units from platoon through corps level. He served two combat tours in Vietnam. Later he was assigned to duty as commander of the joint task force in charge of U.S. forces in the Grenada student rescue operation. Of course, most of us recognize General Schwarzkopf for his services as commander of Operations of Desert Shield and Desert Storm.

His troops affectionately referred to their commander as "The Bear." Perhaps they were referring to his appearance or his emotional outlook on life. On February 27, 1991, when the war was declared over, General Schwarzkopf, the allies, and our best-trained, best-equipped soldiers and officers had stood their ground, accomplished their objectives, and minimized casualties in record time.

When General Schwarzkopf was interviewed by Ted Koppel of *Nightline,* he said something profound: "I would never want to serve under a general who enjoyed war." He spoke about his heroes from World War II: Omar Bradley, Dwight Eisenhower, and George Marshall. He mentioned others who hated war, telling the nation that it made them safe to be generals.

Joshua was a general who loved God and was willing to go to war for the righteous cause of the God he loved. He went to war to claim the Promised Land for the chosen people and to root out the idolatry that was so widespread in the land. No doubt Joshua did not enjoy making war, but he could do no less than serve his God and bring peace to the land.

LISTEN TO ...

Good kings never make war, but for the sake of peace.

—Proverb

DAY 2

Constructive Eviction

A constructive eviction occurs when housing is so substandard that a tenant will want to move out. The landlord may resort to evicting a tenant by refusing to provide light, heat, water, or other essential services, destroying part of the premises, or refusing to clean up an environmental health hazard, such as lead paint dust. Because the premises are unlivable, the tenant has the right to move out and stop paying rent without incurring legal liability for breaking the lease. Usually, the tenant must first bring the problem to the landlord's attention and allow a reasonable amount of time for the landlord to make repairs.

The Canaanite kings and priests had polluted God's land with idolatry, prostitution, and child sacrifice: "They even sacrificed their sons And their daughters to demons, And shed innocent blood, The blood of their sons and daughters, Whom they sacrificed to the idols of Canaan; And the land was polluted with blood" (Ps. 106:37–38). Spiritually, these pagans also represented an environmental health hazard to God's children. Because they persisted in a substandard way of life and refused to clean up their act, they were no longer welcomed. After waiting patiently for over four hundred years, God—the rightful landlord—was about to impose constructive eviction upon these unruly tenants.

LIFT UP ...

Lord, only You can keep track of the things that once kept me from knowing You. Thank You for conquering those areas through Jesus Christ and allowing me to enjoy the inheritance You have for me. Amen.

LOOK AT ...

Joshua exhibited incredible fortitude after vanquishing the Canaanites in the southern kingdom. He quickly turned his full attention to threats in the north. Very little time had passed between these great conquests, leaving the Israelite army little time to recuperate.

Joshua's battles were offensive, not defensive. He never paused long enough to dig a foxhole or build a fortress. If he heard that an enemy attack was imminent, he launched a preemptive strike against them instead. He frequently used the element of surprise, never allowing enemies time to regroup. He wanted to prevent them from reaching their fortified cities.

He was tireless and relentless. It must have been exhausting for the Canaanite kings to face such a formidable opponent. These rulers attempted alliances and evasive measures, but in the end they were vanquished and evicted. Joshua 12 records a long list of the kings of Canaan who were defeated as well as the lands they once possessed. You can take heart knowing that your God has defeated multitudes of principalities and rulers in the heavenly places.

READ JOSHUA 12:1-6

These are the kings of the land whom the children of Israel defeated, and whose land they possessed on the other side of the Jordan toward the rising of the sun, from the River Arnon to Mount Hermon, and all the eastern Jordan plain: One king was Sihon king of the Amorites, who dwelt in Heshbon and ruled half of Gilead, from Aroer, which is on the bank of the River Arnon, from the middle of that river, even as far as the River Jabbok, which is the border of the Ammonites, and the eastern Jordan plain from the Sea of Chinneroth as far as the Sea of the Arabah (the Salt Sea), the road to Beth Jeshimoth, and southward below the slopes of Pisgah. The other king was Og king of Bashan and his territory, who was of the remnant of the giants, who dwelt at Ashtaroth and at Edrei, and reigned over Mount Hermon, over Salcah, over all Bashan, as far as the border of the Geshurites and the Maachathites, and over half of Gilead to the border of Sihon king of Heshbon. These Moses the servant of the LORD and the children of Israel had conquered; and Moses the servant of the LORD had given it as a possession to the Reubenites, the Gadites, and half the tribe of Manasseh. Joshua 12:1–6

1. Describe the land spoken of here in terms of its relation to the Jordan River.

2. Name the two conquered kings mentioned in this passage.

3. Who led the children of Israel during this initial conquest?

4. Who received possession of these conquered lands *east* of the Jordan?

LOOK AT ...

We have recalled the kings and country that God delivered to Moses on the eastern side of the Jordan, including Sihon and Og. The Transjordan tribes of Rueben, Gad, and the half tribe of Manasseh inherited these lands. Now let's turn to the rulers and the real estate on the other side of the Jordan as we review verses 7–24.

And these are the kings of the country which Joshua and the children of Israel conquered on this side of the Jordan, on the west, from Baal Gad in the Valley of Lebanon as far as Mount Halak and the ascent to Seir, which Joshua gave to the tribes of Israel as a possession according to their divisions, in the mountain country, in the lowlands, in the Jordan plain, in the slopes, in the wilderness, and in the South—the Hittites, the Amorites, the Canaanites, the Perizzites, the Hivites, and the Jebusites: the king of Jericho, one; the king of Ai, which is beside Bethel, one; the king of Jerusalem, one; the king of Hebron, one; the king of Jarmuth, one; the king of Lachish, one; the king of Eglon, one; the king of Gezer, one; the king of Debir, one; the king of Geder, one; the king of Hormah, one; the king of Arad, one; the king of Libnah, one; the king of Adullam, one; the king of Makkedah, one; the king of Bethel, one; the king of Tappuah, one; the king of Hepher, one; the king of Aphek, one; the king of Lasharon, one; the king of Madon, one; the king of Hazor, one; the king of Shimron Meron, one; the king of Achshaph, one; the king of Taanach, one; the king of Megiddo, one; the king of Kedesh, one; the king of Jokneam in Carmel, one; the king of Dor in the heights of Dor, one; the king of the people of Gilgal, one; the king of Tirzah, one—all the kings, thirty-one. Joshua 12:7–24

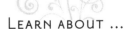

LEARN ABOUT ...

I Crossing Jordan

The Jordan extends from the Sea of Galilee in the north to the Dead Sea in the south and is about seventy miles in length. The zigzag pattern of the river varies from ninety to one hundred feet in width and between three and ten feet in depth. The water is not really navigable by boat.[106]

---

3 Commander Moses

Previously, Commander Moses brought victory. Matthew Henry wrote, "Joshua's achievements are great, but let not those under Moses be overlooked and forgotten, since God was the same who wrought both ... the Alpha and Omega of Israel's great salvation."[107] Moses recounted, "There was not one city too strong for us; the LORD our God delivered all to us" (Deut. 2:36).

LEARN ABOUT ...

6 Conquered Cities

Israel did not occupy all of these cities, as there were not enough soldiers to leave in each place. However, the defensive strength in each city was vanquished. Each tribe would be given the task to fully occupy the cities in their allotment. Joshua likely thought this was an attainable task.

7 Counting Kings

In total there were thirty-one conquered kings. Their land spanned 150 miles from north to south and fifty miles from east to west. Rather than seeing them as rulers of nations, they should be viewed as vassals over city-states. Each possessed limited local authority. Their lack of central government probably accounted for their downfall.

8 Eternal Inheritance

Moses and Joshua gave the children of Israel their inheritance in Canaan. Jesus, our true Commander in Chief, has provided us with spiritual blessings and a heavenly Promised Land: "He is the Mediator of the new covenant ... that those who are called may receive the promise of the eternal inheritance" (Heb. 9:15).

5. Who was leading the children of Israel when the kings west of the Jordan were conquered?

6. Who did Joshua allot the lands to?

7. a. What impression of Joshua do you think chapter 12 is meant to leave us with?

   b. What are we meant to understand about how well the conquest of Canaan succeeded?

   c. What do you learn about God from this chapter?

LIVE OUT ...

8. God deals fairly with all His children. Each tribe and family shared equally in the Promised Land. Review the inheritance "each one" of us has received from God. Check each inheritance you currently enjoy.
   - ❑ "Each one appears before God in Zion" (Ps. 84:7).
   - ❑ "God has dealt to each one a measure of faith" (Rom. 12:3).
   - ❑ "Each one will receive his own reward according to his own labor" (1 Cor. 3:8).
   - ❑ "Each one has his own gift from God, one in this manner and another in that" (1 Cor. 7:7).
   - ❑ "The Spirit is given to each one for the profit of all" (1 Cor. 12:7).

9. Hebrews 11 recounts the great men and women of faith who received God's great promises. Read the chapter then complete the following exercise.

a. Circle the phrase "by faith" and underline the person who possessed that faith.

b. Reread verses 13 and 39. What was the outcome of their faith?

c. According to verses 13 and 40, when will they receive their heavenly inheritance? What is the reason for the delay?

d. According to verse 16, what was the patriarchs' ultimate desire? What was God's response?

10. We saw Joshua conquering earthly kings. But our Savior, the King of Kings, can never be conquered. Rewrite the following verse into a personal praise to King Jesus!

> He who is the blessed and only Potentate, the King of kings and Lord of lords, who alone has immortality, dwelling in unapproachable light, whom no man has seen or can see, to whom be honor and everlasting power. Amen. (1 Tim. 6:15–16)

LEARN ABOUT ...

9 Heavenly City

The children of Israel received earthly cities that represented the coming of a heavenly Jerusalem with pearly gates and golden streets: "But you have come to Mount Zion and to the city of the living God, the heavenly Jerusalem, to an innumerable company of angels" (Heb. 12:22).

º º ● º º

Land ownership in early medieval England depended primarily on possession. You had it; you owned it. You wanted it; you fought for it. You won it; you kept it. There were no courts, real estate agents, title companies, or police agencies ready to recognize or enforce "legal rights" as we know them today. All this changed with the Norman conquest of England in 1066, when King William decreed that he owned all of the land in England by right of conquest. Not one acre of England was exempted. This sudden vacuum of privately held land was promptly filled by a variety of huge land grants the new king gave either to his Norman officers or to those of the Saxon English who were ready to recognize him as king.[108]

The Saxons in England forfeited their land rights to a conquering king. In ancient Canaan the kings relinquished their rights to the Promised Land through the conquest of Joshua's armies. In reality the land belonged to God (see Lev. 25:23). God used the Israelite army to reclaim what rightfully belonged to God.

When Adam and Eve fell to sin in the garden of Eden, the deed to the earth was transferred into the hands of the prince of the power of the air (see Matt. 4:8–9). Through Christ's resurrection, the ruler of darkness was defeated and the earth was redeemed. One day soon, the King of all kings will return to reclaim the title to the earth (see Rev. 5:1–10). At that time we will be a part of God's victorious army coming to conquer the enemy and lay claim to the earth.

LISTEN TO ...

All the armies that ever marched, and all the navies that ever sailed, and all the parliaments that ever sat, and all the kings that ever reigned, put together, have not affected the life of man upon this earth as powerfully as has this one solitary life.

—*Dr. James Allan Francis*

DAY 3
Chain of Title

My [Lenya] great-great-great-grandparents built their own ship in Norway and sailed all the way to the United States of America. They knew full well they would never see their relatives again. The dream of a better life and land to call their own motivated them along their journey. Eventually they settled in Wisconsin and became farmers. To acquire their property, they took advantage of a government homesteading act. To this day, the land grant made out to my ancestor Peter Swansby and signed by Ulysses S. Grant hangs in my grandmother's kitchen. It provides the origination for the chain of title to the land they owned.

A chain of title provides a list of successive owners for a parcel of land, beginning with the original owner to the person who currently possesses the land. This practice is most common in real estate to prove that a piece of land is marketable and free to transfer to another. Additionally, the seller should be able to trace the way in which each person came into the chain of title, whether through purchase, inheritance, or homesteading. Frequently this history appears on public records so that title to land can be checked.

Today we'll be reviewing the chain of title to the Promised Land. Our spiritual forefathers traveled great distances to obtain their property through inheritance as well as victory in battle. God records this transaction so that future generations will know that the Land of Promise truly belongs to Israel.

LIFT UP ...

Lord, no matter how young or old I am, there is always more ground to take in my spiritual life. I want to be open to wherever You send me. I want the work of my hands to be pleasing to You. Amen.

LOOK AT ...

The previous chapter included an impressive list of kings and countries that the Israelites conquered under Joshua's leadership. Even then he was a fairly old man, but he acted like a young man full of vim and vigor. He had been relentless in his pursuit of his enemies, sometimes moving with lightning speed. He was energetic enough to pray that God would lengthen his days. And He did!

Chapter 13 begins with Joshua's confession that he's getting old and much work is still to be done. Leadership takes its toll on an individual and Joshua is no exception. Even though he fought courageously against the Canaanites, they still held on to strongholds, especially the Philistine cities of Gaza, Ashdod, Ashkelon, Gath, and Ekron. These Canaanites would be thorns in Israel's side for three hundred years until King David completed what Joshua couldn't.

Perhaps, like Joshua, you're winding down in years but your work seems to be winding up. It's a wake-up call when we realize that we might not complete everything we've started. Joshua took comfort in the fact that his mentor, Moses, also accomplished great works but ended his life with just a glimpse of the Promised Land. Joshua carried on God's plans in his place. Because the larger wars were completed in the land, and the kings had been conquered, Joshua turned the future over to the tribes. It was their task to finish what he had begun.

READ JOSHUA 13:1–14.

Now Joshua was old, advanced in years. And the LORD said to him: "You are old, advanced in years, and there remains very much land yet to be possessed. This is the land that yet remains: all the territory of the Philistines and all that of the Geshurites, from Sihor, which is east of Egypt, as far as the border of Ekron northward (which is counted as Canaanite); the five lords of the Philistines—the Gazites, the Ashdodites, the Ashkelonites, the Gittites, and the Ekronites; also the Avites; from the south, all the land of the Canaanites, and Mearah that belongs to the Sidonians as far as Aphek, to the border of the Amorites; the land of the Gebalites, and all Lebanon, toward the sunrise, from Baal Gad below Mount Hermon as far as the entrance to Hamath; all the inhabitants of the mountains from Lebanon as far as the Brook Misrephoth, and all the Sidonians—them I will drive out from before the children of Israel; only divide it by lot to Israel as an inheritance, as I have commanded you. Now therefore, divide this land as an inheritance to the nine tribes and half the tribe of Manasseh." With the other half-tribe the Reubenites and the Gadites received their inheritance, which Moses had given them, beyond the

Jordan eastward, as Moses the servant of the LORD had given them: from Aroer which is on the bank of the River Arnon, and the town that is in the midst of the ravine, and all the plain of Medeba as far as Dibon; all the cities of Sihon king of the Amorites, who reigned in Heshbon, as far as the border of the children of Ammon; Gilead, and the border of the Geshurites and Maachathites, all Mount Hermon, and all Bashan as far as Salcah; all the kingdom of Og in Bashan, who reigned in Ashtaroth and Edrei, who remained of the remnant of the giants; for Moses had defeated and cast out these. Nevertheless the children of Israel did not drive out the Geshurites or the Maachathites, but the Geshurites and the Maachathites dwell among the Israelites until this day. Only to the tribe of Levi he had given no inheritance; the sacrifices of the LORD God of Israel made by fire are their inheritance, as He said to them. Joshua 13:1–14

1. Describe Joshua's physical condition at this point.

2. What kind of work was still yet to be done?

3. Who would inherit the land that was yet to be possessed?

4. "Nevertheless," who had the children of Israel failed to drive out?

5. Describe the inheritance the tribe of Levi would receive.

LOOK AT ...

Joshua realized that he was fading into the pages of history, but there were more battles yet to be fought and victories yet to be won. Wisely, he passed the task to the tribes who would inhabit the land. This must have provided great incentive. The verses also record their failure to eradicate all the enemies. We are wise if we learn from their mistake and become ruthless with our enemies: sin, self, and Satan.

LEARN ABOUT ...

2 Driving Force

"I will drive them out" was emphatic, affirming that God would be the driving force in the conquest. He reminded Joshua that He would continue to work even when Joshua was dead and gone. This promise presupposes that the children of Israel must be God's instruments. Otherwise they would be unable to say the enemy was driven out before them.

4 Driven Out

This is the first account that one of the tribes "did not drive out" some of the inhabitants. This failure was on the part of the Transjordan tribes, who had received their inheritance earlier than their brothers. Centuries later they would be the first to be driven out by the Assyrians as judgment for worshipping pagan gods.

Now we examine the territories given by Moses on the east side of the Jordan as we review verses 15–33.

———————————

And Moses had given to the tribe of the children of Reuben an inheritance according to their families. Their territory was from Aroer, which is on the bank of the River Arnon, and the city that is in the midst of the ravine, and all the plain by Medeba; Heshbon and all its cities that are in the plain: Dibon, Bamoth Baal, Beth Baal Meon, Jahaza, Kedemoth, Mephaath, Kirjathaim, Sibmah, Zereth Shahar on the mountain of the valley, Beth Peor, the slopes of Pisgah, and Beth Jeshimoth—all the cities of the plain and all the kingdom of Sihon king of the Amorites, who reigned in Heshbon, whom Moses had struck with the princes of Midian: Evi, Rekem, Zur, Hur, and Reba, who were princes of Sihon dwelling in the country. The children of Israel also killed with the sword Balaam the son of Beor, the soothsayer, among those who were killed by them. And the border of the children of Reuben was the bank of the Jordan. This was the inheritance of the children of Reuben according to their families, the cities and their villages. Moses also had given an inheritance to the tribe of Gad, to the children of Gad according to their families. Their territory was Jazer, and all the cities of Gilead, and half the land of the Ammonites as far as Aroer, which is before Rabbah, and from Heshbon to Ramath Mizpah and Betonim, and from Mahanaim to the border of Debir, and in the valley Beth Haram, Beth Nimrah, Succoth, and Zaphon, the rest of the kingdom of Sihon king of Heshbon, with the Jordan as its border, as far as the edge of the Sea of Chinnereth, on the other side of the Jordan eastward. This is the inheritance of the children of Gad according to their families, the cities and their villages. Moses also had given an inheritance to half the tribe of Manasseh; it was for half the tribe of the children of Manasseh according to their families: Their territory was from Mahanaim, all Bashan, all the kingdom of Og king of Bashan, and all the towns of Jair which are in Bashan, sixty cities; half of Gilead, and Ashtaroth and Edrei, cities of the kingdom of Og in Bashan, were for the children of Machir the son of Manasseh, for half of the children of Machir according to their families. These are the areas which Moses had distributed as an inheritance in the plains of Moab on the other side of the Jordan, by Jericho eastward. But to the tribe of Levi Moses had given no inheritance; the LORD God of Israel was their inheritance, as He had said to them.
Joshua 13:15–33

6. Reread all of today's text and circle the name of "Moses." Then underline those to whom Moses had already given an inheritance.

7. What key figure had the children of Israel killed "with the sword"? In your own words, what was his occupation?

8. Explain again why Moses hadn't given the tribe of Levi an inheritance.

LIVE OUT ...

9. a. Joshua had been single-minded in his efforts to conquer and occupy the Promised Land. Now he would pass on the effort to the next generation. Read Philippians 3:10–16. Describe the goals Paul admitted that he had not reached.

   b. Despite his shortcomings, what were Paul's priorities?

   c. What other people did Paul hope to inspire?

   d. How do Paul's words affect you?

10. Perhaps Joshua hadn't noticed gray hairs, wrinkles, or failing eyesight. Therefore God admonished him to assess his health and his plans for the future. Journal about your current physical and spiritual condition. Have you made plans for those who will follow after you? What are some wise ways to prepare for what comes next?

11. Each section of today's Scripture texts ends with a comment concerning the inheritance for the Levites. Compare and contrast their inheritance with the other tribes. Who do you think got the better deal? Why do you think that?

LEARN ABOUT ...

7 Driven By

Balaam's name means "lord of the people." He was a Canaanite magician or soothsayer who was summoned by the Moabite king Balak to curse the Israelites before they entered Canaan (see Num. 22:5—24:25). Balaam possessed a conflicting mixture of good and evil, but he eventually succumbed to greed.[109]

10 Defining Goals

The truly wise understand that life is but a vapor and should be enjoyed to the last breath. The average life expectancy is seventy-seven years. The oldest recorded human lived to be 122 years old. David wrote, "Teach us to number our days, That we may gain a heart of wisdom" (Ps. 90:12).

11 Different Inheritance

Unlike the other tribes, the Levites received no property as their inheritance. Instead their portion was a person—God Himself (see Num. 18:20). Forty-eight cities were set apart for them, along with pastures for their cattle (see Num. 35:1–8). They received the tithes due God from the fruits of the fields, the flocks and the firstborn.[110]

o o ● o o

Joshua and Caleb were the only old men among the multitude of Israeli citizens. Imagine their gray heads standing out in a crowd. None who had escaped Egypt or wandered the wilderness were now alive except these two. Joshua surely realized that more was to be done and that time was of the essence. So the soldier turned in his marching boots for maps and survey tools to supervise the allotment of the land. Joshua ensured that his final act would be serving the Lord and Israel. Now he would use his brains more than his brawn.

In our pop culture, the aged are marginalized. In fact, youth fear old age more than death. Conversely, God values the aged: "You shall rise before the gray headed and honor the presence of an old man, and fear your God: I am the LORD" (Lev. 19:32). Perhaps this list of active senior citizens will inspire you to get busy:

> Between the ages of seventy and eighty-three, Commodore Vanderbilt added about $100 million to his fortune.
>
> Emmanuel Kant, at seventy-four, wrote his *Anthropology, Metaphysics of Ethics,* and *Strife of the Faculties.*
>
> Tintoretto, at seventy-four, painted the vast *Paradise,* a canvas seventy-four by thirty feet.
>
> Giuseppe Verdi, at seventy-four, produced his masterpiece, "Otello"; at eighty, "Falstaff"; and at eighty-five, the famous "Ave Maria," "Stabat Mater," and Te Deum.
>
> Oliver Wendell Holmes, at seventy-nine, wrote *Over the Teacups.*
>
> Cato, at eighty, began the study of Greek.
>
> Johann Wolfgang von Goethe, at eighty, completed *Faust.*
>
> Alfred Lord Tennyson, at eighty-three, wrote "Crossing the Bar."
>
> Titian, at ninety-eight, painted his historic picture of the *Battle of Lepanto.*

If you're a silver-haired beauty—and even if only your hairdresser knows for sure—don't lose heart. God still has a purpose for you![III]

LISTEN TO ...

If wrinkles must be written upon our brows, let them not be written upon the heart. The spirit should not grow old.

—*James A. Garfield*

DAY 4

Counteroffer

As we continue with Joshua's division of the land, we see that not all of the tribes were content with what Joshua disbursed. One tribe, the tribe of Joseph, made what is called a counteroffer. A counteroffer occurs when someone rejects an offer to buy or sell a piece of property and simultaneously makes a different offer, changing the terms in some way. Though Joseph's descendants were given the land, they wanted to change the terms and made Joshua a counteroffer so they could gain more land.

Perhaps they suffered from a case of sibling rivalry. It happens in all families. Do you remember during the days of the flower-powered sixties *The Smothers Brothers Comedy Hour?* We would watch Dick on bass and Tom on guitar playing folk songs and getting on each other's nerves. We knew they were joined at the hip, but we also knew that there was an undercurrent of tension. The tension would build until Dick would put the "nail in the coffin" with one simple phrase, "Mom always liked you best."

In the book of Genesis, Joseph's brothers always thought Dad liked Joseph best. So they tormented him and sold him into slavery. Joseph prospered in Egypt and even helped his brothers when famine came. The heavenly Father also liked Joseph. Since the Levites were given no share of the land, Joseph's tribe was divided into two branches named for his sons, Manasseh and Ephraim, so there would be twelve tribes who held property in the Land of Promise.

LIFT UP ...

Lord, there is no shortage when it comes to Your gifts and blessings. Thank You for all that You have given me. Help me in my efforts to maintain an attitude of thanksgiving regardless of what I have. Amen.

LOOK AT ...

Yesterday we saw that, despite Joshua's advancing age, God still had tasks for him to accomplish—the land was to be divided among the tribes. Today we move ahead to chapter 16 and see the allotments for the Joseph tribes. Next week we'll go back to chapters 14 and 15 to closely study the portions for Judah and the Levites.

We'll see that the house of Joseph was a powerful house that inherited the rich territory of central Canaan. They began the apportionment where the battle began—at Jericho. Perhaps because Joseph kept the entire nation alive during the famine in Egypt, their territory in Canaan was in many ways some of the most beautiful and fertile in the land. God does indeed bless those who bless others.

READ JOSHUA 16:1–10.

The lot fell to the children of Joseph from the Jordan, by Jericho, to the waters of Jericho on the east, to the wilderness that goes up from Jericho through the mountains to Bethel, then went out from Bethel to Luz, passed along to the border of the Archites at Ataroth, and went down westward to the boundary of the Japhletites, as far as the boundary of Lower Beth Horon to Gezer; and it ended at the sea. So the children of Joseph, Manasseh and Ephraim, took their inheritance. The border of the children of Ephraim, according to their families, was thus: The border of their inheritance on the east side was Ataroth Addar as far as Upper Beth Horon. And the border went out toward the sea on the north side of Michmethath; then the border went around eastward to Taanath Shiloh, and passed by it on the east of Janohah. Then it went down from Janohah to Ataroth and Naarah, reached to Jericho, and came out at the Jordan. The border went out from Tappuah westward to the Brook Kanah, and it ended at the sea. This was the inheritance of the tribe of the children of Ephraim according to their families. The separate cities for the children of Ephraim were among the inheritance of the children of Manasseh, all the cities with their villages. And they did not drive out the Canaanites who dwelt in Gezer; but the Canaanites dwell among the Ephraimites to this day and have become forced laborers. Joshua 16:1–10

1. a. Verses 1–10 explore the lots that fell to the children of Joseph. Provide a general description of where Joseph's inheritance was located.

   b. Describe where Ephraim's inheritance was located and whose cities were within this territory.

2. a. Explain what happened to the Canaanites in Gezer.

  b. What do you think should have happened to them? Why?

LEARN ABOUT …

2 Cohabitating

Though they were powerful, the Ephraimites were materialistic. Rather than killing the Canaanites who lived in Gezer, they put them in bondage. At some point Gezer once again came under Canaanite control. Israel only got it back as part of Solomon's dowry to an Egyptian princess.

LOOK AT …

As we see in the first verses of Joshua 17, the descendants of Machir, Manasseh's firstborn, settled east of the Jordan (the Transjordan) with Reuben and Gad. The remaining heirs settled in Canaan. Now let's see how the rest of the land was divided for this large tribe as we explore Joshua 17:1–9.

———————————

There was also a lot for the tribe of Manasseh, for he was the firstborn of Joseph: namely for Machir the firstborn of Manasseh, the father of Gilead, because he was a man of war; therefore he was given Gilead and Bashan. And there was a lot for the rest of the children of Manasseh according to their families: for the children of Abiezer, the children of Helek, the children of Asriel, the children of Shechem, the children of Hepher, and the children of Shemida; these were the male children of Manasseh the son of Joseph according to their families. But Zelophehad the son of Hepher, the son of Gilead, the son of Machir, the son of Manasseh, had no sons, but only daughters. And these are the names of his daughters: Mahlah, Noah, Hoglah, Milcah, and Tirzah. And they came near before Eleazar the priest, before Joshua the son of Nun, and before the rulers, saying, "The LORD commanded Moses to give us an inheritance among our brothers." Therefore, according to the commandment of the LORD, he gave them an inheritance among their father's brothers. Ten shares fell to Manasseh, besides the land of Gilead and Bashan, which were on the other side of the Jordan, because the daughters of Manasseh received an inheritance among his sons; and the rest of Manasseh's sons had the land of Gilead. And the territory of Manasseh was from Asher to Michmethath, that lies east of Shechem; and the border went along south to the inhabitants of En

4 Daughters' Share

God is not sexist concerning the rights of inheritance. In fact, He's an equal-opportunity Father. When Moses heard the girls' claim, he realized that it was not fair for the heirs of Zelophehad to be left out of the share of the Promised Land just because he had no male heirs. He made provision for the females to inherit, saying, "You must give them a grant of land" (Num. 27:7 NLT).

Tappuah. Manasseh had the land of Tappuah, but Tappuah on the border of Manasseh belonged to the children of Ephraim. And the border descended to the Brook Kanah, southward to the brook. These cities of Ephraim are among the cities of Manasseh. The border of Manasseh was on the north side of the brook; and it ended at the sea. Joshua 17:1–9

3. Describe the lots given to the tribe of Manasseh and any details that stand out to you.

4. What was different about Zelophehad's situation in regard to his descendants?

5. Read Numbers 27:5–7. What did the Lord command regarding Zelophehad's daughters' inheritance?

LOOK AT ...

As we move south, we discover that the decision was made to give the Canaanite fortresses of Dor, En Dor, Taanach, and Megiddo to the strong tribe of Ephraim. Perhaps they thought it would help strengthen the nation militarily. Unfortunately, the people were more concerned with gaining more land than what they had already been given, rather than overcoming the people of the land. Let's look at 17:10–18 to learn more.

Southward it was Ephraim's, northward it was Manasseh's, and the sea was its border. Manasseh's territory was adjoining Asher on the north and Issachar on the east. And in Issachar and in Asher, Manasseh had Beth Shean and its towns, Ibleam and its towns, the inhabitants of Dor and its towns, the inhabitants of En Dor and its towns, the inhabitants of Taanach and its towns, and the inhabitants of Megiddo and its towns—three hilly regions. Yet the children of Manasseh could not drive out the inhabitants of those cities, but the Canaanites were determined to dwell in that land. And it happened, when the children of Israel grew strong, that they put the Canaanites to forced labor, but did not utterly drive them out. Then the children of Joseph spoke to Joshua, saying, "Why have you given us only one lot and one share to inherit, since we are a great people, inasmuch as the LORD has blessed us until now?" So Joshua answered them, "If you are a great people, then go up to the forest country and clear a place for yourself there in the land of the Perizzites and the giants, since the mountains of Ephraim are too confined for you." But the children of Joseph said, "The mountain country is not enough for us; and all the Canaanites who dwell in the land of the valley have chariots of iron, both those who are of Beth Shean and its towns and those who are of the Valley of Jezreel." And Joshua spoke to the house of Joseph—to Ephraim and Manasseh—saying, "You are a great people and have great power; you shall not have only one lot, but the mountain country shall be yours. Although it is wooded, you shall cut it down, and its farthest extent shall be yours; for you shall drive out the Canaanites, though they have iron chariots and are strong." Joshua 17:10–18

LEARN ABOUT …

7 Expanding Territory

The tribe of Ephraim complained to Joseph and he met them with a challenge: Take the hill country! They had seen God destroy the chariots when the northern kings attacked, but didn't trust God to do for them what He had done for Joshua. Beware the sin of self-confidence—it's always eventually exposed. How much better to trust in God than in yourself.

6. The "children of Manasseh could not drive out the inhabitants." What did they do with those who insisted on dwelling among them?

7. Recount what Joshua gave the children of Joseph when they complained about their portion of the inheritance.

LIVE OUT …

8. One common theme throughout the Bible is that of the firstborn heir being displaced by the second-born heir.

   a. Read Genesis 48:14–20 and describe how this happened between Joseph's sons, Ephraim and Manasseh.

LEARN ABOUT ...

Second Birth

Abraham gave Isaac the first son's birthright over Ishmael. Isaac was considered the son of promise (see Gal. 4:28). Israel (Jacob) was the second son who bought his birthright from his brother Esau for a pot of stew. Israel gave birth to the twelve tribes. As believers, our second birth is more important than our first because it gives us eternity. Jesus said, "You must be born again" (John 3:7).

---

9 Bondage

Too often, like the Ephraimites, we think we have things under control. Sadly, there are things that take control of us in the end. John wrote that "the whole world lies under the sway of the wicked one" (1 John 5:19). Thankfully, as believers we are bondservants of Christ and have His power to overcome the wicked one.

b. Now recall your second birth. How did it change your life?

9. Rather than putting the idolatrous Canaanites to death, the Ephraimites allowed them to live among them as slaves. Fill in the chart to discover some things that might put people in bondage.

SCRIPTURE	IN BONDAGE TO
Romans 8:15	
Galatians 4:3	
Hebrews 2:15	
2 Peter 2:18–20	

10. God desires Israel to expand its horizons. In fact, He promises that He will enlarge the spaces for the faithful.

a. What "territory" has God given to you (your home, your workplace, your neighborhood, your ministry, etc.)?

b. Journal Isaiah 54:2 into a personal prayer asking God to expand your horizons: "Enlarge the place of your tent, and let them stretch out the curtains of your dwellings; Do not spare; Lengthen your cords, And strengthen your stakes."

∘ ∘ ● ∘ ∘

London businessman Lindsay Clegg had a warehouse for sale. The building had been empty for months and needed repairs. Vandals had damaged the doors, smashed the windows, and strewn trash all over the place. He took a prospective buyer to show him the property. He promised that if the man bought the place he would replace the broken windows, bring in a crew to correct any structural damage, and clean out the garbage. The buyer said, "Forget about the repairs. When I buy this place, I'm going to build something completely different. I don't want the building; I want the site."

Joshua told the discontent Ephraimites to clean out the hills of the forested hill country. This was clearly not what they wanted to hear, however. They refused to clear out the hill country and did not expand their territory.

Let that not be said of us! When God sent our Joshua, Jesus Christ, the purchase price for our sin, He saw the opportunity to renovate our lives. He inspected the property that is our hearts and decided to do a completely new work. Don't let stubborn pride or spiritual laziness stall your personal renovation. Turn your will and your ways over to Him today. Remember, "if anyone is in Christ, he is a new creation; old things have passed away; behold, all things have become new" (2 Cor. 5:17).

LISTEN TO ...

Hell was our inheritance, now heaven is our possession…. We were bondslaves to Satan, now we are heirs of God and co-heirs with Jesus Christ.

—*James Bisse*

DAY 5

Covenants, Conditions, and Restrictions

We've been looking at the allotment of the Promised Land through modern real-estate terms. In today's society, restrictions govern the use of real estate; these are enforced by homeowners' associations and passed on to new owners of property. For example, covenants, conditions, and restrictions may dictate the size of your house, how you landscape your yard, or whether you can have pets. If your property is subject to covenants, conditions, and restrictions, buyers must be notified before any sale takes place. Once you take up residence, you must abide by these rules.

Sometimes homeowners' associations are very active. They monitor the neighborhood to make sure each house is in compliance with the standards established in the contract. Other associations are more lax and don't follow up on the restrictions they have established.

When God established His covenant with Israel to enter the Promised Land, He expected them to follow His orders to the letter. You might consider Him to be the president of the Hebrew Homeowners' Association. He wanted to make sure that the people followed the contract to the letter by taking possession of every bit of land they inherited.

In a spiritual sense, God is head of your home and your heart. Have you followed His commands to seize every bit of the inheritance He has for you?

LIFT UP ...

Lord, with You, no battle is without its end and its reward. You are faithful to bring rest and blessings. Thank You for seeing me through difficult times. I can always trust You to be there through every trial and with me to enjoy the victory. Amen.

LOOK AT ...

Yesterday we discovered the territories that Joseph's sons Ephraim and Manasseh, would inherit. Remember that Manasseh's tribe had divided into two branches. One received property on the east side of the Jordan, while the other half would obtain fertile lands from the west side of the Jordan all the way to the Mediterranean Sea.

At this juncture, Israel's base camp shifts from Gilgal to Shiloh before Joshua apportioned the final boundaries to the remaining seven tribes. Perhaps the squabble over Joseph's allotment had alarmed Joshua. Strategically, Shiloh (which is centrally located) became the home for the tabernacle. As a result, all seven tribes had equal access to worship and godly motivation to coalesce.

Perhaps we can learn something from Joshua's leadership style: It's better to motivate people with godly, rather than greedy, incentives. Oh, that our jealousy would be for the Lord and His dwelling place! It has been said that "location, location, location" is the number-one real estate motto; if so, then the nearer our homes (where our hearts lie) are to heaven, the more valuable they must be.

LEARN ABOUT ...

I Shiloh

Shiloh is a title of the Messiah (see Gen. 49:10). Although there have been many discussions as to the grammatical interpretation of the word, Jewish officials and the Christian church both agree that the name proclaims the coming of the Messiah. The NIV renders "until he comes to whom it belongs."[112]

READ JOSHUA 18:1–10.

Now the whole congregation of the children of Israel assembled together at Shiloh, and set up the tabernacle of meeting there. And the land was subdued before them. But there remained among the children of Israel seven tribes which had not yet received their inheritance. Then Joshua said to the children of Israel: "How long will you neglect to go and possess the land which the LORD God of your fathers has given you? Pick out from among you three men for each tribe, and I will send them; they shall rise and go through the land, survey it according to their inheritance, and come back to me. And they shall divide it into seven parts. Judah shall remain in their territory on the south, and the house of Joseph shall remain in their territory on the north. You shall therefore survey the land in seven parts and bring the survey here to me, that I may cast lots for you here before the LORD our God. But the Levites have no part among you, for the priesthood of the LORD is their inheritance. And Gad, Reuben, and half the tribe of Manasseh have received

3 Survey

To ensure equality, the surveyors included three men from each of the seven tribes, twenty-one total. They divided themselves into three companies, one of each tribe in each company. This ensured no partiality or suspicion in making up the seven lots so that all might be satisfied. Historians believe the task took nearly seven months.[113]

their inheritance beyond the Jordan on the east, which Moses the servant of the LORD gave them." Then the men arose to go away; and Joshua charged those who went to survey the land, saying, "Go, walk through the land, survey it, and come back to me, that I may cast lots for you here before the LORD in Shiloh." So the men went, passed through the land, and wrote the survey in a book in seven parts by cities; and they came to Joshua at the camp in Shiloh. Then Joshua cast lots for them in Shiloh before the LORD, and there Joshua divided the land to the children of Israel according to their divisions. Joshua 18:1–10

1. What did the children of Israel do when they assembled in Shiloh? Explain in your own words what this meant.

2. Why did Joshua admonish the seven tribes that hadn't received their inheritance?

3. Summarize Joshua's instructions to these tribes.

LOOK AT ...

After Joshua centralized God's house in the midst of the Promised Land, he returned to the task of allocating property to the remaining seven tribes. To do so, he inaugurated a survey committee. Historian Josephus believed that these men were experts in geometry, which they likely mastered in Egypt. Isn't it wonderful to know that God can redeem even the years of captivity for His glory and good? Let's look at 18:11–28 to discover what the tribe of Benjamin would inherit.

———————

Now the lot of the tribe of the children of Benjamin came up according to their families, and the territory of their lot came out between the children of Judah and the children of Joseph. Their border on the north side began at the Jordan, and the border went up to the side of

Jericho on the north, and went up through the mountains westward; it ended at the Wilderness of Beth Aven. The border went over from there toward Luz, to the side of Luz (which is Bethel) southward; and the border descended to Ataroth Addar, near the hill that lies on the south side of Lower Beth Horon. Then the border extended around the west side to the south, from the hill that lies before Beth Horon southward; and it ended at Kirjath Baal (which is Kirjath Jearim), a city of the children of Judah. This was the west side. The south side began at the end of Kirjath Jearim, and the border extended on the west and went out to the spring of the waters of Nephtoah. Then the border came down to the end of the mountain that lies before the Valley of the Son of Hinnom, which is in the Valley of the Rephaim on the north, descended to the Valley of Hinnom, to the side of the Jebusite city on the south, and descended to En Rogel. And it went around from the north, went out to En Shemesh, and extended toward Geliloth, which is before the Ascent of Adummim, and descended to the stone of Bohan the son of Reuben. Then it passed along toward the north side of Arabah, and went down to Arabah. And the border passed along to the north side of Beth Hoglah; then the border ended at the north bay at the Salt Sea, at the south end of the Jordan. This was the southern boundary. The Jordan was its border on the east side. This was the inheritance of the children of Benjamin, according to its boundaries all around, according to their families. Now the cities of the tribe of the children of Benjamin, according to their families, were Jericho, Beth Hoglah, Emek Keziz, Beth Arabah, Zemaraim, Bethel, Avim, Parah, Ophrah, Chephar Haammoni, Ophni, and Gaba: twelve cities with their villages; Gibeon, Ramah, Beeroth, Mizpah, Chephirah, Mozah, Rekem, Irpeel, Taralah, Zelah, Eleph, Jebus (which is Jerusalem), Gibeath, and Kirjath: fourteen cities with their villages. This was the inheritance of the children of Benjamin according to their families.
Joshua 18:11–28

4. a. Benjamin was an important tribe and received its lot first. List some of the things you notice about Benjamin and the cities it included. Note any place names you recognize.

   b. Why do you think Scripture devotes so much attention to the land of the Benjamites? Use other passages of Scripture to back up your answer.

LOOK AT ...

While Benjamin's inheritance seemed small and full of rugged terrain, mountains and ravines, it included many important cities in Israel's history. Of course the greatest city, God's holy city of Jerusalem, was the chief among them. The Benjamites also served as a buffer between the two leading tribes, Judah and Ephraim, which rivaled constantly.

Now turn to Joshua 19:1–23 to examine the lot that fell to Simeon and Zebulun.

———————————

The second lot came out for Simeon, for the tribe of the children of Simeon according to their families. And their inheritance was within the inheritance of the children of Judah. They had in their inheritance Beersheba (Sheba), Moladah, Hazar Shual, Balah, Ezem, Eltolad, Bethul, Hormah, Ziklag, Beth Marcaboth, Hazar Susah, Beth Lebaoth, and Sharuhen: thirteen cities and their villages; Ain, Rimmon, Ether, and Ashan: four cities and their villages; and all the villages that were all around these cities as far as Baalath Beer, Ramah of the South. This was the inheritance of the tribe of the children of Simeon according to their families. The inheritance of the children of Simeon was included in the share of the children of Judah, for the share of the children of Judah was too much for them. Therefore the children of Simeon had their inheritance within the inheritance of that people. The third lot came out for the children of Zebulun according to their families, and the border of their inheritance was as far as Sarid. Their border went toward the west and to Maralah, went to Dabbasheth, and extended along the brook that is east of Jokneam. Then from Sarid it went eastward toward the sunrise along the border of Chisloth Tabor, and went out toward Daberath, bypassing Japhia. And from there it passed along on the east of Gath Hepher, toward Eth Kazin, and extended to Rimmon, which borders on Neah. Then the border went around it on the north side of Hannathon, and it ended in the Valley of Jiphthah El. Included were Kattath, Nahallal, Shimron, Idalah, and Bethlehem: twelve cities with their villages. This was the inheritance of the children of Zebulun according to their families, these cities with their villages. The fourth lot came out to Issachar, for the children of Issachar according to their families. And their territory went to Jezreel, and included Chesulloth, Shunem, Haphraim, Shion, Anaharath, Rabbith, Kishion, Abez, Remeth, En Gannim, En Haddah, and Beth Pazzez. And the border reached to Tabor, Shahazimah, and Beth

Shemesh; their border ended at the Jordan: sixteen cities with their villages. This was the inheritance of the tribe of the children of Issachar according to their families, the cities and their villages. Joshua 19:1–23

LEARN ABOUT ...

5 Simeon

Simeon helped his sibling Judah subdue the land and its inhabitants with Judah's southern borders. Eventually Simeon's tribe would lose its identity and be absorbed by the more predominant Judah. This explains why we count only two tribes in the south, Judah and Benjamin, several centuries later when Solomon's kingdom was divided after his death.

5. List the names of the next three tribes in the order their lots were drawn, give a brief description of each piece of territory, and record anything you find memorable about each lot.

   a. Second lot:

   b. Third lot:

   c. Fourth lot:

LOOK AT ...

Simeon's inheritance was absorbed within the portion Judah received. Because Judah's property proved too vast, that tribe was unable to cope with the task of settlement. Zebulun's inheritance included the lower Galilee and a portion of land along the Mediterranean, making them dwellers of the seashore as Jacob had prophesied (see Gen. 49:5–7). Issachar enjoyed the shores of the Sea of Galilee on its southern coast.

Now, as we review Joshua 18:24–48, we turn our attention to the territory that Asher, Naphtali, and Dan would receive.

———————————

The fifth lot came out for the tribe of the children of Asher according to their families. And their territory included Helkath, Hali, Beten, Achshaph, Alammelech, Amad, and Mishal; it reached to Mount Carmel westward, along the Brook Shihor Libnath. It turned toward the sunrise to Beth Dagon; and it reached to Zebulun and to the Valley of Jiphthah El, then northward beyond Beth Emek and Neiel, bypassing Cabul which was on the left, including Ebron, Rehob, Hammon, and Kanah, as far as Greater Sidon. And the border turned to Ramah and to the fortified city of Tyre; then the border turned to Hosah, and ended at the sea by the region of Achzib. Also Ummah, Aphek, and Rehob were included: twenty-two cities with their villages. This was the inheritance of the tribe of the children of Asher according to their families, these cities with their villages. The sixth lot came out to the children of Naphtali, for the children of Naphtali according to their families. And their border began at Heleph, enclosing the territory from the terebinth tree in Zaanannim, Adami Nekeb, and Jabneel, as far as Lakkum; it ended at the Jordan. From Heleph the border extended westward to Aznoth Tabor, and went out from there toward Hukkok; it adjoined Zebulun on the south side and Asher on the west side, and ended at Judah by the Jordan toward the sunrise. And the fortified cities are Ziddim, Zer, Hammath, Rakkath, Chinnereth, Adamah, Ramah, Hazor, Kedesh, Edrei, En Hazor, Iron, Migdal El, Horem, Beth Anath, and Beth Shemesh: nineteen cities with their villages. This was the inheritance of the tribe of the children of Naphtali according to their families, the cities and their villages. The seventh lot came out for the tribe of the children of Dan according to their families. And the territory of their inheritance was Zorah, Eshtaol, Ir Shemesh, Shaalabbin, Aijalon, Jethlah, Elon, Timnah, Ekron, Eltekeh, Gibbethon, Baalath, Jehud, Bene Berak, Gath Rimmon, Me Jarkon, and Rakkon, with the region near Joppa. And the border of the children of Dan went beyond these, because the children of Dan went up to fight against Leshem and took it; and they struck it with the edge of the sword, took possession of it, and dwelt in it. They called Leshem, Dan, after the name of Dan their father. This is the inheritance of the tribe of the children of Dan according to their families, these cities with their villages. Joshua 19:24-48

6. List the name of the tribes in the order their lots were drawn, give a brief description of each piece of territory, and record anything you find memorable about each lot.

   a. Fifth lot:

   b. Sixth lot:

   c. Seventh lot:

LOOK AT ...

Asher's strategic location on the Mediterranean coast provided them a vital position to protect Israel from northern coastal enemies. Poor Dan seemed to receive the most undesirable location, as it was landlocked by other tribes.

Only after all the tribes received their fair share of the land did the Lord determine special land for Joshua. He was rewarded, like Caleb previously, for being one of the faithful spies from the first generation of Israel's exodus. Let's review 18:49–51 to see what this selfless man possessed.

When they had made an end of dividing the land as an inheritance according to their borders, the children of Israel gave an inheritance among them to Joshua the son of Nun. According to the word of the LORD they gave him the city which he asked for, Timnath Serah in the mountains of Ephraim; and he built the city and dwelt in it. These were the inheritances which Eleazar the priest, Joshua the son of Nun, and the heads of the fathers of the tribes of the children of Israel divided as an inheritance by lot in Shiloh before the LORD, at the door of the tabernacle of meeting. So they made an end of dividing the country. Joshua 19:49–51*

7. a. Describe who received the last piece of land, from whom he received it, and where it was located.

   b. What do you think this says about Joshua's character?

LIVE OUT ...

8. After an argument, Joshua relocated the place of worship from Gilgal to Shiloh in order to unify the nation. Let's examine our motivation for unity in Ephesians 4:3–6 NIV.

   Make every effort to keep the unity of the Spirit through the bond of peace.

LEARN ABOUT ...

8 Staying Together

Biblically, unity means oneness, harmony, or agreement. It signifies a commonality of sentiment, affection, or behavior that should exist among the people of God (see Ps. 133:1). The church is a union despite diversity, a fellowship of faith, of hope, and of love that binds believers together.

---

10 Selfless

Joshua was last but not least to receive his inheritance in the Promised Land that he had helped to conquer. His choice of cities only emphasizes his selflessness. He chose Timnath-Serah, which was located in a rugged, infertile mountain district. He would improve this city with new additions, leaving it better than he'd found it.

There is one body and one Spirit—just as you were called to one hope when you were called—one Lord, one faith, one baptism; one God and Father of all, who is over all and through all and in all.

a. Circle the word *one* wherever it appears, then underline all the ones we share.

b. Now draw a box around the word *all*, then make a squiggle line beneath the person we all have in common.

c. Explain how hard we should strive for unity and through what resource.

9. Joshua wisely assesses that Judah cannot handle settling his allotment alone. Therefore he sends another, Simeon, to assist in the task. With this in mind, rewrite Ecclesiastes 4:9–12 into your own words, extolling the benefits of 1+1 = 2-getherness.

10. Joshua was the last to receive an inheritance. How patiently do you wait for your due? Using the word WAIT as an acrostic, list what you are waiting patiently for God to provide.

W

A

I

T

○ ○ ● ○ ○

A Vacation Bible School teacher had an experience with her primary class she says she will never forget. Her class was interrupted on Wednesday about an hour before dismissal when a new student was brought in. The little boy had one arm missing, and since the class was almost over, she didn't have the chance to learn details about the cause or how he had adjusted to his condition. She was very nervous that one of the other kids would comment on his handicap and embarrass him. There was no opportunity to caution them, so she proceeded as carefully as possible. As the class came to a close, she began to relax. She asked the class to join her in their usual closing ceremony. "Let's make our churches," she said. "Here's the church and here's the steeple, open the doors and see …" As she made the hand gestures to the popular children's teaching on church unity, the awful truth of her actions struck her. The thing she had feared that the children would do, she had done. She stood before the class speechless.

Thankfully, a little girl sitting next to the new boy reached over with her left hand and placed it up to his right hand and said, "Davey, let's make the church together."

When Joshua divided the land, the call for unity was still necessary for the Israelites to survive. For us the clarion call is the same. We are all handicapped by sin. If we do not stretch out our hands to one another and join together in unity, the church will easily be divided by discord and dissension.

LISTEN TO …

There can be no unity, no delight of love, no harmony, no good in being, where there is but one. Two at least are needed for oneness.

—George MacDonald

LESSON TEN

Exploring the New Land
Joshua 14—15

Since grade school we've heard the story of Christopher Columbus beseeching Queen Isabella to finance his quest for a new route to the Indies. We all know this adventure turned into a discovery of the New World. Christopher Columbus's 1492 expedition resulted in the European settlement of America. Eventually, Britain and France also sent groups of people to settle the continent and claim the land as their own. The North American continent was seen as a brave new world, full of adventure and promise, just waiting to be explored.

What is it about unexplored territory that causes some people's blood to pulse with excitement? That beckons them to seize the adventure and search for more? Are there some people who are born to explore the unknown? Perhaps God has hardwired some of us with an innate sense of adventure that longs to climb tall mountains, explore deep seas, and fearlessly take risks that others might not take.

In this week's lesson, we encounter a few such people: Caleb, his daughter Achsah, and his son-in-law Othniel. They were willing to climb mountains, fight giants, and boldly ask for more when they explored the land of their inheritance.

How about you? Are you satisfied with your spiritual inheritance, or do you want more from the living God? Let this week's lesson be a reminder that you always have more territory to gain, more mountains to climb, more giants to conquer. God wants you to have more and more of Him. Don't settle for less.

Day 1: Joshua 14:1–5   CLAIMING THE INHERITANCE

Day 2: Joshua 14:6–15   CLIMBING TO THE TOP

Day 3: Joshua 15:1–12   COAST TO COAST

Day 4: Joshua 15:13–19   COLLECTING WATER RIGHTS

Day 5: Joshua 15:20–63   CHART OF JUDAH

DAY 1
Claiming the Inheritance

LIFT UP ...

Lord, thank You for providing me with a wonderful inheritance. You are a generous God who takes care of all of my needs. Amen.

LOOK AT ...

Last week we saw that Joshua divided the land among the tribes of Israel. However, we did not review chapters 14—15 because they stand on their own as very important chapters, dealing with the royal tribe of Judah and the priestly tribe of Levi. Today we will see that a very specific method was in place for dividing the land for the tribes.

Moses had recorded in the book of Numbers how the land was to be divided, and Joshua faithfully followed his mentor's directions. The principle is clear: Though new leadership takes the helm, it is still necessary to follow some of the established methods of old, especially those written in the Word of God. What about you? When you are faced with a new situation, do you maintain biblical standards and seek the advice of those who have gone before?

READ JOSHUA 14:1–5.

These are the areas which the children of Israel inherited in the land of Canaan, which Eleazar the priest, Joshua the son of Nun, and the heads of the fathers of the tribes of the children of Israel distributed as an inheritance to them. Their inheritance was by lot, as the LORD had commanded by the hand of Moses, for the nine tribes and the half-tribe. For Moses had given the inheritance of the two tribes and the half-tribe on the other side of the Jordan; but to the Levites he had given no inheritance among them. For the children of Joseph were two tribes: Manasseh and Ephraim. And they gave no part to the Levites in the land, except cities to dwell in, with their common-lands for their livestock and their property. As the LORD had commanded Moses, so the children of Israel did; and they divided the land. Joshua 14:1–5

1. What areas of land did the writer discuss here?

2. a. Who were the three parties in charge of distributing the inherited land?

   b. How do you understand the phrase, "the heads of the fathers of the tribes of the children of Israel"? If you don't know, compare it with some other Bible translations.

3. a. Describe the method used for deciding how the land was to be distributed.

   b. Who had commanded that this method be used?

4. How many tribes received their inheritance by casting lots?

5. Based on this text and what we've studied so far in the book of Joshua, explain how and when the other two and a half tribes received their inheritance.

6. a. What did the Levites receive as an inheritance?

   b. Based on what you learned last week, do you think this was fair? Why or why not?

7. Based on the last sentence in today's text, describe the chain of command in the process of land division. What does this tell you about Joshua's priorities?

LEARN ABOUT …

2 Eleazar

This is the first mention of Eleazar the high priest. He was Aaron's third son. He was given the office of high priest after the death of his brothers, Nadab and Abihu, who offered profane fire in the wilderness (see Num. 3:4). The high priesthood is said to have remained in the family of Eleazar until the time of Eli.[114]

3 Casting Lots

Casting lots was a way of making decisions, similar to drawing straws or throwing a pair of dice to determine what course or direction to follow. Most of the occurrences were in the early biblical period when God apparently used this means for determining His will.[115]

5 Inheritance

Inheritance refers to a possession one has received as a legal claim. In the Pentateuch and the book of Joshua, it indicates the possession of land that all of Israel or a tribe or a clan received as their share in the Promised Land. It fell upon Joshua to execute the division of the "possession."

8 High Priest's Power

The high priest was always the people's representative before God. The most important responsibility of the high priest was to conduct the service on the Day of Atonement. This particular service most identifies Jesus with the office of high priest (see Heb. 9). Jesus' powerful sacrifice made further sacrifices unnecessary.

---

9 God's Will

Many people believe that God's will is not easily discovered. However, God's will is clearly revealed in His Word, through His Spirit, and by providential circumstances. The Bible tells us, "Do not be conformed to this world, but be transformed by the renewing of your mind, that you may prove what is that good and acceptable and perfect will of God" (Rom. 12:2).

LIVE OUT ...

8. Eleazar the high priest helped determine the distribution of the land for the Israelites. Fill in the following table to discover some of the things that Jesus, our High Priest, does or has done for us.

SCRIPTURE	JESUS AS HIGH PRIEST
Hebrews 2:17–18	
Hebrews 4:14–16	
Hebrews 7:26–27	
Hebrews 8:1–2	
Hebrews 9:11–14	
Hebrews 10:19–22	

a. What were some preconceived ideas you held if any about the position of high priest, before reading these passages?

b. Now how do you feel knowing that Jesus is your High Priest? How might these insights change your prayer life or thought life about Him?

9. In the Old Testament, God's will was sometimes determined by casting lots using the Urim and Thummim. Today, we don't have such a means of seeking God's will. Talk about some ways you go about finding God's will for your life.

10. Just as God had an inheritance in store for the Israelites, He also has an inheritance for believers today. Read the beginning of Jesus' Sermon on the Mount in Matthew 5:3–10.

> Blessed are the poor in spirit,
> For theirs is the kingdom of heaven.
> Blessed are those who mourn,

For they shall be comforted.

Blessed are the meek,

For they shall inherit the earth.

Blessed are those who hunger and thirst for righteousness,

For they shall be filled.

Blessed are the merciful,

For they shall obtain mercy.

Blessed are the pure in heart,

For they shall see God.

Blessed are the peacemakers,

For they shall be called sons of God.

Blessed are those who are persecuted for righteousness' sake,

For theirs is the kingdom of heaven.

Matthew 5:3–10

a. In each sentence, underline the condition of the one who is inheriting (the blessed one).

b. Circle what they will receive or inherit from the Lord.

c. Put a star by each of these blessings you believe God is offering you.

d. Write a prayer thanking God for bequeathing you this inheritance.

○ ○ ● ○ ○

Before my [Penny's] paternal grandmother died, she began to get her affairs in order. She went around her house and put masking tape with people's names on the bottom of her possessions. When we'd visit her, she'd pick up a piece of china or a piece of jewelry and say, "Look, this has your name on it." It was a sweet gesture, but rather sad. We didn't want to think of our grandmother dying—we'd rather have her with us than have her earthly possessions. Fortunately, no one bickered over the things she left for us. We gratefully accepted her decisions.

On a larger scale, God apportioned the inheritance for the Israelites. But don't you wonder if it was difficult for them to accept the inheritance without questioning who got what? Perhaps the tribe of Judah wanted some of the land that the tribe of Dan received. Or the tribe of Asher was slightly jealous over the property that Naphtali was given. It was a good thing that God told Moses to use the Urim and Thummim to determine the boundaries and locations for the tribes. Just before Moses died, God ordered a census of the people and explained to Moses how to go about dividing the land: "The land shall be divided by lot; they shall inherit according to the names of the tribes of their fathers. According to the lot their inheritance shall be divided between the larger and the smaller" (Num. 26:55–56). In essence, God put the people's names on the portion of the land and made sure their inheritance was assured when the lots were cast.

LISTEN TO ...

I have now disposed of all my property to my family. There is one thing more I wish I could give them and that is the Christian religion. If they had that, and I had not given them one shilling, they would have been rich; and if they had not that, and I had given them all the world, they would be poor.

—*Patrick Henry*

DAY 2

Climbing to the Top

If you asked mountain climbers why they wanted to reach the mountain peak, they'd probably say, "Because it is there!" *TIME* magazine reports, "There had been 32 years of expeditions, and at least 13 lives lost, by the time Edmund Hillary and Tenzing Norgay set off for the world's highest peak in 1953. 'There was much talk about "unjustifiable risk,"' recalled Hillary in his autobiography. 'But I think we all realized that these were attitudes from the past, that nobody was going to get up Everest without a few risks.'"

Everest posed serious dangers: natural risks such as avalanches, ice walls, gaping crevasses, freezing temperatures, and gusting winds. And no one was sure that humans could survive at such great heights. Oxygen deprivation was serious business. Difficulty breathing, nausea, flulike symptoms, lethargy, and light-headedness made reaching the summit difficult. Hillary was undaunted by the obstacles. Upon making the final push to the summit with Norgay, he said, "Even on top of Everest, I was still looking at other mountains and thinking of how one might climb them."[116]

Caleb had wandered in the wilderness forty years knowing there was a mountain to climb and claim. Though he was older than everyone in his tribe, he was unafraid of the obstacles he would face. God had promised him the mountain, and he knew he would reach the summit. He still had the same spirit of adventure he had exhibited as a young man sent to spy out the land forty years earlier. Caleb was ready to reach the summit of God's promises.

LIFT UP ...

Lord, You fulfill all of Your promises. Help me to keep the faith when I go through difficult times. I will wait on You to finish what You have begun in me. Amen.

LOOK AT ...

We've seen that God had a plan to divide the Promised Land for the tribes west of the

Jordan River. The high priest, Joshua, and the heads of the clans in each tribe were to determine lots for the tribes. Today we see that Caleb, one of the two original spies allowed to enter the land, refused to settle for less than what God had promised him.

As we'll see, the pattern for allotment was from south to north. The claims relating to land for the Judah and Joseph tribes were largely based on promises that Moses made while leading the nation. Joshua, always faithful, made sure that Moses' promises were kept. It only seems right that the first allotment begin with one of the original members of the exodus: Caleb.

READ JOSHUA 14:6–11.

Then the children of Judah came to Joshua in Gilgal. And Caleb the son of Jephunneh the Kenizzite said to him: "You know the word which the LORD said to Moses the man of God concerning you and me in Kadesh Barnea. I was forty years old when Moses the servant of the LORD sent me from Kadesh Barnea to spy out the land, and I brought back word to him as it was in my heart. Nevertheless my brethren who went up with me made the heart of the people melt, but I wholly followed the LORD my God. So Moses swore on that day, saying, 'Surely the land where your foot has trodden shall be your inheritance and your children's forever, because you have wholly followed the LORD my God.' And now, behold, the LORD has kept me alive, as He said, these forty-five years, ever since the LORD spoke this word to Moses while Israel wandered in the wilderness; and now, here I am this day, eighty-five years old. As yet I am as strong this day as on the day that Moses sent me; just as my strength was then, so now is my strength for war, both for going out and for coming in." Joshua 14:6–11

1. a. Describe the setting and who first came to Joshua concerning the allotment.

   b. Put yourself in Joshua's sandals: What do you think his emotions may have been upon seeing his old comrade and hearing this request?

2. What did Caleb bring up about Kadesh Barnea that would influence his inheritance?

3. Describe how the Lord had been faithful to Caleb from the time of Kadesh Barnea to the present.

LOOK AT ...

Caleb recounted his history with Joshua as one of two faithful spies willing to conquer the land over four decades earlier at Kadesh Barnea. He also reminded Joshua of God's promises to give Caleb an inheritance in the land of promise and to maintain Caleb's strength. Let's look at 14:12–15 to see what land Caleb requested as his inheritance.

———————

"Now therefore, give me this mountain of which the LORD spoke in that day; for you heard in that day how the Anakim were there, and that the cities were great and fortified. It may be that the LORD will be with me, and I shall be able to drive them out as the LORD said." And Joshua blessed him, and gave Hebron to Caleb the son of Jephunneh as an inheritance. Hebron therefore became the inheritance of Caleb the son of Jephunneh the Kenizzite to this day, because he wholly followed the LORD God of Israel. And the name of Hebron formerly was Kirjath Arba (Arba was the greatest man among the Anakim). Then the land had rest from war. Joshua 14:12–15

4. a. Identify what specific piece of land Caleb asked Joshua to give him, who inhabited it, and what type of cities it contained.

   b. What phrase reveals that Caleb understood his success depended on the Lord?

5. How did Joshua respond to this request?

6. Explain what happened to Hebron and the remainder of the land.

LEARN ABOUT ...

2 Wholly Followed

Caleb had spied out the land he was to inherit forty-five years earlier and had been confident that God was strong enough to lead the people to victory. God had promised, "My servant Caleb, because he has a different spirit in him and has followed Me fully, I will bring into the land where he went, and his descendants shall inherit it" (Num. 14:24).

———————

4 Anakim

The Anakim were a race descended from Arba. Thus, Hebron was named Kirjath Arba when the Anakim took the land. In the spies' time, they were a terror to Israel (see Num. 13:28). After Joshua and Caleb destroyed them, a remnant remained in the Philistine cities of Gaza, Gath, and Ashdod. In David's day there was a giant race among the Philistines in Gath.[117]

———————

6 Hebron

Hebron is one of the most ancient cities in the world. It was the favorite home of Abraham. There he pitched his tent under the oaks of Mamre. At Hebron, Sarah died and was buried in the cave of Machpelah (see Gen. 23:17–20). When David became king, Hebron was his royal residence for seven and a half years. There he was anointed as king over all Israel.[118]

LEARN ABOUT ...

7 Follow Him

Following Christ involves both
sacrifices and blessings. We
might alienate members of
our family who don't understand our desire to follow a
holy God; it might involve
fishing for men in a foreign
country at the expense of
personal luxury. Taking up
our cross to follow Him is
the best choice we can ever
make, but a choice the
world might not understand.

---

9 Blessing

A blessing is the act of
declaring or wishing God's
favor and goodness upon
another; to ask God's
blessing upon a person.
The blessing seeks the
good effect of the words
uttered; it seeks God's
power to bring the good to
pass by consecrating the
blessing with solemn
prayers that the person may
prosper and be happy.[119]

LIVE OUT ...

7. a. The key to Caleb's spiritual success was following God wholeheartedly. Fill in the chart below to learn more about following
Christ.

SCRIPTURE	FOLLOWING CHRIST
Matthew 4:18–20	
Matthew 8:19–22	
Matthew 10:37–39	
Matthew 19:21–22	

   b. In which of the above ways have you followed Christ? How will
you earnestly seek to follow Him more closely in the future?

8. Caleb was never afraid of the giants in the land because he knew
that God was on his side. We may not face literal giants, but there
are spiritual, emotional, and physical giants to conquer.

   a. Check the boxes of some of the giants in your life.

   ❏ Insecurity   ❏ Loneliness   ❏ Work
   ❏ Unbelief   ❏ Body Image   ❏ Marriage
   ❏ Finances   ❏ Health   ❏ Relationships
   ❏ Depression   ❏ Doubt   ❏ Other _____

   b. Now journal a prayer offering yourself wholeheartedly to the
Lord. Ask Him to conquer the giants on your behalf and to
give you a rich inheritance of His joy, grace, and peace.

9. a. Joshua blessed Caleb for his faithful service by giving him the
inheritance he had been promised at Hebron. Name someone
you know who has been faithful in serving the Lord.

b. How will you bless them for being faithful (a prayer of encouragement, a promise to pray for them on a daily basis, a prayer for God's goodness to be evident in their life)?

. . ● . .

Years ago in Marseilles there lived a man named Guyot who had acquired a reputation as a miser. The people treated him with disdain. Walking the streets, gangs of boys followed him and insulted him in every possible way. They even cast stones at him. No one in the town spoke kindly to him, nodded in his direction, or reached out to him. They looked upon him as their town Scrooge—a mean-spirited man devoted to hoarding wealth.

When Guyot died, they learned that he had amassed a fortune. The executors of his will read: "Having observed, from my infancy, that the poor of Marseilles are ill-supplied with water, which can only be procured at a great price, I have cheerfully labored the whole of my life to procure for them this great blessing, and I direct that the whole of my property shall be expended in building an aqueduct for their use."[120]

For years Guyot disregarded the jeers so he could fulfill a promise. Even more amazingly, he went about his task cheerfully. Apparently, Caleb also went about receiving his promise with the same cheerful resolve. He knew he would face giants. But he willingly faced the obstacles to receive the promise. What about you? Do you back down when you encounter a problem? Maybe the promise doesn't come when you expect it. Or people taunt you, tempting you to stop moving forward. Follow the example of these brave men. Move forward in faith. You have mountains to climb and blessings to bestow!

LISTEN TO ...

Never undertake anything for which you wouldn't have the courage to ask the blessings of heaven.

—Georg Christoph Lichtenberg

DAY 3

Coast to Coast

Someone has to do the difficult work of mapping out the territory. After the Louisiana Purchase, President Thomas Jefferson tapped two men, Meriwether Lewis and William Clark, to map the American West. In May 1804 they took a crew of men and one Shoshone Indian woman named Sacagawea to travel from St. Louis, Missouri, to the Oregon coast and back. This trip was the first expedition to cross the continent to the Pacific Ocean. Lewis really traveled from coast to coast, having begun his journey in Philadelphia near the Atlantic Ocean. This expedition lasted two years, four months, and ten days and covered over eight thousand miles. They mapped the land, described the animal life and natural wonders, and encountered native peoples.

As Joshua began to map out the territory of the Judah tribe, he went about the process in a methodical fashion. Just as Lewis and Clark had done in their journals, he described well-known landmarks so the tribe would understand what the boundaries were. The easiest boundaries to understand were west and east: coast to coast. The tribe of Judah would hold the land from the Great Sea to the Dead Sea. The rest of the boundaries were delineated by mountain ranges, brooks, rivers, and other easily discernible landmarks. Though some of this is difficult to imagine, it was vitally important to the tribes. So let's explore the land of Judah and see what nuggets of truth we can dig up.

LIFT UP ...

Lord, I'm amazed at how detailed You are. I know that You have mapped out a plan for my life. Help me to follow Your ways all the days of my life. Amen.

LOOK AT ...

Yesterday we saw that Joshua dealt most graciously with Caleb's request for his portion. Joshua could then move forward with the rest of Judah's allotment. With the eastern border being the Salt Sea (Dead Sea), Joshua started in the south, moved north and west to the

Great Sea (Mediterranean Sea) to determine the borders for Judah.

Jacob had prophesied about the tribe of Judah in Genesis 49, and his prophecy was remarkably fulfilled. In the first place Jacob prophesied that Judah's "hand shall be on the neck of your enemies" (Gen. 49:8) and that "from the prey, my son, you have gone up" (49:9). Judah was indeed hedged in by enemies: The Moabites, the Philistines, the Amalekites, and the Edomites were all strategically emplaced around them. Second, Jacob prophesied that the Judah tribe would be blessed with vineyards: "Binding his donkey to the vine, And his donkey's colt to the choice vine, He washed his garments in wine" (49:11). It was from the Judean valley that the spies brought the large clusters of grapes, and this valley is still ideally suited for vineyards. Third and most important, Jacob prophesied that "the scepter shall not depart from Judah, Nor a lawgiver from between his feet, Until Shiloh comes" (49:10). And indeed, Jesus our Messiah was from the tribe of Judah. When God apportioned the land for Judah, He took all of these factors into account.

Isn't it good to know that when God designates the places you will go, the occupations you will pursue, the people you will meet, He takes everything into account? He truly is a God who loves you and foresees every aspect of your life.

READ JOSHUA 15:1–4.

So this was the lot of the tribe of the children of Judah according to their families: The border of Edom at the Wilderness of Zin southward was the extreme southern boundary. And their southern border began at the shore of the Salt Sea, from the bay that faces southward. Then it went out to the southern side of the Ascent of Akrabbim, passed along to Zin, ascended on the south side of Kadesh Barnea, passed along to Hezron, went up to Adar, and went around to Karkaa. From there it passed toward Azmon and went out to the Brook of Egypt; and the border ended at the sea. This shall be your southern border. Joshua 15:1–4

1. The first sentence explains how the tribe was given their allotment. How was the land divided?

2. The division began with the southern border. Recount the southern division using the key phrases in the passage. You can find some of these places on the map on page 389.

LEARN ABOUT ...

2 Southern Boundary

Though Moses did not enter the land, God showed him at Mt. Nebo "all the land of Judah as far as the Western Sea, the South, and the plain of the Valley of Jericho, the city of palm trees, as far as Zoar" (Deut. 34:2–3).

The extreme southern boundary:

Where the southern border began:

Went out:

Passed along:

Ascended:

Passed along:

Went up:

Went around:

Passed toward:

Went out:

Ended at:

LOOK AT ...

From the southern border, Joshua moved on to describe the eastern and northern borders. Let's look at 15:5–9 and see where the borders were located.

The east border was the Salt Sea as far as the mouth of the Jordan. And the border on the northern quarter began at the bay of the sea at the mouth of the Jordan. The border went up to Beth Hoglah and passed north of Beth Arabah; and the border went up to the stone of Bohan the son of Reuben. Then the border went up toward Debir from the Valley of Achor, and it turned northward toward Gilgal, which is before the Ascent of Adummim, which is on the south side of the valley. The border continued toward the waters of En Shemesh and ended at En Rogel. And the border went up by the Valley of the Son of Hinnom to the southern slope of the Jebusite city (which is Jerusalem). The border went up to the top of the mountain that lies before the Valley of Hinnom westward, which is at the end of the Valley of Rephaim northward. Then the border went around from the top of the hill to the fountain of the water of Nephtoah, and extended to the cities of Mount Ephron. And the border went around to Baalah (which is Kirjath Jearim). Joshua 15:5–9.

3. What was the eastern border of the tribe of Judah?

4. Let's turn our attention to the northern border. Using key phrases from the text, detail the northern boundary. (Compare the map on page 389.)

Began:

Went up:

Passed:

Went up:

Went up:

Turned:

Continued:

Ended:

Went up:

Went up:

Went around:

Extended:

Went around:

5. Based upon this description, what type of terrain do you think the Judah tribe inherited here?

LEARN ABOUT ...

5 Jerusalem

Currently, Jerusalem is considered the "holy city" for three world religions: Christianity, Judaism, and Islam. It is located fourteen miles west of the Dead Sea and thirty-three miles east of the Mediterranean. Bethlehem lies about five miles to the southeast. The psalmist describes it as "beautiful in elevation, The joy of the whole earth" (Ps. 48:2).

LOOK AT ...

As the allotment continued, the borders turned westward. Let's finish our day by focusing on 15:10–12.

Then the border turned westward from Baalah to Mount Seir, passed along to the side of Mount Jearim on the north (which is Chesalon), went down to Beth Shemesh, and passed on to Timnah. And the border went out to the side of Ekron northward. Then the border went around to Shicron,

LEARN ABOUT …

6 Mt. Seir

Mt. Seir is a landmark on the boundary of Judah not far from Kiriath-jearim and Chesalon. The name means "shaggy," and probably here denoted a wooded height. It may be that part of the range that runs northeast from Saris by Karyat el-'Anab and Biddu to the plateau of el-Jib. Traces of an ancient forest still exist.[121]

---

7 Dead Sea

The Dead Sea is nearly surrounded by hills and cliffs that feed it freshwater. Because the Dead Sea has several entrances but no exits, it is indeed a dead sea, containing a very large supply of potash, bromine, magnesium chloride, salt, and other minerals.[122] Spiritually, to really live we need both to take in from God and pour out to Him.

passed along to Mount Baalah, and extended to Jabneel; and the border ended at the sea. The west border was the coastline of the Great Sea. This is the boundary of the children of Judah all around according to their families. Joshua 15:10–12

6. As we continue to follow the border for Judah, let's once again use the key words to follow Joshua's mapping.

Turned westward from–to:

Passed along:

Went down:

Passed on:

Went out:

Went around:

Passed along:

Extended to:

Ended at:

LIVE OUT …

7. One of the boundaries for the tribe's land was the Dead Sea. One reason it is considered dead is that it only takes in without pouring out. In our lives, taking in without pouring out can lead to spiritual necrosis. Read the following verses and choose one of them to "pour" out a prayer to God to maintain a living relationship.

Ps. 42:4—Pour out your soul

Ps. 62:8—Pour out your heart

Ps. 141:1–2—Pour out your trouble

8. Today we saw that the land of Judah did not have straight boundaries but had twists and turns, ascents and descents. The same can be said for the life of a believer. Use some of the words from today's

lesson to describe your journey of faith to date. (For instance, "I began at church camp but went downhill during high school.")

○ ○ ● ○ ○

LEARN ABOUT ...

8 Judah

Judah's inheritance was mostly composed of land taken during Joshua's southern campaign. The southern boundary extended from the south end of the Dead Sea westward to the brook of Egypt (not the Nile but a small river in the Sinai Peninsula). The northern border stretched from the Dead Sea west to the Mediterranean Sea. It included fertile tracts as well as mountainous and barren land.

Historians have named the force that drove settlers west in America. They call it the push/pull factor. In other words, they believe there were specific forces that helped to push settlers west and other factors that helped pull them. For instance, pioneers were often pushed west because they couldn't find high-paying jobs. Some were younger sons who had no hope of inheriting land. In those cases, they were pushed from their family homes to seek their own piece of land in the West. Other settlers felt pushed from their homes in the East because they were uncomfortable with the new industries and larger cities.

On the other hand, some pioneer settlers were pulled west because they hoped to strike gold, like the forty-niners in the Pacific Northwest. Others received enticing letters from friends or family members talking about how good life was in the West. The biggest pull factor was the opportunity to buy land. Pioneers could purchase land for a much smaller price than in states to the east.[123]

Surely the Hebrew people had a pioneering spirit to move into the Land of Promise. They were pushed out of Egypt by the devastating cruelty of slavery. And they were pulled into the Promised Land by the hope of the inheritance that God had given to their ancestor Abraham centuries ago. They were willing to face any hardship to claim the land as their own.

LISTEN TO ...

Prayer serves as an edge and border to preserve the web of life from unraveling.

—Robert Hall

DAY 4
Collecting Water Rights

What good is land without water? Just ask Ponce de Leon. He was a Spanish explorer and soldier who was the first European to set foot in Florida. He also established the oldest European settlement in Puerto Rico and, as he sailed, discovered the Gulf Stream. One of his goals was to discover the legendary Fountain of Youth—a spring that would supposedly give people eternal life and health.

According to history, Ponce de Leon spent his expeditionary life sailing in the Atlantic Ocean and fighting the natives. He was known for exhibiting extreme brutality and was even removed from office as governor for his violent tendencies. Though he searched for riches and eternal life through a spring of water, he was wounded in battle and died in San Juan, Puerto Rico.

As in other desert countries, water rights are extremely important in Israel, since the country has few water sources. Generally speaking, precipitation is the only source of water. The moisture is carried up from the sea in clouds and falls on the hills as rain or snow. This supplies the springs and fountains. Rivers are mostly small and contain little or no water in summer. Springs supply the villages, and ancient peoples used cisterns to collect water. Most of the rain falls on the western slopes of the mountains, and most of the springs are also found there. Limestone found in many places does not hold water, so wells are few and far between and considered valuable property.[124]

Today we'll see just how generous a father was in giving his daughter her water rights. As you study this portion of Scripture, remember how generous your heavenly Father has been in giving you living water that brings eternal life.

LIFT UP ...

Lord, you are the most generous Father of all. Thank You for Your Son, Jesus, who is the living water that springs forth to eternal life. May I pour out refreshment to all I encounter. In His name I pray. Amen.

LOOK AT ...

We've seen the general boundaries given to the land of Judah. Now we return to the story of Caleb and see the inheritance he provided for his daughter.

Some scholars believe Caleb was not born of the tribe of Judah but was given his portion in that tribe by God's special command. By submitting to Jehovah's covenant with Israel, he and his family had become Israelites by adoption. Just as Jethro, Rahab, Ruth, and Naaman were examples of God's mercy to the Gentiles in Old Testament times, Caleb was also a picture of God opening the door of faith to Gentiles.[125]

LEARN ABOUT ...

I Gentile Roots

Caleb's father was a Kenazite, seemingly an Edomite. Kenaz was a duke of Edom (see Gen. 36:15). Other Edomite names occur in Caleb's genealogy, such as Shobal (see I Chron. 2:50, 52). Many conclude that Caleb's family was an Edomite family incorporated into the tribe of Judah.[126]

READ JOSHUA 15:13–19.

Now to Caleb the son of Jephunneh he gave a share among the children of Judah, according to the commandment of the LORD to Joshua, namely, Kirjath Arba, which is Hebron (Arba was the father of Anak). Caleb drove out the three sons of Anak from there: Sheshai, Ahiman, and Talmai, the children of Anak. Then he went up from there to the inhabitants of Debir (formerly the name of Debir was Kirjath Sepher). And Caleb said, "He who attacks Kirjath Sepher and takes it, to him I will give Achsah my daughter as wife." So Othniel the son of Kenaz, the brother of Caleb, took it; and he gave him Achsah his daughter as wife. Now it was so, when she came to him, that she persuaded him to ask her father for a field. So she dismounted from her donkey, and Caleb said to her, "What do you wish?" She answered, "Give me a blessing; since you have given me land in the South, give me also springs of water." So he gave her the upper springs and the lower springs. Joshua 15:13–19

1. Describe Caleb's heritage, which tribe he was apportioned a share among, and exactly where he was given his inheritance.

4 Marriage Plans

In the Middle East, it was customary to offer one's daughter to the victor in a battle. In so doing, Caleb could ensure that his daughter would marry a brave man who would be capable of protecting her and serving his country well. It was not unusual in that day to marry within the family.

---

7 Springs

A spring here refers to a gushing fountain or a deep well. Wherever a spring existed, it was likely to be the nucleus of a village. It furnished sufficient water to be used in irrigation. In many cases, gardens surrounding the village became an oasis in the midst of the parched land. Wherever springs flowed, people considered the water to be "living."

---

8 Grafted In

Caleb never looked back to his biological beginnings but fully embraced his new heritage. He became grafted into the tribe of Judah and the Jewish nation and history. In the same way, as believers in Christ we are grafted into the root of Jewish theocracy, where God is the root and we are branches that bear fruit.

2. What three Anakim did Caleb drive out of Hebron?

3. Where did Caleb go next, and what incentive did he offer to receive help?

4. Who responded to Caleb's challenge, and what was the result?

5. What did Achsah persuade her husband to do?

6. a. Describe what action Achsah took and how Caleb responded.

   b. Why do you think this action showed that Achsah was going to request something?

7. What did Achsah request and how did her father bless her abundantly?

LIVE OUT ...

8. Amazingly, one of the two faithful spies was probably of Gentile blood. This shows the grace of God written throughout the Old Testament toward the Gentile people.

   a. What does Galatians 3:28–29 say about the distinction between Jews and Gentiles, slave and free, male and female in God's eyes?

   b. According to this passage, what is your right of inheritance?

   c. List some of the promises you are most looking forward to inheriting and why.

9. a. Caleb ensured that his daughter married a brave man who

would protect the family heritage. Read 1 Peter 3:1–5 and give a detailed description of a Christian wife.

b. If you're married, how do you think you're doing in this respect? What do you need to work on? If you're unmarried, consider this passage in light of your relationship to your heavenly Husband, Jesus Christ, and answer the same question.

10. a. Caleb gave his daughter living water to sustain her family for generations. Read John 7:37–39. What does Jesus offer to those who thirst?

b. What does He promise those who believe in Him?

c. Can you describe a time when you've experienced living water flowing from you? (If you don't know that you have the Holy Spirit dwelling in your heart, ask Him to come dwell in your heart through faith in Christ. Then talk to your spiritual leader about your prayer.)

LEARN ABOUT ...

9 Submissive Heart

Biblically, to submit means to place in order, to come under, to yield. It does not mean to be subservient, but to come in line like a military ranking. It also does not imply an inferior position but a willingness to place oneself in a lowly position, just as Christ did. All Christians are exhorted to "be submissive to one another" (I Peter 5:5).

○ ○ ● ○ ○

Today we saw that Achsah and her husband, Othniel, received springs of living water from the brave and generous Caleb. Charles Haddon Spurgeon wrote this inspirational piece about the living water offered by Jesus Christ:

The sharp shrill cry of "Acqua! Acqua!" constantly pierces the ear of the wanderer in the towns of Italy. The man who thus invites your attention bears on his back a burden of water, and in his hand glasses to hold the cooling liquid. In the streets of London he would find little patronage, but where fountains are few and the days are hot as an oven, he earns a livelihood and supplies a public need. The water-dealer is a poor old man bent sideways by the weight of his daily burden. He is worn out in all but his voice, which is truly startling in its sharpness and distinctness. At our call he stops immediately, glad to drop his burden on the ground, and smiling in prospect of a customer. He washes out a glass for us, fills it with sparkling water, receives payment with manifest gratitude, and trudges away across the square, crying still, "Acqua! Acqua!"

That cry, shrill as it is, has sounded sweetly in the ears of many a thirsty soul, and will for ages yet to come, if throats and thirst survive so long. How forcibly it calls to mind the Savior's favorite imagery, in which he compares the grace which he bestows on all who diligently seek it to "living water." And how much that old man is like the faithful preacher of the Word, who, having filled his vessel at the well, wears himself out by continually bearing the burden of the Lord, and crying, "Water! Water!" amid crowds of sinners who must drink or die. Instead of the poor Italian water-bearer, we see before us the man of God, whose voice is heard in the chief places of concourse, proclaiming the divine invitation, "Ho, every one that thirsts, come to the waters!" until he grows grey in the service, and people say, "Surely those aged limbs have need of rest." Yet he does not court rest, but pursues his task of mercy, never laying down his charge till he lays down his body, and never ceasing to work until he ceases to live. [127]

May we be found faithful to hold out the fresh mercy of living water to those who are dying of thirst.

LISTEN TO ...

Wherever the Son of God goes, the winds of God are blowing, the streams of living water are flowing, and the sun of God is smiling.

—*Helmut Thielicke*

DAY 5

Chart of Judah

In Shakespeare's *Romeo and Juliet,* the heroine wistfully poses the question, "What's in a name? That which we call a rose by any other name would smell as sweet." But is that really true? Names are vitally important identifiers. A rose might smell as sweet if it were named a pansy, but would it have the same romantic aura? We'll never really know, will we?

In the seventeenth century, French explorer René-Robert Cavelier Sieur de La Salle was commissioned by King Louis XIV to travel south from Canada and sail down the Mississippi River to the Gulf of Mexico. His mission was to explore and establish fur-trade routes along the mighty Mississippi. He and his crew reached the Mississippi River on February 6, 1682, then headed down it in canoes. They reached the Gulf of Mexico on April 9, 1682. To celebrate their success and give credit to God, they built a cross. The expedition claimed the land along the Mississippi River for France. Perhaps one of La Salle's most memorable accomplishments was to name the Mississippi Basin Louisiana, in honor his king. Though Thomas Jefferson ultimately bought the land that the French had claimed, one state still bears the name of Louisiana.

Today, we look at the names of the cities found in the territory of Judah. Some of them are very familiar and even continue to make headlines today—cities like Jerusalem and Gaza. Others hold biblical familiarity. We remember how David hid at En Gedi when Saul was chasing him and how Abraham buried his beloved wife, Sarah, in the town of Hebron. As believers, it is good for us to remember the wisdom of the psalmist who wrote: "Unless the Lord builds the house, They labor in vain who build it; Unless the Lord guards the city, The watchman stays awake in vain" (Ps. 127:1). As a child of God, you can know that, whether you live in the heights or the valley, the mountains or the lowlands, the Lord is watching over you.

Lift up ...

Lord, I know that You have prepared an inheritance for everyone who believes. Help me to show my family the beauty of your salvation. Amen.

Look at ...

We've studied Caleb and his daughter's inheritance; now we return to the tribe of Judah's inheritance. Today we see that God charted the territory of Judah and divided it based on families as well as the natural features of the regions: the southern portion, the lowlands, the mountain country, and the wilderness.

The south is also known as the *Negev*, which literally means "parched and dry." Much of it is desert land. This land became famous as the favorite camping ground of the old patriarchs. The lowland, or *shephelah*, is a broad strip lying between the central highlands and the Mediterranean. The hill country or mountains of Judah is an elevated plateau stretching from below Hebron northward to Jerusalem. The wilderness is the sunken district next to the Dead Sea, averaging ten miles in breadth. A wild, barren, uninhabitable region, it's fit only for pasturing sheep and goats, and providing a secure home for leopards, bears, wild goats, and outlaws.[128] Though some of the cities are difficult to identify, it is good to know that the Lord cared where each family lived and what each family inherited. As we dissect this text, you'll be surprised to find some nuggets to apply to your own life.

Read Joshua 15:20–32.

This was the inheritance of the tribe of the children of Judah according to their families: The cities at the limits of the tribe of the children of Judah, toward the border of Edom in the South, were Kabzeel, Eder, Jagur, Kinah, Dimonah, Adadah, Kedesh, Hazor, Ithnan, Ziph, Telem, Bealoth, Hazor, Hadattah, Kerioth, Hezron (which is Hazor), Amam, Shema, Moladah, Hazar Gaddah, Heshmon, Beth Pelet, Hazar Shual, Beersheba, Bizjothjah, Baalah, Ijim, Ezem, Eltolad, Chesil, Hormah, Ziklag, Madmannah, Sansannah, Lebaoth, Shilhim, Ain, and Rimmon: all the cities are twenty-nine, with their villages. Joshua 15:20–32

1. a. How did Joshua divide the land at this point?

   b. Why might it be important to go into such detail?

2. What geographical area did Joshua address first?

3. How many cities does the text say are in the south? Now count the number of cities. How many are listed?

LOOK AT ...

We've seen the families who inherited land to the south. Now let's explore the territory in the lowland by exploring 15:33–47.

_____

In the lowland: Eshtaol, Zorah, Ashnah, Zanoah, En Gannim, Tappuah, Enam, Jarmuth, Adullam, Socoh, Azekah, Sharaim, Adithaim, Gederah, and Gederothaim: fourteen cities with their villages; Zenan, Hadashah, Migdal Gad, Dilean, Mizpah, Joktheel, Lachish, Bozkath, Eglon, Cabbon, Lahmas, Kithlish, Gederoth, Beth Dagon, Naamah, and Makkedah: sixteen cities with their villages; Libnah, Ether, Ashan, Jiphtah, Ashnah, Nezib, Keilah, Achzib, and Mareshah: nine cities with their villages; Ekron, with its towns and villages; from Ekron to the sea, all that lay near Ashdod, with their villages; Ashdod with its towns and villages, Gaza with its towns and villages—as far as the Brook of Egypt and the Great Sea with its coastline. Joshua 15:33–47

4. How many towns and villages in total did Judah inherit in the lowland?

5. How far did the boundary stretch?

LOOK AT ...

Now let's explore the mountain country and wilderness by looking at 15:48–63.

LEARN ABOUT ...

3 Thirty-eight Cities

Though the text says there are twenty-nine cities, it lists thirty-eight here. Why the discrepancy? Probably because nine of the cities were later transferred to the tribe of Simeon (see Josh. 19:5).

_____

5 Gaza

One of the oldest cities in the world, Gaza was the capital of the Philistines. It was the scene of Samson's prowess and humiliation (see Judg. 16:1–3) and of Philip's Christian service (see Acts 8:26).[129]

And in the mountain country: Shamir, Jattir, Sochoh, Dannah, Kirjath Sannah (which is Debir), Anab, Eshtemoh, Anim, Goshen, Holon, and Giloh: eleven cities with their villages; Arab, Dumah, Eshean, Janum, Beth Tappuah, Aphekah, Humtah, Kirjath Arba (which is Hebron), and Zior: nine cities with their villages; Maon, Carmel, Ziph, Juttah, Jezreel, Jokdeam, Zanoah, Kain, Gibeah, and Timnah: ten cities with their villages; Halhul, Beth Zur, Gedor, Maarath, Beth Anoth, and Eltekon: six cities with their villages; Kirjath Baal (which is Kirjath Jearim) and Rabbah: two cities with their villages. In the wilderness: Beth Arabah, Middin, Secacah, Nibshan, the City of Salt, and En Gedi: six cities with their villages. As for the Jebusites, the inhabitants of Jerusalem, the children of Judah could not drive them out; but the Jebusites dwell with the children of Judah at Jerusalem to this day. Joshua 15:48–63

6. a. How many cities did the tribe of Judah inherit in the mountains?

   b. Which of these cities do you recognize from the book of Joshua or other texts in the Bible?

7. a. How many cities did they receive in the wilderness?

   b. What notable cities are in this area?

8. Describe what happened to the inhabitants of Jerusalem and the long-lasting consequences of this failure.

LIVE OUT ...

9. a. Read 2 Samuel 23:20–23. Describe the actions of Benaniah from Kabzeel.

b. The Negev is the desert or wilderness area of Judah. How do you think living in the Negev might have prepared him for becoming such a valiant man?

c. Have you ever physically or spiritually lived in a place such as the Negev? If so, how has it molded you into the person you are today?

10. a. Gaza was one of the key cities given to the tribe of Judah in the lowlands. The Gaza Strip is currently one of the most disputed areas in the world. What do you know about the situation in the Gaza Strip?

b. Does it make a difference in your everyday life? Why or why not?

c. Does reading about this gift of inheritance change your view of the news articles you read and hear? Why or why not?

11. God had commanded the Israelites to completely cut off the enemies from the land. They were unable to dislodge the Jebusites in Jerusalem.

a. Read Romans 13:12–14 and list those things that God has commanded us to cast off.

b. Have you allowed them to continue to dwell with you in any measure?

c. Journal a prayer asking God to help you be ruthless with the sin in your life. Ask Him to help you be valiant in conquering that sin through the power of the Holy Spirit.

LEARN ABOUT ...

10 Gaza Strip

Modern Gaza (Ghuzzeh) serves as the administrative center of the Gaza Strip under the auspices of the Palestinian Authority. Following Yasser Arafat's death in September 2005, Israel withdrew its settlers and soldiers and dismantled its military facilities in the Gaza Strip and four northern West Bank settlements. Nonetheless, Israel controls maritime, airspace, and most access to the Gaza Strip.

∘ ∘ ● ∘ ∘

John Ashcroft wrote that in order to clean up New York City, "Rudolph Giuliani started by going after the little things. 'I am a firm believer in the theory that "minor" crimes and "quality of life" offenses are all part of the larger picture,' he explains. Among the first elements to go were the 'Squeegee Men,' drug-addicted and shady-looking riffraff who personified New York's rough edge. Armed with a soiled rag and a dirty bottle of watered-down Windex, these men would bully and badger motorists for money.

"Giuliani said, 'We're not going to put up with this anymore,' and he brought this intimidation to an end. He then declared war on graffiti, subway panhandlers, loitering, broken windows, and petty vandalism—minor offenses that would have gone unnoticed in days past while the police force was overwhelmed with homicides and violent crime. But Guiliani had a hunch: If you send out a signal that you won't tolerate these minor offenses, people will get the idea that the major offenses will be treated even more seriously.… It worked. Giuliani has been successful in reducing crime beyond all expectations."[130]

What if we began the same policy concerning the "city" of our hearts? If we declare war on the "minor" sins, surely the major sins won't be able to lodge in our cities and defile the quality of our walk with God.

LISTEN TO …

He who is faithful over a few things is a lord of cities. It does not matter whether you preach in Westminster Abbey, or teach a ragged class, so you be faithful. The faithfulness is all.

—*George MacDonald*

The Cities Different
Joshua 20—21

Santa Fe, New Mexico, bears the nickname "the City Different." How did it earn this label? The Spaniards (not the British or French) founded the city. Established in 1607, it is the oldest city capital in the United States and a famous tourist town. The beautiful setting in the Sangre de Cristo mountains adds to its allure.

The Spaniards and Native Americans have lived side by side for centuries. During the 1820s people of Anglo-European descent joined the melting pot. After the Mexican-American War, Jewish and Lebanese mercantile store builders arrived, ushering in the era of the Santa Fe Railroad. Later, physicists from Los Alamos labs added brainpower to the city different. Artists like Georgia O'Keefe found the lighting in New Mexico perfect to paint by. Writers like D. H. Lawrence were inspired by the setting. Cultural diversity flowed into the city in the hills. No wonder Santa Fe's motto is "Any and all welcome." Today when you visit the city plaza, you get a taste of old Mexico blended with Pueblo Indian architecture and mixed with a touch of New York art gallery flair. There truly is no city quite like Santa Fe.

While the cities of refuge found in Joshua 20—21 may not have borne the same reputation that Santa Fe holds today, they had something in common: They were definitely "the cit[ies] different." Holy cities of faith, they derived their name from a godly concept: asylum offered to manslayers fleeing retaliation from an avenger. Traditionally, these cities were established to provide sanctuary if certain criteria were fulfilled by the accidental perpetrator. They became multicultural cities that opened their arms warmly to citizens who endured painful pasts.

Day 1: Joshua 20:1–4   **CITY OF REFUGE**

Day 2: Joshua 20:5–9   **CITY OF BROTHERLY LOVE**

Day 3: Joshua 21:1–19   **CITY OF HOPE**

Day 4: Joshua 21:20–40   **CITY OF LIGHTS**

Day 5: Joshua 21:41–45   **CITY OF PEACE**

DAY 1
City of Refuge

LIFT UP ...

Lord, thank You that, although my past is painful, You will one day welcome me into Your holy city, the New Jerusalem. I take refuge in You. Amen.

LOOK AT ...

Last week Joshua divided the land among the royal tribe of Judah and the priestly tribe of Levi. We witnessed the faith of Caleb, who in his old age took on giants and conquered mountains.

This week, instead of focusing on regions that encompass large territories, we'll examine some special cities with small boundaries. In these cities of refuge, an accidental manslayer could find sanctuary. Moses had instructed the people to establish these cities to balance justice with mercy. Although the hand was guilty, the heart was not. Those found in such a state would not be punished severely, but with truth and grace.

Isn't it good to know that God does not deal harshly with His people? He understands that sometimes bad things happen to good people. Although accidents occur, we can still find hope and new beginnings. God provides a shelter for us in the midst of pain and persecution.

READ JOSHUA 20:1–4.

The LORD also spoke to Joshua, saying, "Speak to the children of Israel, saying: 'Appoint for yourselves cities of refuge, of which I spoke to you through Moses, that the slayer who kills a person accidentally or unintentionally may flee there; and they shall be your refuge from the avenger of blood. And when he flees to one of those cities, and stands at the entrance of the gate of the city, and declares his case in the hearing of the elders of that city, they shall take him into the

LEARN ABOUT ...

1 God's Spokesman

Joshua, like Moses, was a prophet of God. Prophets spoke courageously on behalf of God to His chosen people. "Joshua the son of Nun was full of the spirit of wisdom, for Moses had laid his hands on him; so the children of Israel heeded him, and did as the LORD had commanded Moses" (Deut. 34:9).

3 City of Refuge

Among the Hebrews, six Levite cities were declared cities of refuge. They provided sanctuary for people who had accidentally or unintentionally committed murder. Upon reaching a city of refuge, a fair trial and asylum was provided. If acquitted, the manslayer must remain in the city until the death of the high priest.

4 Avenger of Blood

Customarily the nearest relative became an "avenger of blood" after a loved one was killed. He was sworn to slay the slayer. An avenger could kill the manslayer if he overtook the perpetrator before reaching the city (see Num. 35:19). If ever found outside the city limits, the manslayer risked death at the hands of the blood avenger (see Num. 35:25–28).[31]

city as one of them, and give him a place, that he may dwell among them.'" Joshua 20:1–4

1. Describe the privileged position Joshua held between God and His people.

2. Explain what Joshua asked the people to do and whose previous advice he upheld.

3. In your own words, describe the purpose for the cities of refuge.

4. a. From whom did the manslayer flee?

   b. What do you think motivated this person?

5. What would take place in the city gates?

6. After the hearing, how were the citizens to respond to the manslayer?

LIVE OUT ...

7. Joshua was a prophet who spoke God's Word to God's people.

   a. List some of those who have spoken God's Word, the Bible, to you.

   b. How was the Scripture they shared inspired by the Holy Spirit? How did it affect your life?

   c. Journal a prayer thanking God for the prophets He has placed in your life. Ask Him to bless them and continue to use them for His glory.

8. God provided cities of refuge for those who had murdered with their hands but not with their hearts. Read Matthew 5:21–26 to discover the New Testament definition of murder and its consequence.

a. List the names of those you have slain in your heart with angry thoughts or cutting words.

b. Describe the activities God asks you to avoid and the commands He asks you to keep if a relationship has been damaged.

c. Have you obeyed God's Word with the people you've listed above? Explain the consequences of disobedience. Please don't engage in further spiritual activity until you've sought reconciliation with those you've verbally slain.

9. Manslayers were provided mercy and grace in the cities of refuge. Fill in the following chart to discover those who find a refuge in God.

SCRIPTURE	THE REFUGEES
Psalm 9:9	
Proverbs 14:26	
Proverbs 14:32	
Isaiah 25:4	

o o ● o o

Two wrongs will never make a right. When tragedy springs from an accident or is unintentional, convicting the innocent will not raise the dead. With manslaughter there are no winners, only victims. That was the reality for Marine pilot Captain Richard Ashby.

LEARN ABOUT …

7 Prophet

More than predicting the future, prophecy is to "speak forth" God's Word. Inspired by the Holy Spirit, it literally means "to bubble forth as a fountain." The main role of the prophet was to bear God's Word for the purpose of teaching, reproving, correcting, and training in righteousness (see 2 Tim. 3:16).[132]

8 Murder or Manslaughter?

Murder is the willful and pre-meditated taking of a human life. Manslaughter is described as accidental killing; killing as an act of war, and lawful executions were not considered murder (see Ex. 21:12–14). Jesus pointed to the spirit of this commandment when He expanded it to forbid hatred, anger, bitter insults, and cursing.[133]

On February 3, 1998, Richard's EA-6B Prowler inadvertently careened into the cable of an Italian gondola in the Alps and plunged twenty people to their deaths. Outraged Italian authorities demanded a trial, accusing the Marine pilot of twenty counts of involuntary manslaughter, with a maximum 206 years in prison if convicted. They blamed the pilot for flying recklessly when his jet sliced through the cable.

Ashby argued that the cables were not on his map, that the jet's altitude-gauging equipment malfunctioned, and that an optical illusion made him believe he was flying higher at the time of the accident. "Basically, all I really want to say is that this has been a tragedy for all involved," Ashby said. "My heart, my thoughts and prayers go out to the families of the victims of this tragedy." After the jury deliberated for nearly seven and a half hours, Captain Ashby was acquitted and all charges were dropped.[134]

In the Old Testament, God differentiates between murder and manslaughter, between sin and transgression. The word *sin* means to miss the mark much like an arrow missing its intended target. *Transgression* implies intentional disobedience, like a child who defiantly rebels against a parent's authority. Sometimes we inadvertently stumble into sin. But other times we blatantly march into rebellion, knowing full well it is wrong. Thankfully, God forgives both the intentional transgressor and the involuntary trespasser. He's willing to drop all charges as we confess all to Him.

Listen to ...

That man is perfect in faith who can come to God in the utter dearth of his feelings and his desires, without a glow or an aspiration, with the weight of low thoughts, failures, neglects, and wandering forgetfulness, and say to him, "Thou art my refuge because thou art my home."

—*George MacDonald*

DAY 2

City of Brotherly Love

Philadelphia was founded in 1682 by the well-known Quaker William Penn. The name of Penn's city was derived from two Greek words translated as "brotherly love." True to his Quaker beliefs, Penn hoped that the capital city founded on principles of freedom and religious tolerance would be a model of his philosophy of brotherly love.

Naming a city takes finesse. Like Philadelphia, ideally it encompasses the city's personality or goals. Here are some helpful hints in naming cities:

CITY SURVEY: Key features like bodies of water or landforms such as hills or mountains are also important. Perhaps Bayview, Riverside, Hillsdale, or Mount Pleasant fits.

CONSIDER FUNCTION: City function could be your inspiration. Is it a farming community? Then name it Wheaton. Sleepy commuter town? Sleepy Hollow. Industrial wasteland? City of Industry.

CHECK YOUR MAP: Are there neighboring cities? Perhaps East Hampton works. If located in the north, then North View is appropriate.

CURRENT EVENT CONSIDERATION: Some towns can be named after celebrities or dignitaries. Lincoln, Pittsburgh, and San Diego tip their hats to famous people.

CRUISE THE NEIGHBORHOOD: You live on Ludington Avenue? Name your city Ludington. Your favorite shop is Cline's at the corner of Second and Oak? Name your city Cline's Corner. The possibilities are endless.

The cities of refuge were named to express their purpose, to offer safe harbor to those seeking asylum from someone motivated by a vendetta. Refuge means a place of shelter, protection, or safety. It's where one finds aid, relief, or escape. These cities were places of refuge and brotherly love.

LIFT UP ...

Lord, You are my hiding place, my strong tower of safety. May I open my heart and home to provide shelter and safety for those running from the storms of life. Help me to offer them the same comfort You have offered to me. Amen.

LOOK AT ...

Yesterday we learned that Joshua had kept Moses' counsel by establishing cities of refuge in the Promised Land. If someone committed an accidental homicide, he or she could flee to these cities for a fair trial within the gates.

Today we discover what was required before a manslayer could be exonerated from guilt. 1) The death must not be premeditated. 2) The crime must not be one of passion, motivated by hate. 3) There must be a trial before the manslayer's peers.

It's apparent that modern laws and courts of our nation are modeled after these same principles. Isn't it wonderful to know that the Bible is the cornerstone of civil justice? It promotes morality as well as spirituality. However, one does not ensure the other. It's possible to be abundantly moral but spiritually bankrupt. One might fulfill the letter of the law yet neglect its very heart and intent.

Remember the story of the Good Samaritan? Like a priest and Levite, this model citizen encountered a victim lying in the street, beaten and stripped of his clothes. The religious men ignored the poor man's plight, but the Samaritan cared for him instead. Each man's actions revealed his true spiritual state. The religious men thought that keeping the law was enough to express God. However, Jesus corrected this erroneous premise by reminding them that loving neighbors must be included in loving the Savior (see Luke 10:25–37).

READ JOSHUA 20:5–9.

"'Then if the avenger of blood pursues him, they shall not deliver the slayer into his hand, because he struck his neighbor unintentionally, but did not hate him beforehand. And he shall dwell in that city until he stands before the congregation for judgment, and until the death of the one who is high priest in those days. Then the slayer may return and come

to his own city and his own house, to the city from which he fled.'" So they appointed Kedesh in Galilee, in the mountains of Naphtali, Shechem in the mountains of Ephraim, and Kirjath Arba (which is Hebron) in the mountains of Judah. And on the other side of the Jordan, by Jericho eastward, they assigned Bezer in the wilderness on the plain, from the tribe of Reuben, Ramoth in Gilead, from the tribe of Gad, and Golan in Bashan, from the tribe of Manasseh. These were the cities appointed for all the children of Israel and for the stranger who dwelt among them, that whoever killed a person accidentally might flee there, and not die by the hand of the avenger of blood until he stood before the congregation.
Joshua 20:5–9

1. What might the "avenger of blood" do and in the hopes of what result?

2. Explain the reasons why the congregation would not deliver the slayer into the hands of the avenger.

3. a. Under what circumstance could the innocent person leave the city of refuge?

   b. What was his likely destination?

4. a. How might this person have felt about internment in the city of refuge?

   b. What might his homecoming have been like?

5. List the six cities of refuge by name and general location. Then find them on the map on page 389.

6. a. Who could access these cities?

LEARN ABOUT ...

1 Hot Pursuit

Often the vendetta for a murder was handed down from one generation to the next. Unfortunately, many innocent people died as a result. Perhaps that explains why this topic is covered in four books of the Old Testament. The Bible places great importance on the sanctity of life. To take another's life, even if unintentionally, carries great weight.

3 High Priest

The high priest's position was at the peak of Israel's hierarchy. Aaron was the first to fill this high position and was succeeded by his son Eleazar. The high priest was required to satisfy all the necessary conditions of his sacred office and had unique attire to represent his position.[135]

LEARN ABOUT ...

7 Heavy Price

The manslayer didn't get away without any consequences. Although the death was accidental, without premeditation or passionate motivation, he bore some responsibility. Spending years away from family, friends, and occupation must have been heart wrenching. The stigma likely followed him upon his homecoming. He probably endured a tender conscience continually.

8 Human Preeminence

God holds man in special regard because he is made in His very image. Even the psalmist wonders at our worth, "What is man that You are mindful of him?" (Ps. 8:4). Humans possess a spiritual nature that ranks them above animals. They alone on earth possess the capability to commune with God.

10 Heavenly Priest

The Old Testament high priest presented the sin offering for himself and the congregation (see Lev. 4:3–21) as occasion required. Jesus is our High Priest: "Seeing then that we have a great High Priest who has passed through the heavens, Jesus the Son of God, let us hold fast our confession" (Heb. 4:14).

b. Why do you think they were placed in these specific locations?

7. What was the manslayers' guarantee?

LIVE OUT ...

8. a. The Bible elevates the value of a human life from conception to death. Read Exodus 21:12–26. List the different situations in which God holds man responsible for the death of another.

b. Journal about some of the ways modern society has diminished the sanctity of life. How can you explain this decline?

9. A city of refuge provided a safe place to hide from those pursuing a person for unjust revenge. The congregation (this probably means the city elders) would judge fairly and then protect those who had fled to them for sanctuary. Using the word HIDE as an acrostic, list some places where you've found safety.

H

I

D

E

10. The manslayer could not leave the city of refuge until the death of the reigning high priest. The Bible teaches that Jesus Christ is our High Priest. Rewrite Hebrews 2:17 into a personal hymn of praise thanking Him for setting you free from death and sin.

Therefore, in all things He had to be made like His brethren, that He might be a merciful and faithful High Priest in things pertaining to God, to make propitiation for the sins of the people. (Heb 2:17)

○ ○ ● ○ ○

"V" is for Vendetta. Vendetta comes from the Latin word for revenge. Also known as a blood feud, it describes a continuing state of conflict between two groups characterized by killings and counterkillings. It exists where an absence of law or a breakdown of legal proceedings fails to negotiate an acceptable grievance between both parties. A famous example includes Celtic feuds between Scottish and Irish clans. Many Celtic immigrants living in the Appalachian region of Kentucky and West Virginia continued this tradition of feuds, the most famous being between the Hatfields and McCoys.

In more modern times, gangs and hip-hop rappers notoriously engage in verbal and violent warfare with one another, sometimes resulting in murder. The most high-profile feud in rap was the Tupac/Notorious B.I.G. Feud, which included several shootings. It culminated with the highly publicized assassinations of Tupac Shakur in 1996 and the Notorious B.I.G. in 1997.

Imagine if today we provided cities of refuge to end feuds and vendettas. Wouldn't the world be a better place? What if each of us served as mediator between enraged and estranged parties? Perhaps we could provide shelter while simultaneously negotiating a truce. God still esteems human life highly and so must we. If we continue to live by the axiom of "eye for eye" and "tooth for tooth," humanity may someday be blind and unable to smile. What can *you* do to stop the cycle? Open your heart, your home, and your hands to end violence and extend sanctuary to those with unjust grievances!

LISTEN TO ...

Discouraged people don't need critics. They hurt enough already. They don't need more guilt or piled-on distress. They need encouragement. They need a refuge. A willing, caring, available someone.

—*Charles R. Swindoll*

DAY 3

City of Hope

"I believe in a place called Hope," Governor Bill Clinton said while completing his acceptance speech at the 1992 Democratic National Convention. He was referring to his birthplace in Hope, Arkansas, which was first settled in 1852. The city received its name in honor of Hope—the daughter of James Loughborough, the Cairo & Fulton (railroad) Land Commissioner—because she drafted the original plat for the city.

Biblically, hope refers to an expectation of some future blessing. Those who possess hope fix their eyes not on temporal but eternal matters. Wouldn't you love to live in a city with heavenly precepts rather than human principles? One where priests, not presidents, dwell? The great men and women of faith "waited for the city which has foundations, whose builder and maker is God" (Heb. 11:10).

The Levites' inheritance in Canaan was not land but the Lord. However, they were to be given cities of hope to dwell in as they cared for the things of God. They waited patiently as all the other people received their inheritance. Yet in chapter 21 their lot remained unassigned until they boldly made their claim. Like the priests, saints hope for their inheritance as God's royal priesthood (see 1 Peter 2:5). But we, too, must petition for it. Jesus assures, "Ask, and it will be given to you; seek, and you will find; knock, and it will be opened to you. For everyone who asks receives, and he who seeks finds, and to him who knocks it will be opened" (Matt. 7:7–8). What are you waiting for?

LIFT UP ...

Lord, please strengthen me as I boldly ask and patiently wait for all the blessings and promises You've given in Your Word. May I fix my eyes on a certain and future hope in You. Amen.

LOOK AT ...

So far we've examined the very different cities of refuge that offered safety to accidental manslayers. Founded on mercy and truth, they ensured that everyone received a fair and balanced trial before a jury of their peers. These cities promoted the sanctity of life among the nation's citizens.

Now we turn to the Levites and the distribution of their cities. Moses had previously stipulated that they would not inherit their own estates, as their possessions were spiritual in nature. Instead, they were promised cities within the boundaries of the other twelve tribes of Israel to raise their families.

We'll see how Joshua responded to their request as he challenged the tribal heads to donate a set number of cities from within their individual boundaries. As a result, God had the opportunity to test their generosity toward the priesthood and the things that pertained to God. They nobly passed this test, and we'll see that many of these cities were the best from within each tribe. Also, they wisely positioned these cities so that no part of the country would be too far from a Levite city of hope.

READ JOSHUA 21:1–8.

Then the heads of the fathers' houses of the Levites came near to Eleazar the priest, to Joshua the son of Nun, and to the heads of the fathers' houses of the tribes of the children of Israel. And they spoke to them at Shiloh in the land of Canaan, saying, "The LORD commanded through Moses to give us cities to dwell in, with their common-lands for our livestock." So the children of Israel gave to the Levites from their inheritance, at the commandment of the LORD, these cities and their common-lands: Now the lot came out for the families of the Kohathites. And the children of Aaron the priest, who were of the Levites, had thirteen cities by lot from the tribe of Judah, from the tribe of Simeon, and from the tribe of Benjamin. The rest of the children of Kohath had ten cities by lot from the families of the tribe of Ephraim, from the tribe of Dan, and from the half-tribe of Manasseh. And the children of Gershon had thirteen cities by lot from the families of the tribe of Issachar, from the tribe of Asher, from the tribe of Naphtali, and from the half-tribe of Manasseh in Bashan. The children of Merari according to their families had twelve cities from the tribe of Reuben, from the tribe of Gad, and from the tribe of Zebulun. And the children of Israel gave these cities with their common-lands by lot to the Levites, as the LORD had commanded by the hand of Moses. Joshua 21:1–8

1. Who did the Levities approach to make a request?

LEARN ABOUT ...

1 Eleazar

Before Aaron's death, his son Eleazar joined Moses on Mt. Hor and was made high priest in his father's stead (see Num. 20:25–29). Moses assigned him overseer of a census as his first official duty. He also participated in the inauguration of Joshua. After the conquest of Canaan he aided in the division of the land (see Josh. 14:1).[136]

2 Priestly Provision

Matthew Henry wrote, "The maintenance of ministers is not an arbitrary thing, left purely to the good-will of the people, who may let them starve. No, as the God of Israel commanded that the Levites should be well provided for, so has the Lord Jesus ... ordained ... 'that those who preach the gospel should live from the gospel' (I Cor. 9:14), and should live comfortably."[137]

2. Explain their request as well as their rationale.

3. Recount the distribution of the forty-eight Levite cities by filling in the following columns.

LEVITE FAMILY:	NUMBER OF CITIES:	FROM WHICH TRIBES:

LOOK AT ...

The Levites evoked their right to receive priestly cities among the tribes of Israel. The tribal heads responded generously by providing forty-eight cities. They were dispersed evenly throughout the country, giving everyone equal access to priestly influence.

The Levites were divided into four families, and each group received its fair share of priestly cities. Read Joshua 21:9–19, then answer the following questions to discover which cities the Kohathites inherited.

So they gave from the tribe of the children of Judah and from the tribe of the children of Simeon these cities which are designated by name, which were for the children of Aaron, one of the families of the Kohathites, who were of the children of Levi; for the lot was theirs first. And they gave them Kirjath Arba (Arba was the father of Anak), which is Hebron, in the mountains of Judah, with the common-land surrounding it. But the fields of the city and its villages they gave to Caleb the son of Jephunneh as his possession. Thus to the children of Aaron the priest they gave Hebron with its common-land (a city of refuge for the slayer), Libnah with its common-land, Jattir with its common-land, Eshtemoa with its common-land, Holon with its common-land, Debir with its common-land, Ain with its common-land, Juttah with its common-land, and Beth Shemesh with its common-land: nine cities from those two tribes; and from the tribe of Benjamin, Gibeon with its common-land, Geba with its common-land, Anathoth with its common-land, and Almon with its common-land: four cities. All the cities of the children of Aaron, the priests, were thirteen cities with their common-lands. Joshua 21:9–19

4. Whose children received the first lot, and from which tribes was it received?

5. Read Numbers 13:22, 28, 33. Describe the descendants of Anak.

6. How was Hebron divided, and to who was it given?

7. Review Joshua 14. Why did Caleb receive part of Hebron as his possession?

Live out ...

8. The Levites' request was biblically based and respectfully addressed. Which of the biblical promises have you asked for, and to whom did you make your requests?

   ❏ Promise of the Holy Spirit (see Acts 1:4–5)
   ❏ Promise of heavenly inheritance (see Eph. 3:6)
   ❏ Promise of rest (see Heb. 4:1)
   ❏ Promise of hope (see Heb. 10:19–23)
   ❏ Promise of eternal life (see 1 John 2:25)

9. In the book of Joshua we learn that God provided for all His children equally, even if each inheritance was not identical. Some tribes received mountaintops; others were given the fertile plains; still others lived near the seashore. The priests did not have land, but they had the Lord.

Learn about ...

4 Aaron's Descendants

Aaron was the first high priest and had four sons: Nadab, Abihu, Eleazar, and Ithamar. The firstborn should have inherited his position. However, Nadab and Abihu offered "profane fire before the LORD" in the Wilderness of Sinai, and both died when "fire went out from the LORD and devoured them" (Lev. 10:1–2).[138]

8 Promises of God

A promise is a solemn pledge to perform or grant a specified thing. God did not have to promise anything to sinful man. Therefore, God's promises reveal His gracious nature.[139] "All the promises of God in Him are Yes, and in Him Amen, to the glory of God" (2 Cor. 1:20).

9 Provision

Not only does God provide for prophets, priests, and kings; He provides for the poor and lowly. "You, O God, provided from Your goodness for the poor" (Ps. 68:10). He promises His children that He will provide all their needs according to His riches in glory (see Phil. 4:19).

    a. Describe what your inheritance includes (people, places, pennies, personality ...).

    b. Describe how your allotment wonderfully differs from others.

    c. Journal a prayer thanking God for His generous provision in your life.

10. God plants us in places where He expects us to bloom. Name the different states, cities, or neighborhoods where you have lived. How do you know that God called you to those places? How did you affect the places in which you lived?

∘ ∘ ● ∘ ∘

Some calculate that no one in Israel lived more than ten miles from a Levite city, making every citizen accessible to a priest well versed in the law. Priests provided counsel regarding family, politics, and religion to the people surrounding their cities. Moses' final blessing over the Levite tribe pronounced, "They shall teach Jacob Your judgments, And Israel Your law" (Deut. 33:10).

Sadly, at the time they were given their cities, many of those cities were still under Canaanite control. The Levities never fully conquered these townships, and unfortunately the other tribes never came to their aid in doing so. Perhaps if they had fully inhabited these cities they could have provided a barrier from future idolatry promoted by the surrounding nations.

How many of us never reach our full potential, failing to appropriate the promises of God? How often do we watch other believers struggle in their faith without offering to lend a hand or bend a knee on their behalf? We need one another. No Christian is intended to go it alone. Think of the metaphors in Scripture that describe God's church: We're the body of Christ; can a body stand on only one leg? We're called the building of God; doesn't it take more than one brick to build a wall? We're also considered the army of God. If you are struggling to be all that you can be, perhaps it's time to call in some reinforcements!

LISTEN TO ...

It takes holy citizens to make a holy city.

—Unknown

DAY 4

City of Lights

"City of Lights" remains the most famous name for Paris. The name was originally derived from the brilliant luminaries who lived in the city and made it a center of education and ideas. Later the name became attached to Paris's early adoption of street lighting. Today if you stroll down the Champs Elysee at night, you'll be dazzled by twinkle lights adorning the trees, headlights glaring from passing traffic, buildings illuminated by spotlights, and the Eiffel Tower sparkling nearby. It's a city full of beauty.

Unfortunately, the reputation of Paris is less than stellar. From bars to bordellos to burlesque halls featuring provocative women dancing the cancan, the city possesses a dark side. Tourists soon discover that all that glitters is not gold. The same lights that beckons can blind them to the dangers all around.

Sprinkling Levite cities throughout the Israelites' land should have had an illuminating effect. These cities would have offered a substitute for the dark and idolatrous high places, shrines, and altars that plagued the Promised Land. Therefore, the Levites were commanded to establish these exemplary cities full of model citizens. Sadly, one day these cities of light would fade as they were clouded by the wickedness all around.

Is there anything like these Levite cities in our society today? Yes, the church is called to be a beacon of light, shining forth purity and truth. Each one of us must add to the glow of God. Let us learn from the Hebrews' mistake. Let us eradicate from our hearts and congregations the pollutants that would suffocate the heavenly flame!

LIFT UP ...

Jesus, You are the light of the world. Your light has exposed all of my dark places and has illuminated my way. Help me to be a bright light attracting others to You. Amen.

LOOK AT ...

So far we've examined the two kinds of cities that God ordained to be placed in Israel. The first were cities of refuge to offer legal safety and compassion. The second were spiritual communities full of religious activity.

The Levite cities were to be surrounded by land for agricultural purposes. These green belts afforded the priests a place to provide for themselves and their families. They would be able to plant crops and graze cattle. Each of the forty-eight cities included enough rural area to make this possible.

The Bible places an emphasis on spiritual leadership and how those who are affected by spiritual leaders are to provide for those leaders' physical needs. Even today people are set apart for full-time ministry—from missionaries to ministers. The apostle Paul wrote, "Let the elders who rule well be counted worthy of double honor, especially those who labor in the word and doctrine. For the Scripture says, 'You shall not muzzle an ox while it treads out the grain,' and, 'The laborer is worthy of his wages'" (1 Tim. 5:17–18).

READ JOSHUA 21:20–26.

And the families of the children of Kohath, the Levites, the rest of the children of Kohath, even they had the cities of their lot from the tribe of Ephraim. For they gave them Shechem with its common-land in the mountains of Ephraim (a city of refuge for the slayer), Gezer with its common-land, Kibzaim with its common-land, and Beth Horon with its common-land: four cities; and from the tribe of Dan, Eltekeh with its common-land, Gibbethon with its common-land, Aijalon with its common-land, and Gath Rimmon with its common-land: four cities; and from the half-tribe of Manasseh, Tanach with its common-land and Gath Rimmon with its common-land: two cities. All the ten cities with their common-lands were for the rest of the families of the children of Kohath. Joshua 21:20–26

1. a. "The children of" whom received their allotted cities next?

   b. Underline the names of tribes who offered them.

2. Scan through the text and circle the name of each city the "children of Kohath" inherited. Find them on the map on page 389.

3. Read 1 Samuel 17:2–10. Who came from Gath? What problem did he present to Israel?

LOOK AT …

Previously we discovered which cities the "children of Kohath" inherited. Now let's see what the "children of Gershon" would receive. Read Joshua 21:27–33.

Also to the children of Gershon, of the families of the Levites, from the other half-tribe of Manasseh, they gave Golan in Bashan with its common-land (a city of refuge for the slayer), and Be Eshterah with its common-land: two cities; and from the tribe of Issachar, Kishion with its common-land, Daberath with its common-land, Jarmuth with its common-land, and En Gannim with its common-land: four cities; and from the tribe of Asher, Mishal with its common-land, Abdon with its common-land, Helkath with its common-land, and Rehob with its common-land: four cities; and from the tribe of Naphtali, Kedesh in Galilee with its common-land (a city of refuge for the slayer), Hammoth Dor with its common-land, and Kartan with its common-land: three cities. All the cities of the Gershonites according to their families were thirteen cities with their common-lands. Joshua 21:27–33

4. a. "The children" of whom were next to receive their allotted cities next?

   b. Underline the names of the tribes who donated them.

5. Scan through the text and circle the name of each city the "children of Gershon" inherited.

I Kohath

Kohath was the second son of Levi. The Kohathites formed one of the three great divisions of the Levites and contained the priestly family descended from Aaron. Their service in the tabernacle was to carry the ark and the other holy objects (see Num. 4:15; 7:9).[140]

---

5 Gershon

Even though Gershon was the eldest of Levi's three sons, apparently the descendants of Kohath outstripped his family in fame. Moses and the priestly line of Aaron were descendants of Kohath. The Gershonites had charge of the fabrics of the tabernacle—the coverings, screen, hangings, and cords (see Num. 3:25–26; 4:24–26).[141]

LEARN ABOUT ...

7 Merari

Merari means "sorrowful." He received this name probably because of the anguish attending his birth (Gen. 46:8, 11). The Merarites took care of the tabernacle boards and frame, so four wagons and eight oxen were assigned them. They shared with the Gershonites and Kohathites the offices of singers and doorkeepers under King David.[142]

---

8 No Compromise

Eventually Goliath would come from Gath, because the city was never completely subdued by the Kohathites. Paul exhorts Christians that "if by the Spirit you put to death the deeds of the body, you will live" (Rom. 8:13). Make sure you do not compromise with your flesh. It may come back to bite you.

LOOK AT ...

Now let's see what the "children of Merari" received. Read Joshua 21:34–40.

And to the families of the children of Merari, the rest of the Levites, from the tribe of Zebulun, Jokneam with its common-land, Kartah with its common-land, Dimnah with its common-land, and Nahalal with its common-land: four cities; and from the tribe of Reuben, Bezer with its common-land, Jahaz with its common-land, Kedemoth with its common-land, and Mephaath with its common-land: four cities; and from the tribe of Gad, Ramoth in Gilead with its common-land (a city of refuge for the slayer), Mahanaim with its common-land, Heshbon with its common-land, and Jazer with its common-land: four cities in all. So all the cities for the children of Merari according to their families, the rest of the families of the Levites, were by their lot twelve cities. Joshua 21:34–40

6. Underline the names of the tribes who donated to the children of Merari.

7. Scan through the text and circle the name of each city the "children of Merari" inherited.

LIVE OUT ...

8. Severe consequences would result from the Levites' failure to conquer the cities they'd inherited. Read Colossians 3:5–9.

Therefore put to death your members which are on the earth: fornication, uncleanness, passion, evil desire, and covetousness, which is idolatry. Because of these things the wrath of God is coming upon the sons of disobedience, in which you yourselves once walked when you lived in them.

But now you yourselves are to put off all these: anger, wrath, malice, blasphemy, filthy language out of your mouth. Do not lie to one another, since you have put off the old man with his deeds. (Col. 3:5–9)

LEARN ABOUT ...

9 No Pollution

The Levites were responsible for maintaining the Hebrew places of worship in both the wilderness tabernacle and later the temple in Jerusalem. Paul likens your body to the temple of God and warns that you are to keep it holy and undefiled (see 1 Cor. 6:19–20). *Defile* means to make unclean or impure.

a. Underline the word *put,* along with the instructions connected to it.

b. Circle the evilness you're to put away.

c. List the actions in "which you [personally] once walked."

9. Today we've discovered which aspects of the tabernacle the individual Levite families were to maintain: Some cared for the ark, some for the articles, and some for the fabrics and covering. Everybody has a ministry. Read Romans 12:4–8.

a. Which words emphasize our diversity of function (see 12:4–5)?

b. Which words emphasize our unity of purpose (see 12:4–5)?

c. Explain why we should not boast in our individual roles (see 12:6).

d. List the various roles Christians are to maintain. What attitude should accompany these functions (see 12:6–8)?

10. One of the functions every Levite priest had in common was singing unto the Lord. Please take time now to sing your favorite praise song to the Lord.

○ ○ ● ○ ○

While delivering the Sermon on the Mount, Jesus spoke of a city of lights set upon a hill. He gave this sermon beside the Sea of Galilee. From this vantage point you can see the lights of the city of Safed shining down from the mountains of Upper Galilee. Some scholars believe that this ancient city was the very one Jesus had in mind.

Safed is one of the four holy cities in Israel, together with Jerusalem, Hebron, and Tiberias. It is believed that the grandsons of Noah settled this city and established a Yeshiva (Bible college) in its midst. Great Hebrew mystics say Safed will play an important role in the final redemption. The Meam Loez, in the name of Rabbi Shimon bar Yochai, says that the Messiah will come from Safed on His way to Jerusalem. The Ari HaKodesh said that until the Third Temple is built, the Shechinah (God's Manifest Presence) rests above Safed.[143]

Did you know that you are called to be a city of light? It was Jesus who said it: "You are the light of the world. A city that is set on a hill cannot be hidden. Nor do they light a lamp and put it under a basket, but on a lampstand, and it gives light to all who are in the house. Let your light so shine before men, that they may see your good works and glorify your Father in heaven" (Matt. 5:14–16). You have the opportunity to shine the light of the gospel to the world around you through the good deeds that you perform. May His holy presence inhabit your life with light and truth.

LISTEN TO ...

The shifting systems of false religion are continually changing their places; but the gospel of Christ is the same forever. While other false lights are extinguished, this true light ever shines.

—Theodore Ledyard Cuyler

DAY 5

City of Peace

In Hebrew minds Jerusalem means "city of peace," but sadly, for centuries it has known very little peace. After King David conquered this Canaanite stronghold, he renamed it. Jebus, its previous name, seems more fitting, because its translation is "trampled underfoot." Jerusalem will become the permanent city of peace when the Prince of Peace returns to reign there. Until then its destiny holds a long period of being trodden down. "Jerusalem will be trampled by Gentiles until the times of the Gentiles are fulfilled" (Luke 21:24).

Ramsey MacDonald, a former prime minister of England, postulated to another government official the possibility of lasting peace. The latter, an expert on foreign affairs, remarked cynically, "The desire for peace does not necessarily ensure it."

This MacDonald admitted, saying, "Quite true. But neither does the desire for food satisfy your hunger, but at least it gets you started toward a restaurant."[144]

God's people had been hoping for a season of peace for centuries. They possessed a futuristic viewpoint and believed that eventually God would deliver them from their enemies. Following the oppression of Egypt, the wandering in the wilderness, and the conquest of Canaan, not one enemy was left to stand against them. Joshua 21 ends with a season of peace for the children of Israel.

Although they had made a good start in inhabiting everything God had promised, they eventually fell short and faced enemies once again. The very next book in the Bible, Judges, stands in startling contrast to Joshua. The obedient nation falls into rebellion and idolatry only to be defeated time and again in punishment for their disobedience. Permanent peace will elude them until the reign of the Messiah.

LIFT UP ...

God, I'm learning that peace isn't a place, but a person—the Prince of Peace. Although I may suffer tribulation in this world, You are with me and Your presence calms my heart. Please help me to rest in You whether times are good or bad. Amen.

LOOK AT ...

Chapter 21 is the culmination of all the previous history of the Hebrew nation. We see the promises and performance combined, bringing about completion. God had promised to give Abraham's seed the land of Canaan for a possession, and now at last He performed this promise. "Though they had often forfeited the benefit of that promise, and God had long delayed the performance of it, yet at last all difficulties were conquered, and Canaan was their own."[145] The people found rest after deliverance from Pharaoh, journeying in the desert, and confronting their enemies. This rest would last as long as they continued to appropriate God's promises through their obedience.

Isn't that the same for Christians, including you and me? Our experience of peace includes both the covenants of God and our conformity to His commands. Matthew Henry wrote, "The promise of the heavenly Canaan is as sure to all God's spiritual Israel, for it is the promise of him that cannot lie.… This rest continued till they by their own sin and folly put thorns into their own beds and their own eyes."[146] Each of us experiences seasons of victory as well as moments of defeat. Yet God remains faithful through them all. "This is a faithful saying: For if we died with Him, We shall also live with Him. If we endure, We shall also reign with Him.… If we are faithless, He remains faithful; He cannot deny Himself" (2 Tim. 2:11–13). If disobedience has brought you to a season of defeat and attack, repentance spells victory once again. Reunite His promises with your performance today!

READ JOSHUA 21:41–45.

All the cities of the Levites within the possession of the children of Israel were forty-eight cities with their common-lands. Every one of these cities had its common-land surrounding it; thus were all these cities. So the LORD gave to Israel all the land of which He had sworn to give to their fathers, and they took possession of it and dwelt in it. The LORD gave them rest all around, according to all that He had sworn to their fathers. And not a man of all their enemies stood against them; the LORD delivered all their enemies into their hand. Not a word failed of any good thing which the LORD had spoken to the house of Israel. All came to pass.
Joshua 21:41–45

1. Sum up the possessions inherited by the Levites.

2. Explain who the land belonged to and who it was given to.

3. What makes you believe that Israel fully received this gift?

4. Besides property, what else did God give His people?

5. Describe the fate of Israel's enemies.

6. Review the text by circling the word *all*. What makes you believe that God's promises were utterly fulfilled?

LIVE OUT …

7. At last, after battles and betrayal, the children of Israel find rest. Fill in the following chart to discover where your rest is found.

SCRIPTURE	WHERE REST IS FOUND
Psalm 37:7	
Proverbs 29:17	
Jeremiah 6:16	
2 Thessalonians 1:6–7	
Hebrews 4:9–11	

8. Although enemies still existed in the Promised Land, they were no longer a threat to the children of Israel.

   a. List some of your enemies that still exist but no longer pose a threat in your life.

   b. How did God deliver these foes into your hands?

LEARN ABOUT …

1 Common Land

The common land or suburbs extended about one mile in all directions. "Measure outside the city on the east side two thousand cubits, on the south side two thousand cubits, on the west side two thousand cubits, and on the north side two thousand cubits. The city shall be in the middle. This shall belong to them as common-land" (Num. 35:5).

4 Real Estate and Rest

The word *rest* comes from a primitive root meaning "to settle down." It also describes giving comfort, a dwelling place, or being let alone.[147] Possessing the real estate made rest possible. Israelites were no longer nomads dwelling in tents, or illegal aliens living in foreign countries. They could now build homes and settle down.

5 No Enemies?

Although some Canaanites still remained and would eventually become problematic, presently they posed no threat. God promised, "Little by little I will drive them out from before you, until you have increased, and you inherit the land" (Ex. 23:30). Currently, the Hebrews had as much of their possession as they could handle. The enemy was relegated to rugged terrain.

7 Promised Rest

How often do we rest in the promises of God? If He says it, then it will come to pass. God promised Joshua He'd give the nation rest: "Remember the word which Moses the servant of the LORD commanded you, saying, 'The LORD your God is giving you rest and is giving you this land'" (Josh. 1:13).

8 Defeated Foes

Wherever Jesus reigns, all enemies are vanquished. Although our foes still exist, our faithful obedience renders them ineffective. "When He delivers the kingdom to God the Father, when He puts an end to all rule and all authority and power. For He must reign till He has put all enemies under His feet" (1 Cor. 15:24–25).

c. Could they present a threat in the future? How can you ensure their continued defeat?

9. a. Joshua 21 culminates with "all" of God's promises being fulfilled for the children of Israel. Check the boxes that represent "all" of the promises you've experience.

☐ "All things" are possible to God (see Matt. 19:26)

☐ "All things" work together for good (see Rom. 8:28)

☐ "All things" have become new (see 2 Cor. 5:17)

☐ "All things" having an abundance for good works (see 2 Cor. 9:8)

☐ "All things" can be done through Christ who strengthens me (see Phil. 4:13)

☐ "All things" given for us to richly enjoy (see 1 Tim. 6:17)

☐"All things" in my life may glorify God (see 1 Peter 4:11)

b. Journal about one of these promises that you most need to possess. What prevents you from inheriting all of His promises? How will you appropriate all that is yours in Christ?

○ ○ ● ○ ○

It's not uncommon to express pride in our hometown with nicknames and slogans. For instance, New Yorkers coined "The Big Apple" to boast that no apple (city) was bigger or better than theirs. Boston embraces the name "Bean Town" to promote its early trade in sugarcane and molasses used in making the famous Boston baked beans. Chicago residents adopted "The Windy City" to lure tourists to its cool, breezy beaches for summer vacation.

My [Lenya] hometown, Ludington, Michigan, doesn't really have a nickname. But that doesn't mean I'm not proud of its great history.

Father Jacques Marquette landed on the narrow peninsula dividing Pere Marquette Lake and Lake Michigan, putting it on the map. Historically, its main industries grew from its rich natural resources. By 1892, Ludington's lumber industry produced 162 million board feet and 52 million wood shingles. The vast stands of white pine became known as "green gold." After the 1900s, the waterfront grew, along with its maritime history, including large car ferries, turning Ludington into a Great Lakes shipping port. Eventually, three lighthouses were erected, and visitors come from distant places to enjoy the sand dune shores and vast state parks.

We've seen the development of two very special kinds of cities in Israel. The inhabitants of these cities could boast in their hometowns for better reasons than most. First, the cities of refuge offered sanctuary to the misunderstood manslayer; these cities were always open to anyone seeking asylum. Second, the Levite cities provided an inheritance and haven for the priestly tribe. It would have been a privilege to call these cities "my hometown." And more important, these were cities where the God of Israel was welcomed.

LISTEN TO ...

Finding God, you have no need to seek peace, for he himself is your peace.

—*Frances J. Roberts*

Family Feud

Joshua 22

The TV game show *Family Feud* has entertained television audiences for decades. Its original host, Richard Dawson, inaugurated the program in 1977. In the fall of 2006, a new host, actor John O'Hurley (Elaine's boss on *Seinfeld* and a *Dancing with the Stars* veteran), took over hosting duties.

The game revolves around two families who go head-to-head trying to guess how a studio audience responded to questions like "Name the smallest breed of dog." Each question has five potential answers. If they wait too long to answer, a buzzer sounds. The families receive points based on how many people in the audience also answered the same way they did.

The grand prize of $20,000 isn't much, especially when Howie Mandel is giving away nearly $1 million on *Deal or No Deal*, and the family members split it five ways. But if you and your family just want to appear on television and get your thirty minutes of fame, this may be your chance.[148]

In Joshua 22 we see a family feud erupt, and it's not a game. Twelve families go head-to-head over a question about a pile of rocks. No funny game-show host mediates to keep things humorous. The feuding families appoint Phinehas, the son of Eleazar the priest, to mediate. Eventually, everyone wins and the prize of peace was awarded.

In God's family there should be no ongoing family feuds. Jesus is our "Mediator of a better covenant, which was established on better promises" (Heb. 8:6). The lesson for us should be clear. Fighting among the brethren is no game. Before going to war with your brother or sister in Christ, consult the Lord, who is our righteous mediator!

Day 1: Joshua 22:1–6   **OTHER TRIBES TO SETTLE**

Day 2: Joshua 22:7–12   **OTHER SIDE OF THE JORDAN**

Day 3: Joshua 22:13–20   **OTHERS UP IN ARMS**

Day 4: Joshua 22:21–29   **OTHER SIDE OF THE STORY**

Day 5: Joshua 22:30–34   **OTHERWORLDLY ENDING**

DAY 1
Other Tribes to Settle

LIFT UP ...

Lord, thank You for rewarding our faithfulness. I know Your promises always come to pass. You are generous and righteous. Help me to remain faithful to all You have called me to do. Amen.

LOOK AT ...

Last week we focused on some special cities with small boundaries. We learned about two different types: 1) cities of refuge where a manslayer could find sanctuary, and 2) Levitical cities within the boundaries of the other twelve tribes, for Levi's inheritance was the Lord and not land.

After seven long years, the Promised Land had finally been subdued and subdivided. Since the Transjordan tribes had fulfilled their promise to help their brothers conquer their enemies, Joshua commissioned them to return to their inheritance across the river. The wanderers had become warriors. It was time for them to settle down and live in peace. Joshua delivered a farewell-to-arms speech as each tribe departed to its respective home.

All of us experience various seasons in life. Solomon said that there's "a time to kill, And a time to heal; A time to break down, And a time to build up" (Eccl. 3:3). For some of us the transition from war to peace, or brokenness to building, comes with great difficulty. It's difficult to let go of a hurt and move on. The pain becomes too familiar; we can't imagine living without it. Sadly, it starts to define us or justify our bitterness. But the Bible does not allow us to wallow in the past. We are to forget those things that are behind and press forward to what lies ahead.

What about you? Are you continually contentious about something that happened a long time ago? Isn't it time to lay down your weapons and cease from strife? Perhaps God longs to give you a farewell-to-arms speech and is calling you to a season of peace. Listen for His still small voice. He may be whispering, "Let it go!"

LEARN ABOUT ...

1 Obedient

To obey is to carry out the word and will of another, especially God. Biblically the word is related to the idea of hearing. Obedience is a positive, active response to what a person hears. In the Old Testament covenant between God and man, obedience was the basis for knowing God's blessing and favor (see Ex. 19:5; 24:1–8).[149]

3 Orderly

The Transjordan tribes were required to lead the charge for all of the battles in Canaan. In total they had sent forty thousand troops to battle. They had tirelessly assisted their brethren without the benefit of having their wives and children easily accessible. They did not return home without receiving discharge orders.

READ JOSHUA 22:1–6.

Then Joshua called the Reubenites, the Gadites, and half the tribe of Manasseh, and said to them: "You have kept all that Moses the servant of the LORD commanded you, and have obeyed my voice in all that I commanded you. You have not left your brethren these many days, up to this day, but have kept the charge of the commandment of the LORD your God. And now the LORD your God has given rest to your brethren, as He promised them; now therefore, return and go to your tents and to the land of your possession, which Moses the servant of the LORD gave you on the other side of the Jordan. But take careful heed to do the commandment and the law which Moses the servant of the LORD commanded you, to love the LORD your God, to walk in all His ways, to keep His commandments, to hold fast to Him, and to serve Him with all your heart and with all your soul." So Joshua blessed them and sent them away, and they went to their tents. Joshua 22:1–6

1. What word would you use to characterize the Reubenites, the Gadites, and half the tribe of Manasseh with regards to the commands they were given by Moses and Joshua?

2. According to this text and what we've seen in the book of Joshua, describe how they demonstrated their faithfulness to the other tribes. What do you think it must have cost them?

3. As a reminder, read Numbers 32:20–22 and describe what the tribes of Reuben, Gad, and half of Manasseh's tribe had agreed to do.

4. a. What had the Lord given the Israelites after all these years of fighting?

b. How were they assured it was coming?

5. In exchange for keeping their commitment to fight with the Israelites, what were the two and a half tribes allowed to do?

6. As a final admonition, what did Joshua tell them to heed?

7. List the five actions Joshua told them to carry out. (Hint: Look for the verbs.)

LIVE OUT ...

8. The Transjordan tribes had displayed godly characteristics throughout their seven-year service in the Lord's army. How would you describe the highs and lows in your Christian experience (use descriptive words such as obedient, disobedient, ardent love, lukewarm love)?

9. The Transjordan tribes made a huge sacrifice to aid their brothers in the conquest of Canaan; they left family, farms, and fortune. As Christians we must make sacrifices to follow our Commander, Jesus Christ. Read Matthew 10:37–39.

   a. List those whom Jesus deems "not worthy of me."

   b. In your own words explain the proper balance of love between God, man, and self.

   c. Explain how Jesus' concept of loss and gain are different from the values of the world.

   d. How have you experienced this in your life?

LEARN ABOUT ...

6 Ardent

The greatest command of all is to love the Lord your God. Love must be our motive, the source of our emotions. We are instructed that if we love God, we'll keep His commands. Obedience must spring from a relationship with Him. It's not that we obey to earn His love; we obey to express our love to Him.

---

9 Benefits

You can't outgive God. For every subtraction there comes an addition: "Give, and it will be given to you: good measure, pressed down, shaken together, and running over will be put into your bosom. For with the same measure that you use, it will be measured back to you" (Luke 6:38).

LEARN ABOUT ...

10 Balancing Act

Josh McDowell says that rules without relationship equal rebellion. Although God gave Ten Commandments as the rules to live by, He did so out of love not legalism. Jesus said, "If you love Me, keep My commandments" (John 14:15). It's the same with parenting; your children are more likely to obey if they are adored.

10. God counterbalances His rules with the offer of relationship. Laws become stabilized with love. Beside each of the Ten Commandments describe how you believe each law emerged from love.

TEN COMMANDMENTS	TEN CALLS TO COMPASSION
No other gods	For example: God is love
No carved images (idols)	
No taking God's name in vain	
Keep the Sabbath holy (rest)	
Honor your parents	
No murder	
No adultery	
No stealing	
No lying	
No coveting	

∘ ∘ ● ∘ ∘

The Reubenites, Gadites, and half tribe of Manasseh displayed admirable qualities throughout the seven-year conquest of Canaan. Joshua stressed three things in his farewell speech: 1) affirmation of obedience to all that Moses had asked, 2) admiration for faithfulness in fighting alongside their brethren, 3) recommendation to continually love God and follow His commands.

They had sacrificed much to aid their brethren, but now they were rewarded with great blessings. They could rest and return to their families. In addition, they would cross the Jordan with their fair share of the booty from the battles with the Canaanites. Most important, they would leave with the blessings of Joshua and Jehovah.

Frances L. Hess wrote this beautiful poem expressing the balance of sacrifice and blessing.

The Master's will, for this I pray, Whatever it may be!

I do not want to miss Your best; Reveal it, Lord, to me.

My own desires may lead me wrong, I must consult my God;

His counsel will be justified, When all the way I've trod.

O soul of mine, delight in Him! His Word discern, obey!

The plan you seek to know will then unfold from day to day.

We do not live our lives alone: If I am in God's will,

The lives of others will be helped, His purpose to fulfill!

My all, O Lord, I give to You, My body, mind and soul;

May all the days that lie ahead, be under Your control.

LISTEN TO ...

Obedience means marching right on whether we feel like it or not. Many times we go against our feelings. Faith is one thing, feeling is another.

—*Dwight L. Moody*

DAY 2
Other Side of the Jordan

Would you like to volunteer your family to be contestants for *Family Feud?* A family team is made up of a captain and three other family members. The members must be related to the captain by either birth or marriage. In-laws, either current or ex, as well as cousins and de facto relationships are all eligible. All members must be at least sixteen years old. Producers recommend that you watch the show a lot. They suggest you even attend a live recording. However, the main thing they look for is a close, fun family who get on well with one another. Remember, the feud is with the *other* family, not your own![150]

Getting along and having fun sounds good in theory, but we all know that eventually every family faces conflict. During times of stress, family members can quickly turn on one another. On many an episode of *Family Feud* an unkind comment, a look that can kill, or an argument ensues. Then the fun really begins. If you've seen the show, you know Richard Dawson was the master at making a facial expression that spoke a thousand words.

The children of Israel were no different. As the war with outside forces ended, a battle within began. The conflict came when a simple gesture was misunderstood. Before they knew it, battle lines were being drawn.

Have you ever experienced a family feud? It probably began with a petty argument that got blown out of proportion. If only the parties involved had asked questions rather than leaving things unspoken and attributing blame, the family feud could have been averted. The next time you have a squabble, remember that "A soft answer turns away wrath, But a harsh word stirs up anger" (Prov. 15:1).

LIFT UP ...

Lord, I love my family so much. Help me to keep peace within my home and within my family. Help me to be a peacemaker. Don't let me make assumptions, but help me to ask the right questions and resolve conflicts quickly. Amen.

LOOK AT ...

Joshua had given the Transjordan tribes a farewell speech and an admonition for the future to continually serve the Lord with all of their hearts. Imagine how emotional their departure must have been. Soldiers who serve together in battle often develop an intimacy that rivals that of family members. These men had been through much together as they had fought battles and sensed the Lord's hand in helping them conquer the enemy. Now it was time to say good-bye.

But they were not leaving empty-handed. God had promised that they could take the plunder of battle with them: livestock, precious metals, and clothing. As the Reubenites, the Gadites, and the half tribe of Manasseh prepared to cross the Jordan, surely they experienced separation anxiety. What if their brethren forgot about them—or worse, disowned them in the future? Therefore, they decided to build an altar of remembrance. However, when the rest of the children of Israel heard about it, they feared that their brothers had forgotten God's command concerning corporate worship: "Three times in the year all your males shall appear before the Lord GOD" (Ex. 23:17). The tribes west of the Jordan mistakenly believed the Transjordan tribes were setting up their own worship system. The ingredients for a battle were brewing.

Have you ever done something with the best of intentions only to be completely misunderstood? Isn't it an awful feeling? Thankfully, "innocent until proven guilty" stands as one of the cornerstones of our society. Everyone deserves a fair hearing. Before you rush to judgment, make sure you get all the facts.

READ JOSHUA 22:7–12.

Now to half the tribe of Manasseh Moses had given a possession in Bashan, but to the other half of it Joshua gave a possession among their brethren on this side of the Jordan, westward. And indeed, when Joshua sent them away to their tents, he blessed them, and spoke to them, saying, "Return with much riches to your tents, with very much livestock, with silver, with gold, with bronze, with iron, and with very much clothing. Divide the spoil of your enemies with your brethren." So the children of Reuben, the children of Gad, and half the tribe of Manasseh returned, and departed from the children of Israel at

LEARN ABOUT ...

1 Warriors' Reward

Joshua instructed those who went to war to share their booty with those who had remained on the other side of the Jordan to protect their families and cultivate crops. Similarly, David commanded, "As his part is who goes down to the battle, so shall his part be who stays by the supplies; they shall share alike" (I Sam. 30:24).

4 Impressive Altar

The river represented a great divide to the Transjordan tribes. Perhaps they feared the adage "Out of sight, out of mind." Their motive might have been right, but the method was clearly wrong. This monument became a stumbling block to future generations, a substitute for the altar at Shiloh. One was built from faith, the other from fear.

6 Gathering War

The general assembly gathered to legislate how this apostasy would be handled. Surely the nation was weary from war and resisted taking up arms again, especially against their own. Emotions ran hot. They needed to be careful to "'be angry, and do not sin': do not let the sun go down on your wrath" (Eph. 4:26).

Shiloh, which is in the land of Canaan, to go to the country of Gilead, to the land of their possession, which they had obtained according to the word of the LORD by the hand of Moses. And when they came to the region of the Jordan which is in the land of Canaan, the children of Reuben, the children of Gad, and half the tribe of Manasseh built an altar there by the Jordan—a great, impressive altar. Now the children of Israel heard someone say, "Behold, the children of Reuben, the children of Gad, and half the tribe of Manasseh have built an altar on the frontier of the land of Canaan, in the region of the Jordan—on the children of Israel's side." And when the children of Israel heard of it, the whole congregation of the children of Israel gathered together at Shiloh to go to war against them. Joshua 22:7–12

1. Describe what each half of Manasseh's tribe received as their possession.

2. List the riches the tribes were blessed to take with them to share with their brethren.

3. To what country did the children of Reuben, Gad, and the half tribe of Manasseh return, and when had they received it?

4. Describe in detail what these two and a half tribes built when they reached the Jordan.

5. Recount how the information reached the children of Israel and what they heard.

6. Explain how the Israelites responded to this news.

LIVE OUT ...

7. The half tribe of Manasseh was exhorted to share the booty with those who had not gone to battle. God rewarded the warriors as well as those who kept guard over things at home.

   a. List some of the benefits and blessings God has bestowed upon you. Why have you received them?

   b. Choose something from the above list and write about how you will share with another person this week.

8. Have you ever done a right thing the wrong way? The Bible warns, "Do not let your good be spoken of as evil" (Rom. 14:16). Read Romans 14:1–17.

   a. Record the situations Paul considered to be disputes over doubtful things.

   b. What labels does Paul give to the parties on each side of the dispute?

   c. Who alone has the right to judge these disputes fairly?

   d. What arguments does Paul give for living in liberty with those who are different from us?

9. Unchecked rumors quickly lead to division. Unbalanced emotions add fuel to the fire. Solomon warned, "A whisperer separates the best of friends" (Prov. 16:28). Journal about a situation where you were involved in gossip and how it divided the parties involved.

LEARN ABOUT ...

7 Shared Blessings

God called the people to a fast so that they could share with those in need: "Is this not the fast that I have chosen...? Is it not to share your bread with the hungry, And that you bring to your house the poor who are cast out...? Then your light shall break forth like the morning" (Is. 58:6–8).

9 Rumors of War

A gossip is a person who spreads rumors or idle, fruitless tales. The apostle Paul described some of the early believers as "not only idle but gossips and busy-bodies" (I Tim. 5:13). Jesus said, "For every idle word men may speak, they will give account of it in the day of judgment" (Matt. 12:36).[5]

o o ● o o

A family feud in Tacoma, Washington, may have sparked a cruel hoax. Laurie Raye owns a rental property that was trashed after someone placed an ad on Craigslist, an advertising Web site. "In the ad, it said come and take what you want," Raye remarked as she looked over what was left of her home.

As a result, many people pulled up in trucks to remove everything of value, including the kitchen sink, window frames, light fixtures, and appliances. Neighbors say they saw strangers drive up and haul away all sorts of things from the house.

"I'm trying to figure out how Craigslist screens people," says Raye, "and how they verify who's placing the ad."

That's where an already-bizarre story takes a bizarre twist. Raye says she recently evicted the tenant who was living there—her own sister—leading to speculation that Raye's own siblings may be behind the ad. The sibling rivalry is one of the reasons Tacoma police are not looking at this as a criminal case. They say it's a civil matter.[152]

Family feuds are nothing new. The very first family got things started when Cain killed Abel for petty reasons: One gave a more acceptable offering to the Lord. Let's be careful of judging others harshly. Your fallen nature left unchecked is capable of committing heinous crimes. Paul warned, "Let him who thinks he stands take heed lest he fall. No temptation has overtaken you except such as is common to man; but God is faithful, who … will also make the way of escape, that you may be able to bear it" (1 Cor. 10:12–13). Before you retaliate or join a feud, humbly look to God for deliverance and clarity concerning the situation.

LISTEN TO ...

Half the evil in the world is gossip started by good people.

—Unknown

DAY 3

Others Up in Arms

The feud between the Hatfields and the McCoys is so iconic that it has come to stand as a metaphor for disputes between rival parties. The disagreement involved two families along the Kentucky–West Virginia border. Their feud started around the time of the Civil War. It has long been believed that the fighting began when an affluent Hatfield wanted to marry a "poor" McCoy, and the marriage was frowned upon. Some believe the feud was because the Hatfields fought for the South while the McCoys sided with the North. Others believe they battled over the production of moonshine.

Scientists now have a new theory about why the families were up in arms. They believe that a rare genetic condition might have contributed to the feud between the Hatfields and the McCoys. A hereditary genetic disorder called Von Hippel–Lindau disease causes a large number of tumors to form on the adrenal glands of the afflicted patient. This in turn causes the body to produce too much adrenaline and activates a fight-or-flight response in the person who is afflicted. People who have Von Hippel–Lindau disease may have a "short fuse when it comes to getting angry."[153]

Apparently, Von Hippel–Lindau runs in the McCoy family. Could it be that a genetic disease is partly responsible for the family feud? We'll never know exactly why the feud started or why it lasted so long. But we do know the families signed a formal truce in June 2003.

All of humanity suffers from a genetic predisposition to sin. We are sinners by birth and by choice. Even if scientists link every disease (such as alcoholism) to a particular DNA strand or genetic link that plagues us, there's no excuse for sin. Science may explain why we sin or which particular sin we're susceptible to, but it cannot absolve us from sin's consequences. Rather than succumbing to sin, we must overcome it. The Bible tells us to "lay aside every weight, and the sin which so easily ensnares us, and let us run with endurance the race that is set before us, looking unto Jesus, the author and finisher of our faith" (Heb. 12:1–2).

LIFT UP ...

Lord, please give me wisdom in identifying sin, especially in my life. I want to be righteous before You. I don't want rebellion to be part of my relationship with You. Amen.

LOOK AT ...

We've seen the Transjordan tribes depart for their homeland, with full hands and heavy hearts. Sadly, they failed to consult Joshua and the tribal leaders at Shiloh with their concerns of being forgotten or cut off. Foolishly, they erected an "impressive" altar on their side of the Jordan hoping it would be a reminder that they were part of the holy nation of Israel. However, it was immediately perceived as apostasy, and the people gathered at Shiloh determined to go to war. Today we see that they formed a delegation to inquire why the tribes would erect an altar without priestly supervision. Their intervention demonstrated both love and concern for God's holiness.

Wouldn't it be wonderful if the body of Christ functioned with such godly haste and concern when one of our own stumbled into sin? Imagine how those who are fading in faith might be rescued if we cared enough to confront in love. Jesus offered us a template in Matthew 18 to restore erring saints. Have you ever taken God at His word by confronting a loved one over a legitimate grievance? If not, why not? You may be the instrument God uses to bring them back into the fold.

READ JOSHUA 22:13–16.

Then the children of Israel sent Phinehas the son of Eleazar the priest to the children of Reuben, to the children of Gad, and to half the tribe of Manasseh, into the land of Gilead, and with him ten rulers, one ruler each from the chief house of every tribe of Israel; and each one was the head of the house of his father among the divisions of Israel. Then they came to the children of Reuben, to the children of Gad, and to half the tribe of Manasseh, to the land of Gilead, and they spoke with them, saying, "Thus says the whole congregation of the LORD: 'What treachery is this that you have committed against the God of Israel, to turn away this day from following the LORD, in that you have built for

yourselves an altar, that you might rebel this day against the LORD?'"
Joshua 22:13–16

1. Who led the delegation that met with the tribes of Reuben, Gad, and half of Manasseh? What was his position among the children of Israel?

2. Who went with him?

3. Describe what the "whole congregation of the LORD" concluded after hearing of the altar that had been built.

2 Ruling Counsel

Here, ten men and a priest went to explore the case. In the New Testament, the Sanhedrin was the highest ruling body or court among the Hebrews. Headed by the high priest, the Sanhedrin was granted limited authority over certain religious, civil, and criminal matters by the foreign nations that ruled over Israel at various times in its history.[154]

4 Iniquity of Peor

Numbers 25 records that Israel indulged in sexual immorality in Moab. In judgment God sent a plague that destroyed twenty-four thousand because one man flaunted his sin by taking a Moabite woman into his tent. Aaron's son Phinehas killed the man and the woman in righteous indignation, thus ending the plague and earning God's favor.

LOOK AT …

The ruling body of Israel went to inquire about the altar before going to war with the two and a half tribes. Now we see them reminded of past events, which brought dreadful consequence. Let's look at 22:17–20 to learn more.

"Is the iniquity of Peor not enough for us, from which we are not cleansed till this day, although there was a plague in the congregation of the LORD, but that you must turn away this day from following the LORD? And it shall be, if you rebel today against the LORD, that tomorrow He will be angry with the whole congregation of Israel. Nevertheless, if the land of your possession is unclean, then cross over to the land of the possession of the LORD, where the LORD's tabernacle stands, and take possession among us; but do not rebel against the LORD, nor rebel against us, by building yourselves an altar besides the altar of the LORD our God. Did not Achan the son of Zerah commit a trespass in the accursed thing, and wrath fell on all the congregation of Israel? And that man did not perish alone in his iniquity.'" Joshua 22:17–20

4. a. Describe what iniquity Phinehas referred to as a comparison? How long lasting were the consequences? How did the Lord

LEARN ABOUT ...

6 Unclean Land

The term *unclean land* refers to the pagan traditions of the peoples of the land. The counsel implied that these traditions were the reason their brethren erected a pagan altar. Generously, the tribal leaders offered their own inheritance as a solution to this perceived rebellion against the Lord. This was costly, sacrificial love.

---

10 Apostasy

Apostasy is falling away from the faith. Israel fell into repeated backslidings. Jeremiah predicted God's judgment: "Your wickedness will chasten you, and your apostasy will reprove you" (Jer. 2:19 RSV). Other infamous apostates are King Saul (see I Sam. 15:11), Hymenaeus and Alexander (see I Tim. 1:19–20), as well as Demas (see 2 Tim. 4:10).[155]

respond to that sin?

b. What did Phinehas demand, and why?

5. Explain the consequences if they continued in their rebellion.

6. What alternative did he offer if their inherited land was unclean?

7. Against whom did Phinehas believe the tribes had sinned?

8. What recent occurrence did Phinehas recall as another example of God's response to disobedience?

LIVE OUT ...

9. a. The tribal leaders felt the situation was serious enough to confront their erring brothers in complete unity. Read Matthew 18:15–20. Describe the three separate steps we're to take when someone sins against us.

   b. Compare and contrast how sinners are to be treated based on their response.

10. a. The leaders believed that pagan practices had caused apostasy within their brethren. Place a check in the boxes that represent the influences in your life that have led to sin.

   ❏ Novels or magazines   ❏ Television or movies

   ❏ Peer pressure   ❏ Hobbies or habits

   ❏ Financial concerns   ❏ Physical illness

   ❏ Laziness or apathy   ❏ Pride or jealousy

b. Now, journal a prayer asking God to help you tear down your idols. Let Him know which sins easily entrap you. Ask Him to replace your bad habits with godly patterns.

11. The leaders recognized that as the people go, so goes the nation. They wanted to stem the tide of rebellion. Although the prophet Daniel was a righteous man, he humbly confessed the nation's sins as his own. Rewrite Daniel's intercession for Israel into a prayer for the country of your birth.

> O Lord, great and awesome God, who keeps His covenant and mercy with those who love Him, and with those who keep His commandments, we have sinned and committed iniquity, we have done wickedly and rebelled, even by departing from Your precepts and Your judgments.... O Lord, righteousness belongs to You, but to us shame of face.... O Lord, to us belongs shame of face, to our kings, our princes, and our fathers, because we have sinned against You. To the Lord our God belong mercy and forgiveness, though we have rebelled against Him. (Dan. 9:4–9)

o o ● o o

11 National Tragedy

The examples of Peor and Achan suggest that one man's sin might bring national tragedy. God's judgment departs, but "if My people who are called by My name will humble themselves, and pray and seek My face, and turn from their wicked ways, then I will hear from heaven, and will forgive their sin and heal their land" (2 Chron. 7:14).

Mr. and Mrs. Alex Chochrane were killed in a firebomb attack on their home in Wythenshawe, England, after a classmate of their daughter, Lucy, developed an obsessive hatred for the seventeen-year-old girl. The feud between the two families came to a head when Natalie Connor's father, Michael, poured £3 worth of petrol through the Cochrane's letter box, sparking a blaze that killed Mr. and Mrs. Cochrane and left their daughter severely burned.

Sadly, the whole thing could have been averted if the Greater

Manchester Police had acted sooner. They failed to visit the family's home after an unsuccessful arson attack five days earlier. The constable who spoke to Mrs. Cochrane by telephone decided that since the fluid poured on the door had disappeared, there was no evidence remaining so no visit to their home was necessary.

Michael Connor and his ex-wife, Jane, were jailed for life for the double murder, and their daughter, Natalie, was jailed for eleven years after being convicted of two counts of manslaughter.[156]

As Christians, we often view sins of commission as more reprehensible than the sins of omission. Sins of commission are when we do the don'ts in Scripture, such as murder, rape, or robbery. Sins of omission are less visible but no less deadly. They occur when we don't fulfill the dos, such as loving our neighbors, praying for the sick, giving to the needy, or sharing the gospel. Thankfully, Joshua's leaders were faithful to avoid both categories of sin. Because they *did* confront sin and *didn't* bear arms against their neighbors too hastily, the nation was rescued from fiery judgment.

LISTEN TO ...

The church does not lead the world nor echo it; she confronts it. Her note is the supernatural note.

—*Oswald Chambers*

DAY 4

Other Side of the Story

Why is it that misunderstandings seem to occur more frequently than understandings? They occur when we fail to understand something correctly or when we develop a false impression of a situation. Often they arise from our faulty presuppositions. Someone once said, "Communicate in a way that it is impossible to be misunderstood." It seems that is easier said than done, even if you are a great communicator.

C. H. Spurgeon was one of nineteenth-century England's most renowned orators. He tells of a misunderstanding he encountered one day while he walked through the countryside with a dear friend. In the distance the preacher noticed an unusual weather vane on the roof of a barn with the words "GOD IS LOVE" written on it. Spurgeon was offended by the message. He told his friend, "I don't agree with those words. Weather vanes are changeable, but God is constant."

"I don't agree with you about those words Charles," his companion replied. "You misunderstood the meaning. That sign is indicating a truth: Regardless of which way the wind blows, God is love."[157] One sign, but two completely different interpretations.

We've seen that the simple sign the Transjordan tribes erected brought about a great misunderstanding among their brethren. What they intended to be a sign of unity effectively became a symbol of division. So the tribal leaders wisely sent mediators to discover what had motivated the Transjordan tribes. They preferred a peaceful solution and offered a sacrificial compromise. Now it was time for them to listen so that they could clear up the misunderstanding and judge fairly.

LIFT UP ...

Lord, it is easy to jump to conclusions when I don't have all the information. Let me extend grace in uncertain situations just as You have extended grace to me. Help me to be as passionate about finding the truth as I am about following You. Amen.

LOOK AT ...

The delegation presented compelling reasons to avoid apostasy. First and foremost, a pagan altar displayed treachery and a turning away from the Lord. Second, there would be a national backlash as the sins of Peor and Achan had illustrated. Third, if the Transjordan inheritance was dissatisfactory, their brothers would gladly share land west of the Jordan.

Now the children of Reuben, Gad, and half the tribe of Manasseh would reveal their reasons for constructing this impressive altar. They affirmed their devotion to the Lord God. They assured that they had not offered profane sacrifices to false gods. They had acted out of fear—a fear of being forgotten. They desired a tangible witness to remind future generations of their connection to Israel.

Fear is a powerful motivator. Those influenced by fear often rush into actions with tragic results. In fact, it is one of Satan's favorite tools. Therefore, fear stands in opposition to faith. It's been said that fear and faith are mutually exclusive. The Bible is full of "fear nots." Hagar was told by the Lord's angel, "Fear not." After Daniel's traumatic vision, he, too, heard, "Fear not." Jesus longs to calm His timid followers. No matter how daunting your situation, He says the comforting words, "Do not fear, little flock, for it is your Father's good pleasure to give you the kingdom" (Luke 12:32).

READ JOSHUA 22:21–25.

Then the children of Reuben, the children of Gad, and half the tribe of Manasseh answered and said to the heads of the divisions of Israel: "The LORD God of gods, the LORD God of gods, He knows, and let Israel itself know—if it is in rebellion, or if in treachery against the LORD, do not save us this day. If we have built ourselves an altar to turn from following the LORD, or if to offer on it burnt offerings or grain offerings, or if to offer peace offerings on it, let the LORD Himself require an account. But in fact we have done it for fear, for a reason, saying, 'In time to come your descendants may speak to our descendants, saying, "What have you to do with the LORD God of Israel? For the LORD has made the Jordan a border between you and us, you children of Reuben and children of Gad. You have no part in the LORD." So your descendants would make our descendants cease fearing the LORD.'" Joshua 22:21–25

1. The two and a half tribes list a number of wrong reasons for building the altar that would have deserved punishment. Describe those reasons.

2. The tribes believed that God knew their hearts in this matter. What in this passage lets you know they were willing to allow the Israelites to understand them and rightly judge them?

3. What, in fact, was the long-term reason they had built the altar?

LOOK AT ...

The two and a half tribes explained their willingness to suffer the death penalty if they had engaged in idolatry. They also described their fear of being cut off from their brethren by the Jordan River. Let's discover more of their reasoning concerning the altar in 22:26–29.

"Therefore we said, 'Let us now prepare to build ourselves an altar, not for burnt offering nor for sacrifice, but that it may be a witness between you and us and our generations after us, that we may perform the service of the LORD before Him with our burnt offerings, with our sacrifices, and with our peace offerings; that your descendants may not say to our descendants in time to come, "You have no part in the LORD."' Therefore we said that it will be, when they say this to us or to our generations in time to come, that we may say, 'Here is the replica of the altar of the LORD which our fathers made, though not for burnt offerings nor for sacrifices; but it is a witness between you and us.' Far be it from us that we should rebel against the LORD, and turn from following the LORD this day, to build an altar for burnt offerings, for grain offerings, or for sacrifices, besides the altar of the LORD our God which is before His tabernacle." Joshua 22:26–29

LEARN ABOUT ...

1 Death Sentence

The Israelites promised they would follow God and keep His commands or face a death sentence. "Whoever rebels against your command and does not heed your words, in all that you command him, shall be put to death" (Josh. 1:18). If found guilty, the Transjordan tribes would bravely accept their punishment.

4 Witness

Among people where writing is not common, transactions are solidified by tangible memorials or ceremonies. Abraham offered seven lambs to Abimelech to prove he owned the well of Beersheba. Jacob raised a heap of stones to be "a witness," a boundary mark between himself and Laban (see Gen. 21:30; 31:48, 52). That was the Transjordan tribes' intent.[158]

LEARN ABOUT ...

6 Forget Me Not

For the two and a half tribes, separation from God was a fate worse than death. Their replica altar was meant to ensure the future right to cross the river to make sacrifices at the true altar in Shiloh. They did not want their heavenly Father or their earthly brothers to forget them in generations to come.

4. What was the altar *not* intended to do?

5. Note the real purpose of the altar. How valid do you think this reason was? Why?

6. What were they afraid the future generations would say about those living east of the Jordan?

7. Where were offerings and sacrifices to be presented to the Lord at this time?

LIVE OUT ...

8. A crisis was averted because the leaders took the time to listen. Listening is a key component to communication. Using the word HEAR as an acrostic, describe your listening abilities.

   H (For example, hard or healthy?)

   E

   A

   R

9. The Transjordan tribes were willing to be put to death rather than deny the Lord. Fill in the following chart to discover what we must put to death rather than deny Christ.

SCRIPTURE	PUT TO DEATH
Matthew 16:24–26	
Romans 8:13	

SCRIPTURE

Colossians 3:5

1 Peter 3:18

PUT TO DEATH

10. The delegation discovered that their brethren had erected the altar to express their faith rather than deny it. It represented an alliance to God and His people. To build your own monument of remembrance, fill in the twelve stones of faith below with some of the ways God has blessed you. (For example, you might write that He's given you peace in some trial you've faced.)

○ ○ ● ○ ○

Henry Ward Beecher, the son of evangelist Lyman Beecher, was a prominent clergyman, social reformer, and abolitionist during the nineteenth century. His sister, Harriet Beecher Stowe, authored *Uncle Tom's Cabin.* He was once accused of having an affair, but the woman recanted. The Plymouth Church board, where Beecher pastored, held an inquiry and exonerated him of the charges. In 1875 the woman's husband took him to court, but after the jurors deliberated for six days, they couldn't reach a verdict. Henry's wife, Eunice, loyally supported him throughout the ordeal.[159]

Henry Beecher shared an incident from his youth that taught him the key to conflict resolution. One time an enraged acquaintance barged into their home. "He was in a terrible rage, supposing he had a serious grievance against us," recalled Beecher. "As the man aired all of his complaints, my father listened in complete silence. He then said in a low tone, 'You only want to do what is right, don't you?' 'Certainly,' replied the visitor. But he flew into a rage again, restating his charge. Father then inquired gently, 'Brother, you are misinformed, wouldn't you be interested in knowing the true facts in the case?' When calmness was restored, our side of the story was quietly presented. The man cooled down and meekly said, 'Sir, forgive me! I was wrong!' My father had won a great victory. It was a lesson I never forgot, for it gave me an insight into the calming effect of Christian self-control."[160]

The leaders of the tribes listened calmly and rationally before making their final judgment, as well. Solomon wrote, "He who answers a matter before he hears it, It is folly and shame to him" (Prov. 18:13). Do you decide a matter before hearing both sides of the story? If so, that's foolish. How much better to listen with equanimity and make a rational judgment.

LISTEN TO ...

Listening is a magnetic and strange thing, a creative force. The friends who listen to us are the ones we move toward, and we want to sit in their radius. When we are listened to, it creates us, makes us unfold and expand.

—*Karl Augustus Menninger*

DAY 5

Otherworldly Ending

Sure, your kids love each other, but there are times they can't stand each other. Why can't they get along? Well, children don't have the coping skills that adults have. They compete over limited resources such as food and parental attention. And let's face it, sometimes provoking a sibling is just plain fun. Psychologist Dr. George Holden gives these tips to deal with squabbling siblings:

1. **MONITOR THE PROBLEM FROM AFAR:** Eavesdrop to make sure a quarrel doesn't get out of control. But as much as possible, stay out of it. It teaches your kids to work out their own problems.

2. **AVOID TAKING SIDES:** Be impartial, or you'll be accused of favoritism, which leads to jealousy. Avoid laying blame.

3. **DON'T DISMISS CHILDREN'S FEELINGS:** Encourage them to express emotions, since talking about it is better than taking it out physically on a sibling.

4. **DON'T MAKE COMPARISONS:** Comparing inevitably leads to lack of self-worth. Instead, focus on each child's individuality.

5. **STICK TO THE CONSEQUENCES:** Establish punishment (no TV, no friends, no phone, etc.), then follow through if rules are broken. Keeping your word will help them keep theirs.

6. **MAKE INDIVIDUAL TIME FOR EACH CHILD:** Take time to treat them as individuals with distinct identities. It reduces rivalry especially if they're acting up for more attention.[61]

The ruling counsel handled the situation with the tribes east of the Jordan like pros. They didn't take sides, but instead validated the feelings of those involved, avoided comparisons, established consequences, and gave the situation the attention it required. As a result, they had an otherworldly ending: peace and praise unto the Lord.

LIFT UP ...

Lord, let my life be a witness of what You have done. May I encourage others to seek and trust You. I want my children and those who come after me to be drawn to You because of the life I've led. Amen.

LOOK AT ...

Both sides had expressed a zeal for God that was balanced by a desire for peace. Admirably, the delegation did not chastise their brethren for their suspicious actions. They didn't taunt "I told you so." Nor did they seek evidence to prove that the testimony was true. They credited the witnesses as honest and sincere. This revealed that the ambassadors held no preconceived notions or prejudice in the matter.

When the delegation returned to report the matter to their anxious brethren, all heaven broke loose. The Israelites laid down their arms as well as their angry intentions. They buried the hatchet and decided not to speak of the matter again. What's more, they agreed to leave the altar intact as a witness between themselves and God.

We can learn a great deal from these godly leaders. How often do we enter a conflict with bias or downright bigotry? We all view what happens in life through the lens of our own past. But if we are to judge fairly, we must view things from God's point of view. We must be willing to believe what sincere people tell us without reproach or further research. And after a situation is resolved, we should make a covenant with our lips to refrain from mentioning the conflict again. Imagine how both parties in a conflict would feel if we treated one another in this manner!

READ JOSHUA 22:30–34.

Now when Phinehas the priest and the rulers of the congregation, the heads of the divisions of Israel who were with him, heard the words that the children of Reuben, the children of Gad, and the children of Manasseh spoke, it pleased them. Then Phinehas the son of Eleazar the priest said to the children of Reuben, the children of Gad, and the children of Manasseh, "This day we perceive that the LORD is among us, because you have not committed this treachery against the LORD. Now you have delivered the children of Israel out of the hand of the LORD." And Phinehas the son of Eleazar the priest, and the rulers, returned from the children of Reuben and the children of Gad, from the land of Gilead to the land of Canaan, to the children of Israel, and brought back word to them. So the thing pleased the children of Israel, and the children of Israel blessed God; they spoke no more of going against them in battle, to destroy the land where the children of Reuben and Gad dwelt. The children of

Reuben and the children of Gad called the altar, Witness, "For it is a witness between us that the LORD is God." Joshua 22:30–34

1. How did Phinehas and the rulers of the congregation react when they heard the response?

2. Who did Phinehas conclude was among them?

3. Because there was no treachery, what were they delivered from?

4. Where did Phinehas and the rest of the delegation return to?

5. What plans did the children of Israel abandon after hearing there was no rebellion or treachery?

6. What did they name the altar? Why?

LIVE OUT ...

7. The words that the Transjordan tribes spoke were pleasing to their brethren. Our words can hurt or heal. Write down examples of things you've said that fit into each column.

HEALING WORDS   **HURTFUL WORDS**

8. a. We hope you know what it's like to sense God's presence. Fill in the following chart to discover the emotions others have felt

LEARN ABOUT ...

1 Pleasant Words

The word *pleasant* means agreeable, enjoyable, or socially acceptable. Many things bring pleasure, but one of the greatest is harmony in the home. David wrote, "Behold, how good and how pleasant it is For brethren to dwell together in unity! ... There the LORD commanded the blessing—Life forevermore" (Ps. 133:1, 3).

2 God's Presence

Matthew Henry wrote, "They looked upon their innocence as a token of God's presence, especially when they found that what was done was so far from being an indication of their growing cool to the altar of God that, on the contrary, it was a fruit of their zealous affection to it."[162]

3 God's Hand

The expression "hand of God" refers to His great power. Often it emphasizes His power in creation (see Ps. 8:6). Sometimes it refers to His power in judgment (see Ruth 1:13). However, God may also extend His hand to express His mercy and forgiveness (see Ps. 37:24).[163] In this text it refers to His open rather than closed hand.

LEARN ABOUT …

7 Nourishing Words

"The tongue that brings healing is a tree of life, but a deceitful tongue crushes the spirit" (Prov. 15:4 NIV). Our words can bring either life or death to those who hear them. What a gift to nourish hungry hearts with the "tree of life" by bearing the fruit of healing. What nourishing words will you utter today?

---

9 Good News

The way we deliver a message is important. Solomon wrote, "Like the cold of snow in time of harvest Is a faithful messenger to those who send him, For he refreshes the soul of his masters" (Prov. 25:13). Are you known as a "refresher of the soul" who brings a drink of "good news" at just the right moment?

in God's presence. Think about the reasons for this variety of responses.

SCRIPTURE	FEELINGS IN GOD'S PRESENCE
Job 23:15–16	
Psalm 16:11	
Isaiah 6:1–5	
1 Corinthians 1:27–29	

b. Journal about a time when you felt God invade your space. How did it make you feel? What was your response?

9. a. The Israelites at Shiloh were relieved when they received great news from the faithful delegation. Solomon warned, "A wicked messenger falls into trouble, But a faithful ambassador brings health" (Prov. 13:17). Tell about a time you received either a wicked or faithful messenger. What were the results?

b. Examine your own life. Have you ever been a wicked or faithful messenger? How did your involvement affect the situation?

○ ○ ● ○ ○

Healthy debate can be a good thing. However, when opposing parties refuse to budge and become immovable, debate can lead to division. Anna's story illustrates the point.

One day, Anna was happily playing in the street when she was hit by a bus and rushed to the hospital. Her divorced parents stood on either side of the bed. The scene was eerily reminiscent of their estrangement—he standing on one side; she on the other. With Anna's last bit of strength, the girl painfully raised her arm from under the hospital sheet and reached for her father. "Daddy," she whispered, "give me your hand." She painfully turned toward her mother: "Mommy," she said, "give me your hand." With one last effort, she drew them together.[164]

Anna's heart reflects Christ on the cross. In His death throes, Jesus reached out His hands on the cross to draw us to God. He stretched one hand to the Father and one hand to humanity. Through the ultimate sacrifice, Christ drew us together.

In the same way, though they faced estrangement, the Israelites reached out in peace to their brothers. Perhaps a debate has turned into a division with someone in your life. Is Jesus nudging you to make peace with them? Remember His words: "Blessed are the peacemakers, For they shall be called sons of God" (Matt. 5:9). When you stretch out your hand in a gesture of peace, you will be blessed.

LISTEN TO ...

Take everything that comes into your life as being from the hand of God, not from the hand of man.

—*Madame Jeanne Marie de la Mothe Guyon*

Parting Is Such Sweet Sorrow

Joshua 23—24

Whether we are saying good-bye to a nation's leader who has led us through good times and bad, or bidding adieu to a lover who holds the key to our heart, Shakespeare was right when he put the words in Juliet's mouth, "Parting is such sweet sorrow." During the famous balcony scene, Juliet said good-bye to Romeo with sweet anticipation that she would see her beloved on the morrow. Thus, their parting was bittersweet. They had no idea that tragedy lay just around the corner.

This week's lesson is also touchingly bittersweet as we read Joshua's farewell address to his beloved nation. Surely the people's hearts were filled with sorrow as they bid good-bye to their longtime leader. They must have wondered who would lead them into tomorrow. They must have wondered how their government would function. Their hearts must have filled with grief as they faced a future without the steadfast leadership of Joshua the son of Nun. But as children of the living God, surely they had hope. They knew that God had brought them this far and would provide for them in the future. As a good leader, Joshua made sure the people knew how to move into the future without him. The people would be comforted so long as they remembered and heeded his words of advice.

As those who follow the living God, we can trust that parting through death is only temporary—it is simply a sweet sorrow until we meet in God's good and perfect time. The challenge is to faithfully live according to God's standards while we walk on earth.

Day 1: Joshua 23:1–10	HOLD FAST TO THE LORD
Day 2: Joshua 23:11–16	LOVE THE LORD
Day 3: Joshua 24:1–13	REMEMBER THE LORD
Day 4: Joshua 24:14–28	FEAR THE LORD
Day 5: Joshua 24:29–33	SERVE THE LORD

DAY 1

Hold Fast to the Lord

LIFT UP ...

Lord, like Joshua, help me to faithfully serve You all the days of my life. Help me to pass on Your will and Your ways to the next generation. Amen.

LOOK AT ...

Ten to twenty years had passed since the conquest and distribution of the Promised Land. The people had babies, built homes, and planted crops. It was time for Joshua to bid farewell to his people. His first act was to call for the leaders and remind them of their duty to hold fast to the Lord.

Following in the tradition of Jacob and Moses, Joshua reminded the people of what the Lord had done for them. He clearly wanted the nation to remain faithful to the living God, especially since the people had failed to drive out all of their enemies. Joshua's words hold true for us today. We are surrounded by those things the world idolizes. Will we cling to God or follow the ways of the world?

JOSHUA 23:1–5.

Now it came to pass, a long time after the LORD had given rest to Israel from all their enemies round about, that Joshua was old, advanced in age. And Joshua called for all Israel, for their elders, for their heads, for their judges, and for their officers, and said to them: "I am old, advanced in age. You have seen all that the LORD your God has done to all these nations because of you, for the LORD your God is He who has fought for you. See, I have divided to you by lot these nations that remain, to be an inheritance for your tribes, from the Jordan, with all the nations that I have cut off, as far as the Great Sea westward. And the LORD your God will expel them from before you and drive them out of your sight. So you

*shall possess their land, as the L*ORD *your God promised you."* Joshua 23:1–5

1. Describe what came to pass and when it came to pass.

2. a. Who did Joshua gather together? Why?

   b. How did he describe himself? Why did that matter?

3. Describe what they had seen God do and why God had done this.

4. Describe the tribes' inheritance.

5. a. How would God help them possess their inheritance?

   b. Why was Joshua telling them all this?

LOOK AT ...

Joshua reminded the leaders of what God had done in the past so they could move forward into the future. Now let's look at 23:6–10 to hear more of Joshua's instructions to the leaders about courageously possessing the land of their inheritance.

_____

*"Therefore be very courageous to keep and to do all that is written in the Book of the Law of Moses, lest you turn aside from it to the right hand or to the left, and lest you go among these nations, these who remain among you. You shall not make mention of the name of their gods, nor cause anyone to swear by them; you shall not serve them nor bow down to them, but you shall hold fast to the L*ORD *your God, as you have done to this day. For the L*ORD *has driven out from before you great and strong nations; but as for you, no one has been able to stand against you to this day. One man of you shall chase a*

LEARN ABOUT ...

I Rest

To rest is to settle down at some particular place; to be quiet or rest after work; to rest from one's enemies, from trouble, or in death. It can mean to leave at rest or allow to remain: "Wisdom rests in the heart of him who has understanding" (Prov. 14:33).[165]

_____

3 Refuge

In earlier lessons, we learned that God had patiently waited over four hundred years before allowing the Israelites to enter the Promised Land. When Joshua and his troops entered the land it was because the iniquity of the inhabitants was complete (see Gen. 15:16). Now we learn that God rebuked the Canaanites while offering refuge to the Israelites.

LEARN ABOUT ...

7 Reverence

Two of the Ten Commandments warned against idolatry: "You shall have no other gods before Me. You shall not make for yourself a carved image" (Ex. 20:3–4). God wanted the people to revere Him rather than follow false gods. Joshua knew that the Canaanites could cause the Israelites to lose their fear of the Lord.

9 Refreshment

Here, the word *rest* is used for Sabbath. This rest speaks of finding rest in God. We will fully rest in heaven but can enter into divine rest now through prayer, reading Scripture, and worship; finding peace and joy through our relationship with God.[166]

10 Revenge

Even uttering the word *revenge* leaves a sour taste in the mouth. Thankfully, when we follow God, we don't need to seek revenge in the midst of a battle. God is the one who metes out perfect justice: "Do not avenge yourselves, but rather give place to wrath; for it is written, 'Vengeance is Mine, I will repay'" (Rom. 12:19).

thousand, for the LORD your God is He who fights for you, as He promised you." Joshua 23:6–10

6. "Therefore" what did Joshua admonish the leaders to be? What would happen if they were not?

7. List the four things the Israelites *should not* do with the Canaanite gods and the one thing they *should* do.

YOU SHALL NOT　　　　　　　　　　**YOU SHALL**

8. With God on their side, describe how the Israelites would measure up to the enemy.

LIVE OUT ...

9. a. Read Hebrews 4:8–10. Did Joshua provide his people lasting rest? Why or why not?

   b. Based on this passage, explain how Jesus—our Joshua—provides a permanent rest for His people.

   c. Describe some ways in which you have experienced this rest.

10. Joshua reminded the leaders that God had fought many battles on their behalf. Journal about some of the battles God has fought for you as you have studied the book of Joshua. How has He shown Himself strong and just on your behalf?

11. Joshua warned the leaders against the sin of idolatry. Though our idols may look different from the idols of ancient Canaan, they still exist today. Talk about what idols exist in modern society and how they lure people into worshipping them today. Have you ever been tempted to bow down to these idols? How did you break their spell?

○ ○ ● ○ ○

Martin Luther wrote "A Simple Way to Pray" because he believed that if Christians prayed the Ten Commandments, they would not fall into the sins that so easily beset us. Concerning idolatry he wrote:

> I am the Lord your God.… You shall have no other gods before me.… Here I earnestly consider that God expects and teaches me to trust him sincerely in all things and that it is his most earnest purpose to be my God.…
>
> Second, I give thanks for his infinite compassion by which he has come to me in such a fatherly way and, unasked, unbidden, and unmerited, has offered to be my God, to care for me, and to be my comfort, guardian, help, and strength in every time of need. We poor mortals have sought so many gods and would have to seek them still if he did not enable us to hear him openly tell us in our own language that he intends to be our God. How could we ever—in all eternity—thank him enough!
>
> Third, I confess and acknowledge my great sin and ingratitude for having so shamefully despised such sublime teachings and such a precious gift through-out my whole life, and for having fearfully provoked his wrath by countless acts of idolatry. I repent of these and ask for his grace.
>
> Fourth, I pray and say, "O my God and Lord, help me by thy grace to learn and understand thy commandments more fully every day and to live by them in sincere confidence… Amen, dear Lord and Father. Amen."[167]

LISTEN TO ...

Idolatry is not only the adoration of images ... but also trust in one's own righteousness, works and merits, and putting confidence in riches and power.

—*Martin Luther*

DAY 2
love the lord

General Douglas MacArthur fought in three wars and played a prominent role in the Pacific theater in World War II. For a tough old soldier, his farewell speech to the West Point cadets in 1962 was beautifully poignant:

> The shadows are lengthening for me. The twilight is here. My days of old have vanished—tone and tints. They have gone glimmering through the dreams of things that were. Their memory is one of wondrous beauty, watered by tears and coaxed and caressed by the smiles of yesterday. I listen then, but with thirsty ear, for the witching melody of faint bugles blowing reveille, of far drums beating the long roll.
>
> In my dreams I hear again the crash of guns, the rattle of musketry, the strange, mournful mutter of the battlefield. But in the evening of my memory I come back to West Point. Always there echoes and re-echoes: Duty, Honor, Country.
>
> Today marks my final roll call with you. But I want you to know that when I cross the river, my last conscious thoughts will be of the Corps, and the Corps, and the Corps.
>
> I bid you farewell.[168]

In his final speech, General Joshua knew that he, too, was calling the final roll call. Joshua also reminded his troops of duty, honor, and country. But he also reminded them of the cement that could hold the people together once he was gone—love for the Lord. He solemnly reminded his troops that the true Commander would never leave nor retire. He asked them to focus on the Lord, the Lord, the Lord.

LIFT UP ...

Lord, You are so good to us when we are faithful to love and serve You with our lives. Your justice is certain when we turn away from You. Help me to live in obedience to You. Amen.

LOOK AT ...

We've seen Joshua issue a solemn warning against idolatry. In this portion of Scripture, we see him continue his speech to the council and issue a solemn warning against intermarriage with the people of the nations remaining in the land.

Clearly Joshua knew he was dying, but he did not indulge in self-pity or self-eulogy. Instead, he kept his focus on the people he had led these many years. As a spiritual father he wanted to make sure they understood the clear consequences of their behavior. In decisive language, he spelled out what would happen if the Israelites failed to love the Lord and were drawn into marriage with unbelievers and away from the Lord. Let's learn the lesson from this passage: God has called us to be people who are separate from the world. Let's not compromise by making "marriages of convenience" with the world and leaving our true love.

READ JOSHUA 23:11–13.

"Therefore take careful heed to yourselves, that you love the LORD your God. Or else, if indeed you do go back, and cling to the remnant of these nations—these that remain among you—and make marriages with them, and go in to them and they to you, know for certain that the LORD your God will no longer drive out these nations from before you. But they shall be snares and traps to you, and scourges on your sides and thorns in your eyes, until you perish from this good land which the LORD your God has given you." Joshua 23:11–13

1. Describe what the Israelites should "therefore" do.

2. Describe what God would no longer do if the Israelites failed to heed His words.

3. Describe the painful effect the Canaanites would have on the Israelites if they intermarried with them.

4. What prophecy did Joshua make about Israel?

LOOK AT ...

Joshua made a dire prophecy concerning Israel's fate if they chose to intermarry with the Canaanites. Now let's see what he had to say about his own destiny in 23:14–16.

———————

"Behold, this day I am going the way of all the earth. And you know in all your hearts and in all your souls that not one thing has failed of all the good things which the LORD your God spoke concerning you. All have come to pass for you; not one word of them has failed. Therefore it shall come to pass, that as all the good things have come upon you which the LORD your God promised you, so the LORD will bring upon you all harmful things, until He has destroyed you from this good land which the LORD your God has given you. When you have transgressed the covenant of the LORD your God, which He commanded you, and have gone and served other gods, and bowed down to them, then the anger of the LORD will burn against you, and you shall perish quickly from the good land which He has given you."
Joshua 23:14–16

5. What was Joshua's imminent fate?

6. Recount what the council knew in their hearts and souls.

7. "Therefore" describe what would happen when the Israelites transgressed their covenant with God. How could they be assured this would happen?

LEARN ABOUT ...

1 Love

The Old Testament word *love* can depict the attachment of a servant toward a master. It also speaks of familial love such as a father toward his son. In some cases the word is used to describe the relationship between friends or in a political relationship between a vassal and his subordinate.[169]

———————

4 Leave

The Israelites had already experienced one period of captivity in Egypt. Now Joshua was predicting a second period if the children of Israel did not keep God's Word and fell into idolatry. Sadly, during the time of the kings, Joshua's words were fulfilled and the people were taken captive to Assyria and Babylon.

———————

5 Live

Knowing his life was ending, Joshua spent his final hours warning others to love the Lord and obey God's Word. We don't know when death will come, but we can treat each day as if it is our last, proclaiming the good news of the gospel. When we meet the Lord may He say, "Well done, good and faithful servant" (Matt. 25:21).

8 Love One Another

Love is the godly virtue held in highest esteem: "Now abide faith, hope, love, these three; but the greatest of these is love" (I Cor. 13:13). When we love one another, we are most like God because "God is love" (I John 4:16). The absence of love invalidates all claims to the true Christianity.

9 Lovely Promises

God's promises are gifts graciously bestowed, not knick-knacks secured through negotiation. You don't have to beg your heavenly Father for the things you need—He knows you need them. In the New Testament, promises most often refer to our eternal inheritance. One of His best promises was to send the Holy Spirit.

LIVE OUT ...

8. a. Joshua reminded his people to love the Lord. Fill in the following chart to discover how Jesus, our Joshua, also commands us to love the Lord.

SCRIPTURE	HOW TO LOVE THE LORD
Matthew 22:37–40	
John 14:15	
John 15:9	
John 21:17	

   b. Talk about some of the ways you have shown your love for the Lord throughout this study in Joshua.

   c. How will you show your love for Him in the future?

9. Joshua reminded the council that "not one good thing has failed" of all that God had promised the people. Think back over the study of Joshua and remember some of the promises God has given to you. List them, and beside each one write how God has answered: Yes or Wait.

GOD'S PROMISE TO ME	GOD'S ANSWER

10. Joshua realized it wasn't a matter of *if* but *when* the people intermarried and served other gods. Read Luke 22:31–33 and talk about Jesus Christ's compassion toward those of us who will fail. (Hint: Key in on the word *when* in Christ's discussion with Peter.)

○ ○ ● ○ ○

What a fearful thing to hear that the Lord's anger would be directed at His own people. After all, Israel had seen God fight the Canaanites by tearing down city walls, sending hailstones from heaven, and making the sun stand still. Surely the people would heed Joshua's words and follow the Lord—wouldn't they? Sadly, they did not. Israel fell into a cycle of sin, continually falling away from the Lord until their captivity. This is a somber warning for us all.

The story is told that the apostle John visited a church and saw a young man filled with God's love. John placed the young man into a local pastor's care. The young man was baptized and lived as a Christian. Sadly, the young man fell into bad company and was corrupted by their ways. He grew so dishonest that he became captain of a band of robbers.

Sometime afterward, John returned and inquired about his young friend. When the pastor told him how far he had fallen from God, John went and allowed himself to be captured by the robbers. "Take me to your captain," John demanded. The young robber saw John coming and fled in shame. John cried out, "My son, fear not; Christ has sent me." Hearing this, the young man stopped and wept bitterly. John prayed for the young man and brought him back to the fellowship of Christians. Though we are all one step away from the Lord, thankfully we are only one step back *to* our loving God.

LISTEN TO ...

So many people think themselves no longer capable to be Christians because they are unchaste, weak, and backsliding. But in fact there is a far greater number of people who will never be Christians because they think themselves just, honorable, and pure.

—*Louis Evely*

DAY 3

Remember the Lord

Beloit College releases a "MindsetList," offering insight into the worldview of kids entering college. Here are some things to know about the Class of 2009:

> Andy Warhol, Liberace, Jackie Gleason, and Lee Marvin have always been dead.
>
> They don't remember when "cut and paste" involved scissors.
>
> Pay-Per-View television has always been an option.
>
> They never had the fun of being thrown into the back of a station wagon with six others.
>
> Jimmy Swaggart and Jim Bakker have never preached on television.
>
> Voicemail has always been available.
>
> "Whatever" is not part of a question but an expression of apathy.
>
> For daily caffeine emergencies, Starbucks has always been around the corner.
>
> Michael Jackson has always been creepy, not cool.
>
> The Starship *Enterprise* has always looked dated.[170]

Trying to relate to an eighteen-year-old by talking about Liberace is clearly ineffective. So how do we talk to these kids who share such different mind-sets from us? Beginning a dialogue is the most important part.

Joshua called all the Israelites together to remind them of the Lord's faithfulness. Though he knew many would fall away, he planted the lessons deep in their hearts so they could pass them on to the next generation.

We have the same responsibility to the generations following us. Let's tell them what the Lord has done in the past so they can look to Him for strength in the future.

LIFT UP ...

Lord, there are many reminders of what You have done for us. Please keep me mindful of all that You have done. Thank You for sending Your Son to deliver us from darkness. Amen.

LOOK AT ...

We've seen Joshua gather the elders, heads, judges, and officers together for his official farewell address. Many scholars believe that the first farewell speech took place at Shiloh and that following it God granted Joshua more time on earth in order to give another farewell speech that included not only the leaders of the people, but the tribes as well. He called them to Shechem, a central location in the country and home to a natural amphitheater. This time he spoke in the prophetic voice on God's behalf, using God's very words.

Shechem is famous in the history of the patriarchs. Abraham settled in Shechem at the terebinth tree of Moreh when he first came to Canaan (see Gen. 12:6–7). The patriarchs, including Joseph, were buried at Shechem. Since Shechem lay between Mt. Ebal and Mt. Gerizim where Joshua had made a covenant with the people, it was an appropriate place for him to speak to them again about his longing that they remember the Lord.

READ JOSHUA 24:1–7.

Then Joshua gathered all the tribes of Israel to Shechem and called for the elders of Israel, for their heads, for their judges, and for their officers; and they presented themselves before God. And Joshua said to all the people, "Thus says the LORD God of Israel: 'Your fathers, including Terah, the father of Abraham and the father of Nahor, dwelt on the other side of the River in old times; and they served other gods. Then I took your father Abraham from the other side of the River, led him throughout all the land of Canaan, and multiplied his descendants and gave him Isaac. To Isaac I gave Jacob and Esau. To Esau I gave the mountains of Seir to possess, but Jacob and his children went down to Egypt. Also I sent Moses and Aaron, and I plagued Egypt, according to what I did among them. Afterward I brought you out. Then I brought your fathers out of Egypt, and you came to the sea; and the Egyptians pursued your fathers with chariots and horsemen to the Red Sea. So they cried out to the LORD; and He put darkness between you and the Egyptians, brought the sea upon them, and covered them. And your eyes saw what I did in Egypt. Then you dwelt in the wilderness a long time.'" Joshua 24: 1–7

1. List those who assembled in Shechem.

LEARN ABOUT ...

2 Homeless

Joshua reminded the Israelites that Abraham's father, Terah, had "served other gods" but that God had called Abraham to leave his home to serve God alone. The worship of one supreme God is an important characteristic of the Hebrew people's worship system. One of their central tenets is Deuteronomy 6:4: "Hear, O Israel: The LORD our God, the LORD is one!"

---

7 Hornets

Swarms of hornets first appeared when the Israelites first encountered Sihon and Og, the two kings of the Amorites. Apparently, God continued to use this tactic throughout the battles. He had promised: "I will send hornets before you, which shall drive out the Hivite, the Canaanite, and the Hittite from before you" (Ex. 23:28).

2. Describe how Terah, Abraham, and Nahor lived before God led Abraham to Canaan.

3. Recount the history of Abraham's descendants.

4. Describe how God liberated His people from slavery in Egypt and what happened after they were freed.

LOOK AT ...

Through Joshua, God reminded the people of their history from the time of Abraham to the time of the exodus and on to the history of the conquest. Let's read more in 24:8–13.

"And I brought you into the land of the Amorites, who dwelt on the other side of the Jordan, and they fought with you. But I gave them into your hand, that you might possess their land, and I destroyed them from before you. Then Balak the son of Zippor, king of Moab, arose to make war against Israel, and sent and called Balaam the son of Beor to curse you. But I would not listen to Balaam; therefore he continued to bless you. So I delivered you out of his hand. Then you went over the Jordan and came to Jericho. And the men of Jericho fought against you—also the Amorites, the Perizzites, the Canaanites, the Hittites, the Girgashites, the Hivites, and the Jebusites. But I delivered them into your hand. I sent the hornet before you which drove them out from before you, also the two kings of the Amorites, but not with your sword or with your bow. I have given you a land for which you did not labor, and cities which you did not build, and you dwell in them; you eat of the vineyards and olive groves which you did not plant.'" Joshua 24:8–13

5. Describe the Israelites' encounter with the Amorites and the role God played in their victory.

6. Recount what happened when Balak came against Israel and God's role in the deliverance.

7. Describe how God conquered the other nations on behalf of Israel. How much credit did He give to the people?

8. List the things God gave them for which they did not labor, did not build, and did not plant.

LIVE OUT ...

9. God called Abraham from idolatry to follow the one true God. The New Testament reveals in more depth that God is One in three Persons. Read the passages below and explain what you learn about God as three Persons: Father, Son, and Spirit.
   Genesis 1:1–2
   John 1:1–5
   John 14:13–17

10. God recounted His mighty deeds for Israel through Joshua. Over and over He used the pronoun *I* connected with a verb—for example, "I brought," "I destroyed," etc. Go back to today's passage and underline all of the *I* passages concerning what God had done for Israel. Talk about why you think He emphasized His actions on their behalf.

11. Now write your own personal history with God, not you, as the central character. Try to look through His eyes and see how He has led you where you are today. (For example, "I saw she was lonely and I rescued her.")

LEARN ABOUT ...

8 Homes

Everything was ready for the people when they reached the Promised Land. The fields were plowed and planted, the cities were built. When they first entered the land, there was even a harvest so they could eat of the fruit of the land. Any prosperity Israel achieved was because of God's good hand.

9 Triunity

The Judeo-Christian tradition is monotheistic at its core. God is the one true God. Yet woven throughout the Bible we see that God is also one God manifested in three Persons: Father, Son, and Holy Spirit. The triune God is united in will, purpose, holiness, and love. Christianity is both monotheistic and Trinitarian.

11 I Am

God revealed Himself to Moses as "I AM WHO I AM" (Ex. 3:14). This simple yet profound name of God encapsulates the essence of God. He is all we need. He will be who He will be. He alone defines Himself. He is never changing. He is everlasting. He is under no one's orders. He is God and reigns supreme.

○ ○ ● ○ ○

Little Timmy's mother faithfully sent him to Sunday school every week, but she rarely talked to him about God the rest of the time. One week, she asked him what he learned in Sunday school. He said, "Well, Mom, today we learned about the time Moses was leading the people of Israel out of captivity in Egypt across the Red Sea. They got to the Red Sea, and Moses realized the Israelites couldn't make their way over. So he asked the Israeli corp of engineers to erect a pontoon bridge over the Red Sea. Then all the people of Israel walked over that pontoon bridge. But when the Egyptians got there, they sent in their tanks and their guns and all their heavy artillery and they sank in the mud. So Moses had the Israeli air force come over, and they bombed them and they wiped out all the Egyptians!"

The mother was astounded and said, "Is that really what they taught you in Sunday school this morning?"

Timmy said, "Well, not exactly. But if I told you what our teacher told us, you'd never believe it!"

Do you live your life as if you believe in miracles? Do you tell your children and grandchildren about the miracles God has performed, not just in the Bible, but in your own life? Perhaps what is lacking in our culture is a sense of the wonder of God. Let's recapture the beauty of knowing that the great I AM is alive and well and working wonders in our lives.

LISTEN TO ...

Those who cannot remember the past are doomed to repeat it.

—George Santayana

DAY 4
Fear the Lord

Have you ever wondered what you would do if you were persecuted for your faith? Would you, like Peter, deny the Lord? Or would you be able to stand strong in your convictions and face the wrath of the world?

In AD 304, three sisters named Irene, Chione, and Agape learned the depths of their faith when they faced persecution. The Roman Emperor Diocletian was virulently anti-Christian and sought to persecute anyone who proclaimed faith in Christ. He deprived citizens of the right to read Scripture. Anyone found proclaiming the gospel or reading God's Word would be sentenced to death.

The sisters retreated from the town of Thessalonica to a nearby mountain cave with parchments filled with God's Word. They gave themselves over to a quiet life of prayer. Legend has it that an old woman brought them food, but a robber followed her and turned the women over to authorities, thinking they had treasure hidden in the cave.

When Agape stood before Dalatius the governor, she was asked whether she would obey the laws imposed by Rome. Her reply was firm: "Not any laws that command the worship of idols and devils." For this defiance, she was burned to death.

Our society is growing more and more hostile to the Word of God. Will we have the faith and the bravery to take a stand for what we believe in? Will we proclaim Christ regardless of the consequences? Truly, we have nothing to fear when we fear the Lord.

LIFT UP ...

Lord, Your awesome and mighty nature strikes fear in my heart. I respect who You are and what You are able to do. Please bless my desire to obey You always. Amen.

LOOK AT ...

Yesterday we saw Joshua end his prophetic message from the Lord reminding the people of

His works on their behalf. Now we see Joshua challenge the people in his own words to fear the Lord and serve Him by putting away foreign gods.

The fear of the Lord is a strand of theology that runs throughout Scripture. This fear does not mean simple fear as in terror. Rather, it means to stand in awe of a person of greater standing. It means that we recognize that the Lord is far superior in every aspect and that we give Him the respect and honor He is due. The Proverbs tell us that "the fear of the LORD is the beginning of knowledge" (Prov. 1:7). Only by fearing God do we grow in the wisdom and understanding of Him.

READ JOSHUA 24:14–18.

"Now therefore, fear the LORD, serve Him in sincerity and in truth, and put away the gods which your fathers served on the other side of the River and in Egypt. Serve the LORD! And if it seems evil to you to serve the LORD, choose for yourselves this day whom you will serve, whether the gods which your fathers served that were on the other side of the River, or the gods of the Amorites, in whose land you dwell. But as for me and my house, we will serve the LORD." So the people answered and said: "Far be it from us that we should forsake the LORD to serve other gods; for the LORD our God is He who brought us and our fathers up out of the land of Egypt, from the house of bondage, who did those great signs in our sight, and preserved us in all the way that we went and among all the people through whom we passed. And the LORD drove out from before us all the people, including the Amorites who dwelt in the land. We also will serve the LORD, for He is our God." Joshua 24:14–18

1. According to Joshua, fearing the Lord meant serving the Lord. Give some examples of how the people could show they genuinely feared the Lord.

2. What choice did Joshua offer to the people?

3. What choice had Joshua already made?

4. Recount the reasons why the Israelites chose the Lord as their God.

LOOK AT ...

Joshua entered into a dialogue with the people encouraging them to choose which god they would serve. The people of Israel promised to serve the Lord their God. Let's read the rest of this conversation in 24:19–28.

But Joshua said to the people, "You cannot serve the LORD, for He is a holy God. He is a jealous God; He will not forgive your transgressions nor your sins. If you forsake the LORD and serve foreign gods, then He will turn and do you harm and consume you, after He has done you good." And the people said to Joshua, "No, but we will serve the LORD!" So Joshua said to the people, "You are witnesses against yourselves that you have chosen the LORD for yourselves, to serve Him." And they said, "We are witnesses!" "Now therefore," he said, "put away the foreign gods which are among you, and incline your heart to the LORD God of Israel." And the people said to Joshua, "The LORD our God we will serve, and His voice we will obey!" So Joshua made a covenant with the people that day, and made for them a statute and an ordinance in Shechem. Then Joshua wrote these words in the Book of the Law of God. And he took a large stone, and set it up there under the oak that was by the sanctuary of the LORD. And Joshua said to all the people, "Behold, this stone shall be a witness to us, for it has heard all the words of the LORD which He spoke to us. It shall therefore be a witness to you, lest you deny your God." So Joshua let the people depart, each to his own inheritance. Joshua 24:19–28

5. a. Joshua seemed to be convincing the people not to follow the Lord. What aspects of God's character did he reveal?

   b. Why do you think he used this tactic with them?

6. What did the people insist?

8 Witness the Truth

A transaction was witnessed in tangible ways through objects and ceremonies. Abraham gave lambs to Abimelech to prove ownership of the well at Beersheba (see Gen. 21:30); Jacob raised a heap of stones to witness the boundary between himself and Laban (see Gen. 31:48). Reuben and Gad raised an altar as witness of the covenant between themselves and the rest of the nation (see Josh. 22:10).

---

10 Service

The apostle Paul frequently spoke of himself as a "servant." This word is often translated as "bondservant" but is also translated as "slave." As Christians, we are not hired servants but bondservants committed to wholeheartedly serving Jesus. Since a slave doesn't manage his own life, the person who calls himself a slave of Christ realizes that He has ultimate authority.

7. Recount the verbal contract between Joshua and the people. Who were the witnesses and what were the conditions of this contract?

8. Describe the three things Joshua physically did to commemorate the people's covenant and how they would help the people remember their contract.

9. What did Joshua do after renewing the covenant?

LIVE OUT ...

10. a. Joshua exhorted the Israelites to serve the Lord in sincerity and truth. Fill in the chart below to discover some New Testament lessons about service.

SCRIPTURE	LESSON ON SERVICE
Matthew 6:24	
Luke 4:8	
Romans 7:6	
Galatians 5:13–14	

b. Talk about some ways you have served the Lord. In what ways do you sense God wanting you to serve Him in the future?

11. a Joshua made a faithful declaration concerning his household's desire to follow the Lord. In your own words, make a declaration of faith for yourself and your household, beginning with the words "But as for me ..."

b. Describe some of the difficulties you encounter in maintaining godly values in the world today.

12. Joshua asked the people to "incline their hearts" to God. Solomon also used this beautiful phrase before dedicating the temple. Rewrite Solomon's prayer into a personal prayer asking God to incline *your* heart toward Him. Underline the familiar phrases from this week's lesson, which Solomon repeated in this beautiful prayer.

LEARN ABOUT …

12 Incline Your Heart

Incline means to bend, to stretch out, or bend toward. The beautiful truth is that when we reach out our hearts to God, He bends down to us. He is inclined to incline His heart to our hearts. God not only inclines His heart, but also He inclines His ear. The psalmist wrote, "Incline Your ear to me, and hear my speech" (Ps. 17:6).

> Blessed be the LORD, who has given rest to His people Israel, according to all that He promised. There has not failed one word of all His good promise, which He promised through His servant Moses. May the LORD our God be with us, as He was with our fathers. May He not leave us nor forsake us, that He may incline our hearts to Himself, to walk in all His ways, and to keep His commandments and His statutes and His judgments, which He commanded our fathers. 1 Kings 8:56–58

o o ● o o

There is an old story about Abraham Lincoln going down to the slave block to buy a slave girl's freedom. As she looked at the tall white man bidding on her, she thought he was probably another white man who would buy her only to abuse her. When Lincoln won the bidding, he went to claim the girl as his property and told her, "Young lady, you are free."

She asked him, "What does that mean?"

He solemnly told her, "It means you are free."

"Does that mean," she asked, "that I can say whatever I want to say?"

Lincoln replied, "Yes, my dear, you can say whatever you want to say."

"Does that mean," she asked, "that I can be whatever I want to be?"

Lincoln said, "Yes, you can be whatever you want to be."

"Does that mean I can go wherever I want to go?" she asked.

He patiently responded, "Yes, you can go wherever you want to go."

So the girl said, with tears streaming down her face, "Then I choose to go with you."

Just as Lincoln went to the slave block to pay the slave price for one life, God willingly came to earth in the form of a man to pay the price for our sins. As He conveyed through Joshua, He is jealous for us with a godly jealousy. He is so deeply in love with us that He willingly offers us the freedom to choose life with Him. Have you chosen this day who *you* will serve?

LISTEN TO ...

The Lord is very jealous over any saint who is utterly abandoned to him. He does not let that believer have any pleasures at all, outside of himself.

—*Madame Jeanne Marie de La Mothe Guyon*

DAY 5

Serve the Lord

One morning in 1888, Alfred Nobel awoke to find his own obituary in the newspaper. The obituary was printed as a result of a simple journalistic error. Alfred's brother had died, and the reporter had carelessly reported the death of the wrong brother.

Any man would be disturbed under the circumstances, but to Alfred the shock was overwhelming because he saw himself as the world saw him. The obituary proclaimed that Alfred was known as "Dynamite King," a great industrialist who had made an immense fortune from explosives. As far as the general public was concerned, this was the entire purpose of Alfred's life. None of Alfred's true intentions to seek peace were recognized. In the world's eyes, Alfred was a merchant of death. He realized that was how he would be remembered.

Alfred resolved to change his reputation and let the world know the true meaning and purpose of his life. He conveyed his wishes via his last will and testament to build a lasting memorial that would stand for what he *really* believed in. The result was the most prestigious prize given to those who had furthered the cause of world peace: The Nobel Peace Prize.

If you had the chance to read your obituary, would you be sad or glad at what you read? Would you be eulogized as one who had an explosive temper? Or maybe you'd be remembered as one who selfishly hoarded her gold. Or could it be that you, like Joshua, will be remembered as the servant of the Lord. Take stock of your life today and purpose to live every day serving Him and serving others. Then your life will be prizewinning.

LIFT UP ...

Lord, I want it to be said of me, "She served the Lord." Help me to take advantage of the opportunities You give me to serve You and Your people. Amen.

LOOK AT ...

Joshua said good-bye to the leaders of the people and offered prophetic words of warning from the Lord. He then led the people in a recommitment covenant with God. Today we

LEARN ABOUT …

2 Mt. Gaash

Joshua was buried in the land he had conquered, on a hill called Mount Gaash. Legend says the mountain is called Mt. Gaash or "quaking" because the people did not properly mourn the passing of their leader as they had mourned the death of Moses and God made the mountain shake to reprimand them.[171]

---

3 Out of Sight, Out of Mind

Apparently, for the Israelites, out of sight was out of mind. Once their leader died, the people as a whole followed the Lord only until the generation who led them into the land died. The next generation, the people developed a new motto for living where "everyone did what was right in his own eyes" (Judg. 17:6).

---

6 High Priest

Phinehas was the grandson of Aaron and the son of Eleazar. He first appeared in biblical history during the exodus, where his zeal and action secured the end of a plague that was destroying the nation (see Num. 25:7–8). He was rewarded by a promise that the priesthood would remain in his family forever.[172]

witness the end of Joshua's story.

Joshua's story began in Egypt where he lived in slavery. He served faithfully under Moses for forty years as the people wandered in the wilderness. And he led the people as their commander and governor throughout the conquest of the land. By all standards Joshua was a great man of God. Perhaps a lesser man would have extolled himself, but Joshua let his actions speak for themselves and allowed God to receive the glory for conquering the Promised Land. He truly lived up to his name Joshua—the Lord is Salvation.

READ JOSHUA 24:29–33.

Now it came to pass after these things that Joshua the son of Nun, the servant of the LORD, died, being one hundred and ten years old. And they buried him within the border of his inheritance at Timnath Serah, which is in the mountains of Ephraim, on the north side of Mount Gaash. Israel served the LORD all the days of Joshua, and all the days of the elders who outlived Joshua, who had known all the works of the LORD which He had done for Israel. The bones of Joseph, which the children of Israel had brought up out of Egypt, they buried at Shechem, in the plot of ground which Jacob had bought from the sons of Hamor the father of Shechem for one hundred pieces of silver, and which had become an inheritance of the children of Joseph. And Eleazar the son of Aaron died. They buried him in a hill belonging to Phinehas his son, which was given to him in the mountains of Ephraim. Joshua 24:29–33

1. Describe what happened after these things came to pass.

2. Where did they bury Joshua?

3. Recount how long Israel served the Lord.

4. Describe where Joseph's bones were buried.

5. Read Genesis 50:24 and explain how this action fulfilled Joseph's request.

6. Who else died, and where was he buried?

LIVE OUT ...

7. a. Supposedly, the land quaked when Joshua was buried. Read Matthew 27:50–54. What supernatural happenings occurred after Jesus, our Joshua, yielded His spirit?

   b. What did the centurion proclaim upon witnessing these events?

   c. When did you make this personal declaration? How and when did you discover this truth?

8. We saw today that those in the generation following Joshua's did what was right in their own eyes. According to Proverbs 3:7, what is the better way to live?

9. Journal about the most valuable lesson you learned in the book of Joshua. How did God help you to be strong and courageous?

∘ ∘ ● ∘ ∘

Billy Graham tells how nearly two hundred years ago there were two Scottish brothers named John and David Livingstone. John had set his mind on making money and becoming wealthy, and he did. But under his name in an old edition of the *Encyclopaedia Britannica*, John Livingstone is listed simply as "the brother of David Livingstone."

LEARN ABOUT ...

7 Son of God

Jesus was called the Son of God at His baptism (see Mark 1:11). He was also given this title by the angel Gabriel at the annunciation (see Luke 1:35). The Father-Son relationship belongs to eternity. The Son reveals the grace and truth of the Father since He is "in the bosom of the Father" (John 1:18).[173]

8 Wisdom

Wisdom is not just knowledge. Rather, wisdom is the ability to follow the best course of action based upon the things one has learned. In other words, wisdom isn't what you know, it is what you do with what you know. The truly wise person follows the precepts of Christ. "Hear instruction and be wise, And do not disdain it" (Prov. 8:33).

And who was David Livingstone? While John had dedicated himself to making money, David had knelt and prayed. Surrendering himself to Christ, he resolved, "I will place no value on anything I have or possess unless it is in relationship to the Kingdom of God." The inscription over his burial place in Westminster Abbey reads, "For thirty years his life was spent in an unwearied effort to evangelize."

On his fifty-ninth birthday David Livingstone wrote, "My Jesus, my King, my Life, my All; I again dedicate my whole self to Thee."[174] David Livingstone died having chosen to live for Christ. Joshua also died having made the right choice to serve the Lord all the days of his life.

As you end the book of Joshua, purpose in your heart to continue serving the Lord. May you remember the lessons you have learned throughout this study. May you "be strong and very courageous, that you may observe to do according to all the law" (Josh. 1:7).

LISTEN TO ...

Resolved: that all men should live for the glory of God. Resolved second: that whether others do or not, I will.

—*Jonathan Edwards*

Notes

1 Herbert Lockyer, *Nelson's Bible Dictionary*, in *PC Study Bible*, version 4.2b (Seattle: Biblesoft, 2004).

2 W. Phillip Keller, *Joshua: Man of Fearless Faith* (Waco, TX: Word Books, 1983), 178.

3 "William Pitt, The Younger," http://www.number-10.gov.uk/output/Page161.asp (accessed December 28, 2006).

4 "Supersonic Bail-Out," November 21, 1955, TIME.com (accessed December 30, 2006).

5 "Courage," Index #849-852, *Bible Illustrator for Windows*, version 3.0F, (Parsons Technology, 1998), adapted.

6 *Israel Insider*, "The War Against the People of the Book," October 8, 2001, http://web.israelinsider.com/Editorials/118.htm (accessed December 29, 2006).

7 Herbert Lockyer, *Nelson's Illustrated Bible Dictionary*, in *PC Study Bible*, version 4.2b (Seattle: Biblesoft, 2004).

8 *Strong's Greek/Hebrew Dictionary*, in *PC Study Bible*, version 4.2b (Seattle: Biblesoft, 2004).

9 *McClintock and Strong Encyclopedia*, Electronic Database Biblesoft (Seattle: Biblesoft, 2000).

10 Amos N. Guiora, "Teaching Morality in Armed Conflict: The Israel Defense Forces Model," June 2006, http://www.jewishvirtuallibrary.org/jsource/Society_&_Culture/IDFmorals.html (accessed January 2, 2007).

11 Alan Redpath, *Victorious Christian Living, Studies in the Book of Joshua* (Old Tappan, NJ: Fleming H. Revell, 1955), 21.

12 *Strong's Greek/Hebrew Dictionary*, in *PC Study Bible*, version 4.2b (Seattle: Biblesoft, 2004), and *Vine's Expository Dictionary of Old Testament Words*, in *PC Study Bible*, version 4.2b (Seattle: Biblesoft, 2004).

13 *The American Heritage® Dictionary of the English Language*, Fourth Edition, adapted.

14 Matthew Henry, *Matthew Henry's Commentary on the Whole Bible: New Modern Edition*,

Electronic Database, (Hendrickson Publishers, Inc., 1991), adapted.

15 Quickverse SermonBuilder, version 4.0, (Build Of June 2005) adapted.

16 Stephen Crane, *The Red Badge of Courage*, (New York: Chelsea House, 1996).

17 Merrill F. Unger, *The New Unger's Bible Dictionary*, in *PC Study Bible*, version 4.2b (Seattle: Biblesoft, 2004), adapted.

18 "Eli Cohen: Hero Of Israel," www.saveisrael.com/martyred/elicohen.htm (accessed January 10, 2007), adapted.

19 Cheryl Cheek, "Corrie Ten Boom," http://www.usoe.k12.ut.us/curr/char_ed/stories/sketches/tenboom.html (accessed January 10, 2007), adapted.

20 Herbert Lockyer, *Nelson's Bible Dictionary*, in *PC Study Bible*, version 4.2b (Seattle: Biblesoft, 2004).

21 Cecil Adams, "Frightfully Fatal," *Salt Lake City Weekly*, slweekly.com, January 5, 2006.

22 Merrill F. Under, *The New Unger's Bible Dictionary*. (Chicago: Moody Press, 1988), adapted.

23 Ibid.

24 Christine Vendel, "KC man rescues two girls from apartment fire," *The Kansas City Star*, http://www.kansascity.com/mld/kansascity/news/local/16450363.htm (accessed January 14, 2007).

25 W. E. Vine, *Vine's Expository Dictionary of New Testament Words*, in *PC Study Bible*, version 4.2b (Seattle: Biblesoft, 2004), adapted.

26 "Military Intelligence," licensed under the GNU Free Documentation License, wikipedia.com (accessed January 15, 2007), adapted.

27 Margaret B. Pumpfrey, "Stories of the Pilgrims," www.mainlessons.com, (accessed January 15, 2007).

28 Herbert Lockyer, *Nelson's Bible Dictionary*, in *PC Study Bible*, version 4.2b (Seattle: Biblesoft, 2004).

29 *Fausett's Dictionary* in *PC Study Bible*, version 4.2b (Seattle: Biblesoft, 2004), adapted.

30 Herbert Lockyer, *Nelson's Bible Dictionary*, in *PC Study Bible*, version 4.2b (Seattle: Biblesoft, 2004).

31 *Fausett's Dictionary*, in *PC Study Bible*, version 4.2b (Seattle: Biblesoft, 2004) adapted.

32 "The Road to Hana," Frommers, Maui Driving Tours, http:/www.frommers.com/destinations (accessed January 19, 2007).

33 Herbert Lockyer, *Nelson's Bible Dictionary,* in *PC Study Bible,* version 4.2b (Seattle: Biblesoft, 2004).

34 Herbert Lockyer, *Nelson's Bible Dictionary,* in *PC Study Bible,* version 4.2b (Seattle: Biblesoft, 2004).

35 H. A. Ironside, *Joshua, Ezra, Nehemiah, Esther* (Neptune, NJ: Loizeaux Brothers, 1950), 40.

36 W. E. Vine, *Vine's Expository Dictionary of Old and New Testament Words,* in *PC Study Bible,* version 4.2b (Seattle: Biblesoft, 2004).

37 J. Vernon McGee, *Joshua and Judges: History of Israel* (Nashville: Thomas Nelson), 34.

38 Herbert Lockyer, *Nelson's Bible Dictionary,* in *PC Study Bible,* version 4.2b (Seattle: Biblesoft, 2004).

39 Merrill F. Unger, *The New Unger's Bible Dictionary,* in *PC Study Bible,* version 4.2b (Seattle: Biblesoft, 2004), adapted.

40 Merrill F. Unger, *The New Unger's Bible Dictionary,* in *PC Study Bible,* version 4.2b (Seattle: Biblesoft, 2004), adapted.

41 Herbert Lockyer, *Nelson's Bible Dictionary,* in *PC Study Bible,* version 4.2b (Seattle: Biblesoft, 2004).

42 *Easton's Bible Dictionary,* in *PC Study Bible,* version 4.2b (Seattle: Biblesoft, 2004), adapted.

43 Herbert Lockyer, *Nelson's Bible Dictionary,* in *PC Study Bible,* version 4.2b (Seattle: Biblesoft, 2004).

44 W. E. Vine, *Vine's Expository Dictionary of New Testament Words,* in *PC Study Bible,* version 4.2b (Seattle: Biblesoft, 2004), adapted..

45 Alan Redpath, *Victorious Christian Living* (Westwood, NJ: Fleming H. Revell), 78.

46 Lisa Katz, "Bris: Jewish Ritual Circumcision," http://judaism.about.com/library/3_life-cycles/bris/blbrit2.htm (accessed January 26, 2007).

47 "Faithfulness of God," Index #1228, *Bible Illustrator for Windows,* version 3.0F, (Parsons Technology, 1998), adapted.

48 "Passover," *International Standard Bible Encyclopaedia,* Electronic Database (Seattle: Biblesoft, 1996), adapted.

49 Herbert Lockyer, *Nelson's Bible Dictionary,* in *PC Study Bible,* version 4.2b (Seattle: Biblesoft, 2004).

50 Ibid.

51 Herbert Lockyer, *Nelson's Illustrated Bible Dictionary* (Nashville: Thomas Nelson, 1986), adapted.

52 "Testimony: A Great Allegiance," Index #3599-3605, *Bible Illustrator for Windows,* version 3.0F, (Parsons Technology, 1998), adapted.

53 Herbert Lockyer, *Nelson's Bible Dictionary,* in *PC Study Bible*, version 4.2b (Seattle: Biblesoft, 2004).

54 Merrill F. Unger, *The New Unger's Bible Dictionary*, in *PC Study Bible*, version 4.2b (Seattle: Biblesoft, 2004), adapted.

55 "The Corruptible Made Incorruptible," in Quickverse SermonBuilder, version 4.0, (Build Of, 2005), adapted.

56 Herbert Lockyer, *Nelson's Bible Dictionary,* in *PC Study Bible*, version 4.2b (Seattle: Biblesoft, 2004).

57 W. E. Vine, *Vine's Expository Dictionary of New Testament Words,* in *PC Study Bible,* version 4.2b (Seattle: Biblesoft, 2004), adapted.

58 *International Standard Bible Encyclopedia,* in *PC Study Bible*, version 4.2b (Seattle: Biblesoft, 2004), adapted.

59 "Loving Devotion to Leader," in *Quickverse SermonBuilder*, version 4.0, (Build Of, 2005) adapted.

60 howstuffworks.comhttp://home.howstuffworks.com/question603.htm (accessed on February 5, 2007).

61 Matthew Henry, *Matthew Henry's Commentary on the Whole Bible: New Modern Edition,* Electronic Database, (Hendrickson Publishers, Inc., 1991), adapted.

62 James S. Hewett, *Illustrations Unlimited* (Wheaton, IL: Tyndale House, 1988) 167. Victor Shepherd, *William Edward Sangster,* June 23, 1998, http://www.victorshepherd. on.ca/Heritage/Sangster.htm (accessed February 5. 2007).

63 Adam Clarke, *Adam Clarke's Commentary*, Electronic Database. (Biblesoft, 1996), adapted.

64 Matthew Henry, *Matthew Henry's Commentary on the Whole Bible: New Modern Edition,* Electronic Database, (Hendrickson Publishers, Inc., 1991), adapted.

65 Angela Doland, "Mime Legend Marcel Marceau Dies at 85," Associated Press, Sept. 22, 2007, ap.google.com/article (accessed September 23, 2007).

66 Judy Wall, "Military Use of Silent Sound," *Nexus* Volume 5, Issue 6, October/November 1998, http://www.raven1.net/silsoun2.htm (accessed February 9, 2007).

67 Dr. Bryant Wood, "The Walls of Jericho," Vol. 21, no. 5 (March–May, 1999), http://biblicalstudies.qldwide.net.au/cs-walls_of_jericho.html, (accessed February 9, 2007).

68 Merrill F. Unger, *The New Unger's Bible Dictionary*, in *PC Study Bible*, version 4.2b (Seattle: Biblesoft, 2004), adapted.

69 *International Standard Bible Encyclopedia*, in *PC Study Bible*, version 4.2b (Seattle: Biblesoft, 2004), adapted.

70 W. E. Vine, *Vine's Expository Dictionary of Old Testament Words*, in *PC Study Bible*, version 4.2b (Seattle: Biblesoft, 2004), adapted.

71 Nancy Redd, "History of Cheerleading," http://www.nancyredd.com/cheerleading/history.html, accessed February 11, 2007.

72 Mark Sherman, "An Inside Look at Witness Protection," cbsnews.com, July 18, 2006, (accessed February 11, 2007).

73 Bryant Wood, "The Walls of Jericho," *Creation*, Vol. 21, Issue 2, answersingenesis.com (accessed February 11, 2007).

74 Warren W. Wiersbe, *Be Strong: Putting God's Power to Work in Your Life* (Wheaton, IL: Victor Books, 1993), 78.

75 "The Walls of Jericho: Archeological Evidence," http://biblia.com/jesusbible/joshua4.htm (accessed February 11, 2007).

76 Herbert Lockyer, *Nelson's Bible Dictionary*, in *PC Study Bible*, version 4.2b (Seattle: Biblesoft, 2004).

77 Lynnita Brown, "Buddy Search - Korean/Japanese/Amerasian Search," Korean War Educator, http://www.koreanwar-educator.org/buddy_search/search_amerasian.htm (accessed February 13, 2007), adapted.

78 "To Know God or Be Known By Man," in Quickverse SermonBuilder, version 4.0, (Build Of, 2005), adapted.

79 Herbert Lockyer, *Nelson's Bible Dictionary*, in *PC Study Bible*, version 4.2b (Seattle: Biblesoft, 2004).

80 W. E. Vine, *Vine's Dictionary of Old Testament Words* and *Nelson's Bible Dictionary*, in

PC Study Bible, version 4.2b (Seattle: Biblesoft, 2004), adapted.

81 Botany 4400, Lecture 34, University of Wyoming, April 12, 2006, http://www.uwyo.edu/botany4400/Lecture%2034.htm (accessed February 18, 2007).

82 Merrill F. Unger, The New Unger's Bible Dictionary, in PC Study Bible, version 4.2b (Seattle: Biblesoft, 2004), adapted.

83 "Greed," Bible Illustrator for Windows, version 3.0F, (Parsons Technology, 1998), adapted.

84 "Unity," Index #3725, Bible Illustrator for Windows, version 3.0F, (Parsons Technology, 1998), adapted.

85 Robert Britt, "Amazing Ants Ambush Prey from Foxholes," April 20, 2005 http://www.livescience.com/animal/050420_ant_trap.html (accessed February 21, 2007).

86 Matthew Henry, Matthew Henry's Bible Commentary, in PC Study Bible, version 4.2b (Seattle: Biblesoft, 2004), adapted.

87 Herbert Lockyer, Nelson's Illustrated Bible Dictionary (Nashville: Thomas Nelson, 1986), adapted.

88 "Pride," Index #1723, Bible Illustrator for Windows, version 3.0F, (Parsons Technology, 1998), adapted.

89 Reader's Digest, July 1979, 87.

90 Trent C. Butler, Word Biblical Commentary: Joshua, vol. 7, (Dallas: Word, 2002), 102, adapted.

91 "The Wiles of the Devil," "Trick," InfoSearch, version 4.11d, 1996, adapted.

92 Alan Redpath, Victorious Christian Living: Studies in the Book of Joshua (Westwood, NJ: Fleming H. Revell, 1955), 142.

93 W. E. Vine, Vine's Expository Dictionary of Old Testament Words, in PC Study Bible, version 4.2b (Seattle: Biblesoft, 2004), adapted.

94 Ibid.

95 Warren W. Wiersbe, Be Strong (Wheaton, IL: Victor Books, 1993), 111.

96 "The Willing Slave," Bible Illustrator for Windows, version 3.0F, (Parsons Technology, 1998), adapted.

97 International Standard Bible Encyclopedia, in PC Study Bible, version 4.2b (Seattle: Biblesoft, 2004), adapted.

98 Russell Grigg, "Joshua's Long Day," *Creation*, June 1997, http://www.answersingenesis.org/creation (accessed March 8, 2007).

99 Merril F. Unger, *The New Unger's Bible Dictionary.* (Chicago: Moody Press, 1988), adapted.

100 "Shoichi Yokoi," *InfoSearch*, version 4.11d, 1996, adapted.

101 Matthew Henry, *Matthew Henry's Commentary on the Whole Bible: New Modern Edition*, Electronic Database, (Hendrickson Publishers, Inc., 1991), adapted.

102 Herbert Lockyer, *Nelson's Illustrated Bible Dictionary* (Nashville: Thomas Nelson, 1986), adapted.

103 "Hindered by Satan," *InfoSearch,* version 4.11d, 1996, adapted.

104 Herbert Lockyer, *Nelson's Illustrated Bible Dictionary* (Nashville: Thomas Nelson, 1986), adapted.

105 Stan Hoig, "Land Run of 1889," Encyclopedia of Oklahoma History and Culture, http://digital.library.okstate.edu/encyclopedia (accessed March 14, 2007).

106 Herbert Lockyer, *Nelson's Illustrated Bible Dictionary* (Nashville: Thomas Nelson, 1986), adapted.

107 Matthew Henry, *Matthew Henry's Commentary on the Whole Bible: New Modern Edition*, Electronic Database, (Hendrickson Publishers, Inc., 1991), adapted.

108 Lloyd Duhaime, "History of Real Estate Law: The Old English Landholding System," October 20, 2006, http://www.duhaime.org/Real-estate/rehist1.aspx (accessed March 9, 2007), adapted.

109 Herbert Lockyer, *Nelson's Illustrated Bible Dictionary* (Nashville: Thomas Nelson, 1986), adapted.

110 Ibid.

111 Edythe Draper, *Draper's Book of Quotations for the Christian World* (Wheaton, IL: Tyndale House, 1992), Entry 8128.

112 Merril F. Unger, *The New Unger's Bible Dictionary.* (Chicago: Moody Press, 1988), adapted.

113 Matthew Henry, *Matthew Henry's Commentary on the Whole Bible: New Modern Edition*, Electronic Database, (Hendrickson Publishers, Inc., 1991), adapted.

114 Merrill F. Unger, *The New Unger's Bible Dictionary*, in *PC Study Bible*, version 4.2b (Seattle: Biblesoft, 2004), adapted.

115 Herbert Lockyer, *Nelson's Bible Dictionary*, in *PC Study Bible*, version 4.2b (Seattle: Biblesoft, 2004).

116 Robert Sullivan, "The Greatest Adventures of All Time," *TIME*, September 12, 2003, http://www.time.com/time/2003/adventures/interview.html (accessed March 30, 2007).

117 Andrew Fausset, *Fausset's Dictionary*, in *PC Study Bible*, version 4.2b (Seattle: Biblesoft, 2004), adapted.

118 Matthew Easton, *Easton's Bible Dictionary*, in *PC Study Bible*, version 4.2b (Seattle: Biblesoft, 2004), adapted.

119 Herbert Lockyer, *Nelson's Bible Dictionary*, in *PC Study Bible*, version 4.2b (Seattle: Biblesoft, 2004).

120 F. Somner Merryweather, "Misers," *Harper's New Monthly Magazine*, Volume 3, Issue 17, October 1851, 614–619, "The 19th Century in Print," http://rs6.loc.gov/ammem/ndlpcoop/moahtml/snchome.html (accessed March 31, 2007), adapted.

121 *International Standard Bible Encyclopedia*, in *PC Study Bible*, version 4.2b (Seattle: Biblesoft, 2004), adapted.

122 Herbert Lockyer, *Nelson's Bible Dictionary*, in *PC Study Bible*, version 4.2b (Seattle: Biblesoft, 2004).

123 "Life as a Pioneer," Camp Silos, http://www.campsilos.org/mod2/students/life.shtml (accessed April 2, 2007).

124 *International Standard Bible Encyclopedia*, in *PC Study Bible*, version 4.2b (Seattle: Biblesoft, 2004), adapted.

125 Andrew Fausset, *Fausset's Dictionary*, in *PC Study Bible*, version 4.2b (Seattle: Biblesoft, 2004), adapted.

126 Andrew Fausset, *Fausset's Dictionary*, in *PC Study Bible*, version 4.2b (Seattle: Biblesoft, 2004), adapted.

127 "Water That Satisfies," in Quickverse SermonBuilder, version 4.0, (Build Of 2005) adapted.

128 Matthew Easton, *Easton's Bible Dictionary*, in *PC Study Bible*, version 4.2b (Seattle: Biblesoft, 2004), adapted.

129 Merrill F. Unger, *The New Unger's Bible Dictionary*, in *PC Study Bible*, version 4.2b (Seattle: Biblesoft, 2004), adapted.

130 "Start Small," in Quickverse SermonBuilder, version 4.0, (Build Of 2005) adapted.

131 Merril F. Unger, *The New Unger's Bible Dictionary.* (Chicago: Moody Press, 1988), adapted.

132 Herbert Lockyer, *Nelson's Illustrated Bible Dictionary* (Nashville: Thomas Nelson, 1986), adapted.

133 Ibid.

134 Estes Thompson, "Pilot Acquitted in Cable Car Death," *Associated Press*, March 5, 1999, http://archive.southcoasttoday.com/daily/03-99/03-05-99/a06wn024.htm (accessed April 7, 2007).

135 Merril F. Unger, *The New Unger's Bible Dictionary.* (Chicago: Moody Press, 1988), adapted.

136 Ibid.

137 Matthew Henry, *Matthew Henry's Commentary on the Whole Bible: New Modern Edition*, Electronic Database, (Hendrickson Publishers, Inc., 1991), adapted.

138 Herbert Lockyer, *Nelson's Illustrated Bible Dictionary* (Nashville: Thomas Nelson, 1986), adapted.

139 Ibid.

140 *The New Unger's Bible Dictionary.* (Chicago: Moody Press, 1988), adapted.

141 Ibid.

142 Andrew Fausset, *Fausset's Dictionary,* in *PC Study Bible*, version 4.2b (Seattle: Biblesoft, 2004), adapted.

143 *Safed,* http://www.safed.co.il/, adapted (accessed April 10, 2007).

144 James S. Hewett, *Illustrations Unlimited* (Wheaton, IL: Tyndale House 1988), 403.

145 Matthew Henry, *Matthew Henry's Commentary on the Whole Bible: New Modern Edition*, Electronic Database, (Hendrickson Publishers, Inc., 1991), adapted.

146 Ibid.

147 *Biblesoft's New Exhaustive Strong's Numbers and Concordance with Expanded Greek-Hebrew Dictionary* (Biblesoft and International Bible Translators, Inc., 1994).

148 http://www.seeing-stars.com/ShowBiz/FamilyFeud.shtml (accessed April 13, 2007).

149 Herbert Lockyer, *Nelson's Illustrated Bible Dictionary* (Nashville: Thomas Nelson, 1986), adapted.

150 "Bert's Family Feud," http://channelnine.ninemsn.com.au/article.aspx?id=90349 (accessed April 13, 2007).

151 Herbert Lockyer, *Nelson's Illustrated Bible Dictionary* (Nashville: Thomas Nelson,

1986), adapted.

152 Ray Lane, "Family feud may have sparked cruel Craigslist hoax," KING 5 News, April 9, 2007, http://www.nwcn.com/topstories/stories/NW_040507 WABcraigslistadLJ.34e92f1d.html (accessed April 13, 2007).

153 Jonathan M. Gitlin, "Famous Family Feud Fueled by Rare Genetic Disease," April 6, 2007, http://arstechnica.com/journals/science.ars/2007/04/06/famous-family-feud-fueled-by-rare-genetic-disease (accessed April 12, 2007).

154 Herbert Lockyer, *Nelson's Illustrated Bible Dictionary* (Nashville: Thomas Nelson, 1986), adapted.

155 Ibid.

156 "Police accused of failings in family feud arson deaths," *Telegraph* April 5, 2007, http://www.telegraph.co.uk/news/main.jhtml?xml=/news/2007/04/04/ncochrane104.xml (accessed on April 13, 2007).

157 "Love of God," Index #2206, *Bible Illustrator for Windows*, version 3.0F, (Parsons Technology, 1998), adapted.

158 Merril F. Unger, *The New Unger's Bible Dictionary.* (Chicago: Moody Press, 1988), adapted.

159 "Henry Ward Beecher" http://en.wikipedia.org/wiki/Henry_Ward_Beecher (accessed April 15, 2007), adapted.

160 "Fruits: Self-Control," Index #1337–1339, *Bible Illustrator for Windows*, version 3.0F, (Parsons Technology, 1998), adapted.

161 George W. Holden, Ph.D., "No More Family Feud: Putting a Stop to Sibling Rivalry," June 15, 2006, http://utopia.utexas.edu/articles/yout/parent/feud.html?sec= parents&sub=elem (accessed April 15, 2007).

162 Matthew Henry, *Matthew Henry's Commentary on the Whole Bible: New Modern Edition*, Electronic Database, (Hendrickson Publishers, Inc., 1991), adapted.

163 Herbert Lockyer, *Nelson's Illustrated Bible Dictionary* (Nashville: Thomas Nelson, 1986), adapted.

164 James S. Hewett, *Illustrations Unlimited* (Wheaton IL: Tyndale House, 1988) 38–39.

165 W. E. Vine, *Vine's Expository Dictionary of Old Testament Words*, in *PC Study Bible*, version 4.2b (Seattle: Biblesoft, 2004), adapted.

166 Ibid.

167 "Praying the Ten Commandments," in Quickverse SermonBuilder, version 4.0, (Build Of 2005) adapted.

168 "General Douglas MacArthur's Farewell Address," http://www.nationalcenter.org/MacArthurFarewell.html (accessed April 21, 2007).

169 *Vine's Expository Dictionary of New Testament Words,* in *PC Study Bible*, version 4.2b (Seattle: Biblesoft, 2004), adapted.

170 "What's Ahead for Generation Y," Lifecourse Associates, February 5, 2006, http://www.lifecourse.com/news/lib-clips/060205_ral.html (accessed April 22, 2007).

171 Matthew Henry, *Matthew Henry's Commentary*, in *PC Study Bible*, version 4.2b (Seattle: Biblesoft, 2004).

172 Merrill F. Unger, *The New Unger's Bible Dictionary*, in *PC Study Bible*, version 4.2b (Seattle: Biblesoft, 2004), adapted.

173 Herbert Lockyer, *Nelson's Bible Dictionary*, in *PC Study Bible*, version 4.2b (Seattle: Biblesoft, 2004).

174 "Two Lives, Two Goals," in *Quickverse SermonBuilder*, version 4.0, (Build Of 2005) adapted.

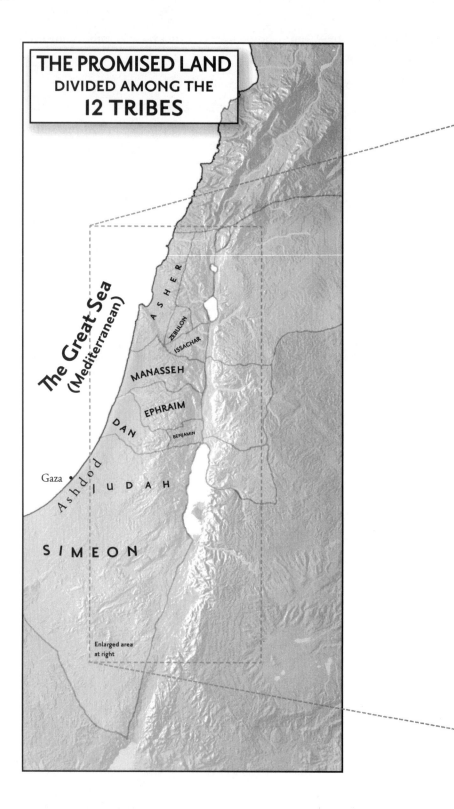

THE PROMISED LAND
DIVIDED AMONG THE
12 TRIBES

The Great Sea
(Mediterranean)

ASHER

ZEBULON

ISSACHAR

MANASSEH

EPHRAIM

BENJAMIN

DAN

Gaza

Ashdod

JUDAH

SIMEON

Enlarged area
at right

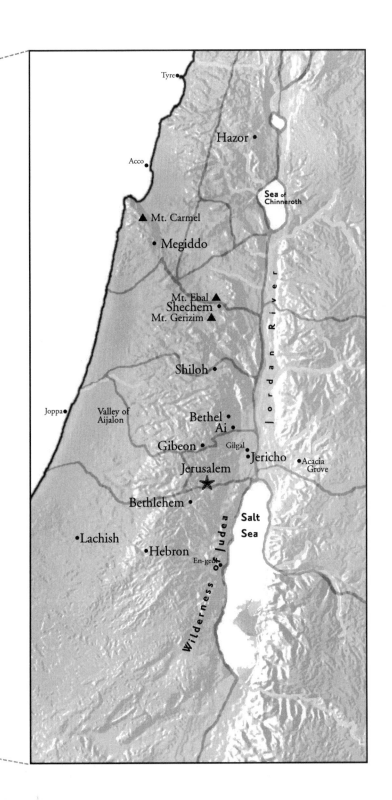

ʠive ʠntimately

Lessons from the Upper Room

Live Intimately
Lenya Heitzig & Penny Rose
978-1-4347-6790-5

This is it. After three years of ministry, traveling the countryside, encountering thousands of desperate people, and delivering a radical new message, Jesus has one last night to spend with His disciples. And He knows it.

This ten-week study puts you in the upper room with Jesus and His closest companions as He gave them His final instructions (John 13—17). Imagine what it would have been like to hear His voice, mere hours before His death. There at the table, foïr all eternity, life was changed. What did the chosen Twelve need to hear and what do we need to take from it today?

1.800.323.7543 • www.DavidCCook.com

David C Cook

About the Authors

Lenya Heitzig is an award-winning author and sought-after speaker at conferences and retreats worldwide. Serving as the director of Women at Calvary, one of the core ministries at Calvary Albuquerque, she delights in seeing God's Word do His work in the lives of women. Her husband, Skip Heitzig, is the senior pastor of the fourteen-thousand-member congregation that has been ranked one of the fastest-growing churches in America. She received the Gold Medallion Award for coauthoring *Pathway to God's Treasure: Ephesians*, which also includes *Pathway to God's Plan: Esther* and *Pathway to Living Faith: James* in this same series. She also contributed a number of devotionals to *The New Women's Devotional Bible*, which was a finalist in the 2007 Christian Book Awards. Her most recent book, *Holy Moments*, published by Regal, enlightens the reader to see God's hand of providence move miraculously in daily life. Lenya loves jogging with her dog, Winston, as well as sampling pastries wherever she goes, fulfilling her motto, "Run so you can eat!" She lives in Albuquerque, New Mexico, with her husband, Skip, and their adult son, Nathan, who is a youth pastor.

Penny Rose is the Gold Medallion Award–winning coauthor of *Pathway to God's Treasure: Ephesians*, as well as *Pathway to God's Plan: Esther* and *Pathway to Living Faith: James* published by Tyndale House. She contributed to Zondervan's *True Identity: The Bible for Women* and was the general editor and a devotional writer for their *New Women's Devotional Bible*, a finalist for the 2007 Christian Book Awards. She wrote *A Garden of Friends* published by Regal as an ode to biblical friendship. A longtime member of the Women at Calvary Steering Committee, Penny thrives on teaching at conferences and retreats nationwide. Penny lives in Albuquerque, New Mexico, with her husband, Kerry, a pastor at Calvary Albuquerque. They have two daughters, Erin and Ryan, and one son, Kristian. She loves to spend time with family and friends, read, travel, and take naps.